# SMALL YACHTS

# SMALL YACHTS

## THEIR DESIGN
## AND CONSTRUCTION
## EXEMPLIFIED BY
## THE RULING TYPES
## OF MODERN PRACTICE.

With numerous plates and illustrations
by
C. P. KUNHARDT

Edited, abridged, and with a preface
by
THE EDITORS OF *WOODENBOAT* MAGAZINE
from
the new enlarged edition of 1891

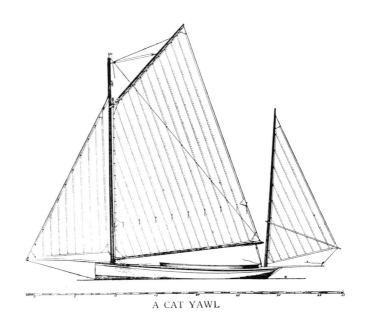

A CAT YAWL

Published by WoodenBoat Books
Naskeag Road, PO Box 78
Brooklin, Maine 04616 USA
www.woodenboat.com

This edition, first published in 1985, is an edited and abridged
republication of the "new and revised edition, " as published by
Forest and Stream Publishing Company in 1891. Preface copyright
© 1985 by WoodenBoat Publications, Inc.

**Library of Congress Cataloging in Publication Data**

Kundhardt, C.P. (Charles P.), 1848 or 9-1889.
    Small yachts

    1. Yachts and yachting—Design and construction.
I. Woodenboat.   II. Title
VM331.K963  1985        623.8'223        84-26984
ISBN 10: 0-937822-00-0
ISBN 13: 978-0-937822-00-5

Printed in USA by Maple-Vail, 2007

10 9 8 7 6 5 4 3 2

# PREFACE TO THE 1985 EDITION

I T IS one hundred years since the first edition of *Small Yachts* appeared, and its purpose, so briefly stated, was expressed in the author's preface:

> The subject matter of this volume is intended to cover the whole range of type in small yachts, but embracing only those which have received sufficiently wide recognition to entitle them to public confidence.
>
> All that which possesses only a distant affinity, or which is still in the experimental stage, is purposely excluded from this volume.
>
> The division separating small yachts from large has been drawn between craft requiring one owner and friend with one paid hand for ordinary control and those demanding the shipping of a crew and a professional skipper.          —C.P.K.

It is remarkable to consider that the range of type in small yachts could have been collected (even then) in one volume. Undoubtedly, there were some additional types that could or should have been included. Yet, it is certain that the most significant contemporary types have been assembled, and that the collection represents the first American study in yacht design. Indeed, the historical significance of the study is profound. As a permanent body of work, it provided a grounding for the devotees of the emergent sport of yachting, and a framework within which to understand the rapid evolutions in the sport which were so thoroughly discussed in *Forest and Stream*, the weekly paper for sportsmen.

*Small Yachts* was, in the best sense, the work of an educator, for C.P. Kunhardt was far more than the Editor of *Forest and Stream's* "Yachting" section, and far more than the fanatic he was considered by many to be. He was an impassioned champion of wisdom and good sense in yacht design, and though he was opinionated in the extreme, he was also remarkably open to the expression of opposing views. Moreover, he believed in the ultimate good judgement of the reading public, and he endeavored, in his work, to provide as broad a forum as possible so that such judgement could be well informed.

The original editions of *Small Yachts* contain a great deal of text material relating to the processes of yacht design and construction, and to numerous other areas of pleasure boating. It is interesting and informative material, but less germane, in our opinion, to the evolution of specific types in yacht design. Since a re-publication of the whole original work was financially unfeasible, we chose to include only that material which was immediately pertinent to a study of the range of type in small yachts. That study was, after all, the primary purpose of the original work. We apologize for the few references to material not included in this edition.

It is strange indeed for a student of the history of yacht design to participate in the abridging of one of the most important works on that history. Yet, by so doing, we have provided wider access to some of the most difficult-to-find material extant, and distilled the essence of some of the most historically significant material ever collected. *Small Yachts* marked the beginning of the serious study of yacht design in this country. The re-publication of this material affirms a long-standing tradition of informed appreciation for the history of yacht design.

Jonathan Wilson
Brooklin, Maine

# CONTENTS

Preface to the 1985 edition     iii
About C.P. Kunhardt     vi
Illustrations of Type     1
Classification by Type     2

## I - CENTREBOARD CATBOATS
I. A Portable Catboat     3
II. A Newport Catboat     4
III. An Eastern Catboat     7
    Rigs of Eastern C.B. Catboats     9
IV. The Catboat Coot     10
    Dimensions of Some New Jersey Catboats     17
V. The Chas. Cohill     19

## II - KEEL CATBOATS
I. The Caprice     21
II. The Dodge No. 2     26
    Rigs of Keel Catboats     30

## III - LIGHT DRAFT CENTREBOARD SLOOPS
I. The Cruiser     31
II. The Trident     35
III. The Schemer     38
IV. A Skipjack     40
V. A German Light-Draft     42

## IV - DEEP CENTREBOARD SLOOPS
I. The Gleam     44
II. The Midge     48

## V - LIGHT DRAFT KEEL YACHTS
I. The Mignonette     51
II. A Small Cruiser     56
III. The Carmita     61
IV. The Dart     64
V. The Nuckel     67
VI. The Alice     70
VII. The Lark     73
VIII. The Gipsy     75
IX. The Yawl Sylvia     78

## VI - DEEP DRAFT KEEL YACHTS
I. The Neva     82
II. The Nyssa     85
III. The Columbine     88
IV. The Cruiser Mermaid     91

VII - COMPROMISE KEEL AND CENTREBOARD
     YACHTS
    I. The Gannet           97
    II. Improved Open Boat    102

VIII - BEAMY CUTTERS
    I. The Daisy          105
    II. The Vayu         110
    III. The Windward     113
    IV. The Aneto       122
    V. The Deuce       126

IX - CUTTERS OF MODERATE BEAM
    I. The Petrel        130
    II. The Merlin       135
    III. The Rajah      139
    IV. The Yolande    141
    V. A Cruising Yacht  146
    VI. The Rondina    151
    VII. The Indra      156

X - CUTTERS OF SMALL BEAM
    I. The Mamie      161
    The Fendeur Model  163
    II. A Six Beam Cutter  169
    Development of the Cutter  171
    III. The Surf       173
    IV. The Spankadillo  185
    V. The Madge     187
    VI. A Cutter by W. Fife, Jr.  195
    VII. The Jenny Wren  198

XI - YACHTS OF SPECIAL CLASS
    A Cruising Schooner  200
    Yawl and Schooner Compared  203
    Sharpies of Long Island Sound  208
    A Large Sharpie  210
    A Small Sharpie  218
    The Buckeye  220
    The Sneakbox  224
    A Lifeboat Yacht  230
    The Canoe Yawl  234
    Combination Row and Sail Boats  242
    The Heathen Chinee  248
    The Chesapeake Flattie  250

XII - GENERAL INFORMATION
    Yachts' Boats  255
    Standing Rigging  261
    Running Gear  268

# ABOUT C.P. KUNHARDT

CHARLES P. KUNHARDT was born on Staten Island, New York, in 1848 or 1849. His father was the head of the large shipping firm of Kunhardt & Co. The family home was a stone house which occupied a commanding position overlooking the water; and here young Kunhardt gave early manifestation of those tastes for which in after life he was to become noted. It was the most natural thing in the world that he should take to the sea, and in 1866 he was appointed midshipman in the Naval Academy at Annapolis, from which he graduated in 1870, eighteenth in a very large class. While stationed at Panama in 1873 he contracted the coast fever and resigned from the service. Then as a naval architect he built two gunboats for the Haitian government, and took them down and delivered them. He spent several years abroad; then, in 1878, he joined the staff of *Forest and Stream* as editor of its yachting department, a position which he held until 1884.

When he first took command of the few columns of *Forest and Stream* then devoted to yachting, the alleged merits and defects of the modern cutter type were being generally discussed. The writers of the day were unanimous in praise of the existing craft—the GRACIE, FANNY, and similar skimming dish types—and loud in their condemnation of the cutter. With them were arrayed the great body of American yachtsmen as well as the general public. Against all these Kunhardt took his stand firmly in favor of deeper yachts, better and lower ballast, seamanlike rigs, and more extended and venturesome cruising.

Kunhardt's sharp and trenchant pen made some enemies, the truths he told were unpalatable, and time alone can bring a true recognition of the pioneer work he did, not alone for the yachts themselves, but for the literature of yachting. That he was extreme in his views, and vigorous and uncompromising in his methods, must be admitted. But he was a reformer, moved to his self-appointed work by a sense of many existing evils, and his justification lies in the fact that he succeeded where most others would have failed. The fruit of his labors is seen and recognized today in the presence of a fleet of magnificent new yachts and the utter disappearance of the once popular national type.

In addition to his work for *Forest and Stream*, Mr. Kunhardt found time to prepare for the press an elaborate and indeed monumental work, *Small Yachts*, and this was supplemented by another volume, *Steam Yachts and Launches*. In 1886 he made a cruise in a catboat from New York to Beaufort, S.C. The spectacle of this sturdy champion of deep keel cutters going to sea in a catboat was naturally one at which there was much amusement. But Kunhardt justified himself by the plea, which was quite true, that under the circumstances it was a catboat or nothing, and he took the catboat.

The rest is told in a few words. Mr. Kunhardt bought the iron steamship MADRID, made her over into a gunboat, and rechristened her the CONSERVA. On Monday, March 25, 1889, the steamship COLORADO reported the finding of a wreck with two dead seamen, and a great quantity of wreckage, off Cape Charles. The next day a pilot boat reported at Philadelphia that she had picked up one of the CONSERVA's lifeboats off Wenwick's Island; and then came word from a New York pilot boat of the finding of another of the CONSERVA's lifeboats. It is now generally conceded that the CONSERVA had gone to the bottom following a collision with another vessel.

Mr. Kunhardt was unmarried. One brother was a captain in the Royal Artillery of England, and another one he expected to meet upon his arrival in CONSERVA at Samana, Dominican Republic. He was a man who held a very warm place in the affections of those who knew him well. His life of adventure had taught him a practical philosophy; and if it was his fate to have gone down with the CONSERVA, perhaps such an end is that which would have been chosen by one who loved the sea as he did.

—Excerpted from *Forest and Stream*, April 4, 1889.

AN AMERICAN YAWL

A CUTTER BEFORE THE WIND

# ILLUSTRATIONS OF TYPE

## FROM ONE EXTREME TO THE OTHER

# CLASSIFICATION
# OF TYPE

THE classification adopted in the following pages has no reference to rig. The sloop, cutter and yawl being interchangeable, an arrangement according to sail plan would have been without purpose.

The yachts have therefore been grouped according to the *type* of their hulls.

The terms cutter and sloop apply strictly to differences in rig, in the same way that we designate large vessels as schooners, brigs, barks or ships.

Owing to the competition between certain prevailing forms, usually accompanied by well-defined peculiarities of rig, the terms cutter and sloop have, by common consent, been invested with a wider meaning, grasping characteristics of hull hitherto found under those rigs. To avoid circumlocution, the broader signification has been recognized in the succeeding collection.

The line between cutter and sloop is drawn with reference to the shape of midship section, a more rational division than one grounded on the proportion of beam to length, because performance is more truly interpreted through the influence of the governing section.

It is the custom at times to insist that an assignment to the genus "cutter" is justified only by close analogy in proportions to some yacht of that class whose widely known record has focused attention to her extreme typification, ignoring the existence of numerous cutters of other ratio in their cardinal dimensions.

Small beam has through such acceptation been heretofore ranked as the proper index to classification as a "cutter" and large beam as the sole prerogative of a "sloop."

But it is readily understood that a pinched middle body, if associated with flat floor and high, flaring bilge, may be attended with the behavior of the sloop, and a liberal allowance of width with the idiosyncrasies of the cutter to a great extent, if deadrise, low bilge and plumb sides be incorporated in the midship section. Hence, the mould of the latter should be deemed the ascendant exponent of type.

The blending of both classes can, however, be accomplished in an average, refusing decided analysis one way or the other. It would be impossible to declare, for instance, to what family the COLUMBINE (Plate XXXII) can claim the closest likeness. Such boats are perhaps best shunted off by themselves under the cognomen of "compromises."

# I

# CENTREBOARD CATBOATS

## I.  A PORTABLE CATBOAT

### PLATE IV

TEN FEET LONG ON THE LOAD-LINE

THE catboat (Plate IV) was designed by Mr. H. W. Eaton, of New York and built by W. P. Stephens, of Staten Island, in 1881, with the object of producing as able a boat as the condition of portability would permit. Being of necessity very small, good floor and great beam had to be preserved for the required displacement for boat and crew, while stiffness followed from these features without resorting to shifting ballast. With one hand aboard a 30 lb. bag in the eyes regulated the trim. The hull weighed 125 lbs., and was readily hauled up a staging into a boathouse after use. She met expectations very well, being a smart sailer, handy and certain in stays in reasonably smooth water. A chop, however, was not to her liking.

The construction was light, but thoroughly riveted, lap-streak canoe style. Keel of close-grained oak, 1 in. thick, 3½ across centre, and tapered to 1¼ at ends. Frames, oak steam-bent, ½ × ¼ in., spaced 6 in. between centres. These and the laps of the ¼ in. cedar streaks are fastened with ¾ copper, riveted up on No. 15 burrs, the rest of the work being fastened with 1 in. copper boat nails, except the wood ends, which are secured with brass screws, as also the ¼ in. mahogany deck. An inside gunwale of spruce, 1⅛ × ¾ in., is run round, jogging over timber heads, and receives the deck beams, which are of spruce 1 × 1¼ in. No caulking was required. The cockpit is 6½ ft. long, 3½ ft. wide, with oak coamings 2 × ¼ in. Thwarts of ½ in. mahogany. Centreboard of oak. Floor boards ⁵⁄₁₆ in. thick. The rudder is 20 in. wide, drops 6 in. below the keel, and is worked by a straight oak tiller 15 in. long. It is shipped sailboat fashion, with braces and a ½ in. brass rod passing through, the heel screw-

3

ing into lower brace. Stem and heel of boat protected by ¼ in. brass strap. For pulling, 8 ft. oars are worked over standards on gunwale.

| | | | | |
|---|---|---|---|---|
| Length over all | | 10 ft. | | |
| Length on water-line | | 9 " | 10 in. | |
| Depth at side, No. 6 | | | 13 " | |
| Extreme beam | | 5 " | | |
| Breadth across transom | | 4 " | 6 " | |
| Sheer forward | | | 7 " | |
| Sheer aft | | | 4 " | |
| Mast from stem | | 1 " | | |
| Mast over all | | 12 " | | |
| Diameter at deck | | | 2½ " | |
| Diameter at truck | | | 1¼ " | |
| Boom over all | | 11 " | 6 " | |
| Diameter in slings | | | 2 " | |
| Yard over all | | 5 " | 6 " | |
| Diameter of yard | | | 1¼ " | |
| Length of board | | 2 " | 4 " | |
| Drop of board | | 1 " | 6 " | |
| Pin of board from stem | | 4 " | | |
| Sail area | | 76 sq. ft. | | |

The sail is a standing lug, the boom having jaws and a tack lashing.

The halliards are bent to the yard, rove through sheave in masthead and down through fair leader into the cockpit to brass cleat. The mainsheet is fast on the quarter, passes up through single block on boom, and again through block on opposite quarter to the hand. For material of sail, heavy 27 in. muslin was used, bighted every 6 in., and hemmed with stiff duck, three seams being stitched in place of bolt rope. Total cost, $150.

## II. A NEWPORT CATBOAT

### *PLATE IV*

#### TWENTY FEET LONG ON LOAD-LINE

THE Newport Catboat, illustrated on Plate IV, is of the local variety, uncolored by late invasion of Narragansett waters by ideas from the outer world of yachting. It possesses buoyancy and stiffness, and is remarkable for the long tapering after-end, "raking" midship section and easy body throughout.

# PLATE IV

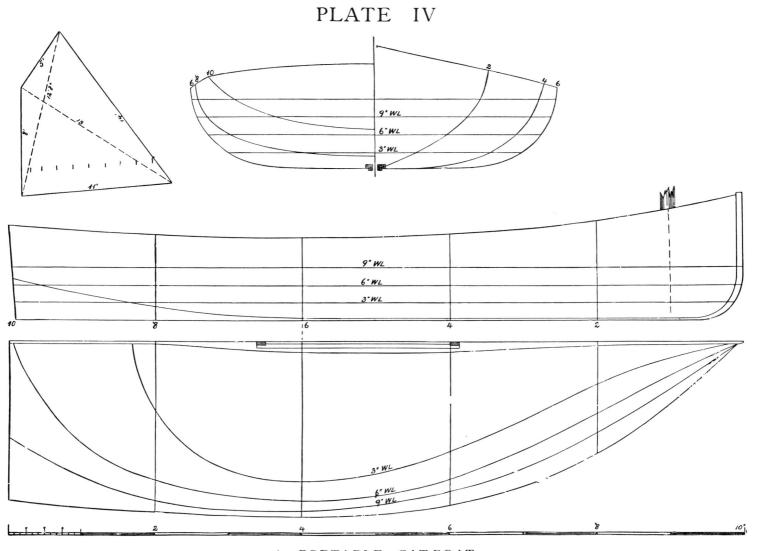

A PORTABLE CAT-BOAT

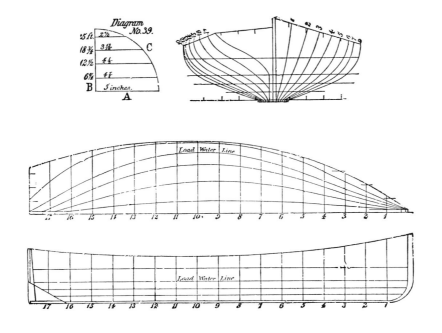

A NEWPORT CAT-BOAT

# Small Yachts

Distance of mast from stem is reckoned from the fore side to centre of mast, and depth at side from rabbet to top of planksheer. The rise of the boom at after-end, above goose-neck at mast, is 2 ft. 6 in. Peak of the sail, 7 ft. 3 in. from mast and 25 ft 4 in. from tack to peak. Luff of sail, 16 ft. 9 in. This will be for a snug cruising sail. Small jibs set flying to a boomkin are occasionally shown in quartering winds, and a spinnaker for running, the clew of the latter being simply "boomed out" by a light pole in any feasible manner.

| | | | | | |
|---|---|---|---|---|---|
| Length over all | 20 | ft. | | | |
| Length on water-line | 20 | " | | | |
| Extreme beam | 7 | " | 9 | in. | |
| Beam on water-line | 6 | " | 8 | " | |
| Breadth across transom | 4 | " | 10 | " | |
| Depth at side, No. 11 | 2 | " | 4 | " | |
| Least freeboard | 1 | " | 4 | " | |
| Draft without board | 1 | " | 2½ | " | |
| Draft with board | 5 | " | | | |
| Sheer forward, | 1 | " | | | |
| Sheer aft | | | 7 | " | |
| Length of board | 6 | " | | | |
| Breadth after-end | 3 | " | | | |
| Pin from stem | 6 | " | | | |
| Mast from stem | 1 | " | 3 | " | |
| Mast over all | 27 | " | 6 | " | |
| Rake in one foot | | | ¾ | " | |
| Diameter at deck | | | 6 | " | |
| Diameter at head | | | 2¾ | " | |
| Boom over all | 24 | " | | | |
| Diameter in slings | | | 4½ | " | |
| Gaff over all | 11 | " | | | |
| Diameter of gaff | | | 2½ | " | |
| Sail area | 350 sq. ft. | | | | |

The keel is of flitch, 2 in. thick and 12 in. wide amidships, tapering as per body plan. Frames 1½ x ¾ in. at heel, the moulding size tapering to ¾ in. at head; spaced 14 in. Stem and post 2½ in. sided at rabbet. Bed pieces of trunk 2 in. thick; plank, ¾ to 1 in. thick. Deck usually of wide stuff ¾ in. thick, covered with canvas. Cockpit 12 x 5 ft. 6 in.

The method of lining out spars is shown in one of the diagrams for a mast 5 in. at deck and 2½ at head. With the dividers scribe a quarter circle. Call the base 5 in., and draw in an ordinate of half the length for the head of 2½ in. The space between this and the base divide into four equal parts. Apply the scale to the ordinates for the diameter of the spar at each quarter length respectively. Sail of 8 oz. duck, roped, and with two rows of reef knittles. The rudder will be 2 ft. across face.

## III. AN EASTERN CATBOAT

### *PLATE V*

#### FIFTEEN FEET WATER-LINE

CATBOATS in Eastern waters are of an abler type than those for smooth water service, and are distinguished by larger bodies, greater draft, fuller lines and higher bows. Like many of the Newport boats, a small cuddy with sliding hatch gives some stowage under cover, and in larger cats the chance for a low berth into which the belated cruiser may creep. In the milder latitude of New York, tents or "shifting" canvas cabin roofs are more common.

| | | | | | |
|---|---|---|---|---|---|
| Length over all | 15 | ft. | 6 | in. | |
| Length on water-line | 15 | " | | | |
| Extreme beam moulded | 5 | " | 6 | " | |
| Beam moulded at *L W L* | 5 | " | | | |
| Breadth across counter | 4 | " | | | |
| Depth at side, No. 10 | 1 | " | 11 | " | |
| Least freeboard | | | 10 | " | |
| Draft without board | 1 | " | 5 | " | |
| Draft with board | 4 | " | | | |
| Sheer forward | 1 | " | 3 | " | |
| Sheer aft | | | 3 | " | |
| Length of board | 3 | " | 4 | " | |
| Breadth after end | 2 | " | 4 | " | |
| Pin from end *L W L* | 6 | " | | | |
| Mast from fore side stem | 1 | " | 11 | " | |
| Mast over all | 20 | " | | | |
| Diameter at deck | | | 4½ | " | |
| Boom over all | 18 | " | 6 | " | |
| Diameter in slings | | | 3½ | " | |
| Gaff over all | 8 | " | | | |
| Diameter of gaff | | | 2 | " | |
| Luff of sail | 14 | " | 6 | " | |
| Cruising sail | 250 | sq. ft. | | | |

The example in Plate V shows the lines of a boat hailing from Duxbury. It will be noticed that the model from which the lines were taken was built up of lifts parallel to the keel, and that true water-lines would show finer forward and fuller in the run than those dotted in the Half Breadth. The boat is in reality much shorter aft with more hollow to the entrance. The *L W L* has been drawn in heavy line in Sheer and Body and could be transferred to the

PLATE V

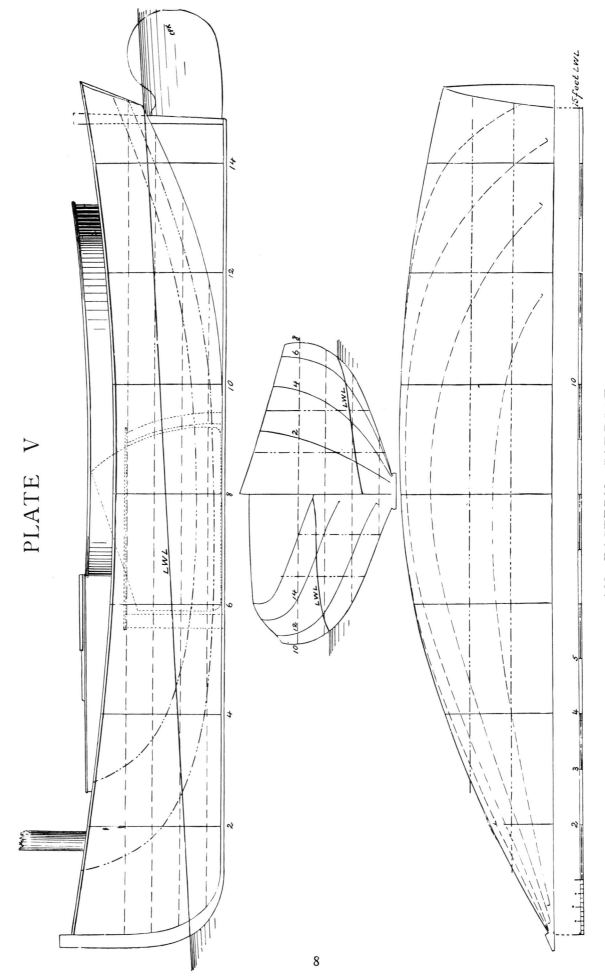

AN EASTERN CAT-BOAT

third plan by taking off half breadths from the Body. The bow and buttocks in the Sheer indicate long floor. The finish aft is a peculiar compromise between the square transom of the Newport cat and a regular yacht's overhang, in vogue to escape tax for over-all measurement. The board is small for cruising purposes, the draft helping out lateral resistance. Frames and lift lines are to moulded breadth only.

## RIGS OF EASTERN C. B. CATBOATS,

### Sailed with Fixed Ballast

| Water-line | Beam | Hoist | Foot | Head |
|---|---|---|---|---|
| 11 ft. 3 in. | 5 ft. 3 in. | 11 ft. 0 in. | 12 ft 0 in. | 6 ft. 6 in. |
| 12 " 7 " | 4 " 10 " | 14 " 4 " | 16 " | 6 " 7 " |
| 14 " 8 " | 6 " 10 " | 16 " | 18 " 7 " | 8 " 9 " |
| 15 " 1 " | 7 " 4 " | 16 " | 17 " 3 " | 6 " 10 " |
| 15 " 6 " | 7 " 6 " | 17 " | 19 " 6 " | 10 " |
| 16 " | 7 " 4 " | 16 " | 21 " | 9 " |
| 16 " 9 " | 7 " 6 " | 18 " | 22 " | 9 " |
| 17 " | 8 " | 20 " | 22 " | 12 " |
| 17 " 11 " | 8 " 1 " | 21 " | 20 " 9 " | 13 " 3 " |
| 18 " 4 " | 8 " | 21 " | 23 " | 13 " |
| 18 " 9 " | 8 " | 22 " | 23 " | 13 " |
| 18 " 11 " | 8 " 5 " | 20 " | 23 " | 14 " 6 " |
| 19 " 3 " | 9 " 1 " | 18 " 4 " | 24 " | 12 " 5 " |
| 19 " 9 " | 9 " 10 " | 22 " 6 " | 25 " 6 " | 15 " 6 " |
| 20 " 11 " | 10 " 3 " | 19 " | 32 " | 17 " |
| 21 " 4 " | 10 " 3 " | 22 " 6 " | 28 " 6 " | 15 " 6 " |
| 22 " 9 " | 10 " | 19 " 6 " | 30 " 6 " | 17 " |
| 24 " 4 " | 11 " 8 " | 22 " | 33 " | 18 " |
| 25 " 1 " | 11 " 6 " | 25 " | 32 " 6 " | 16 " |

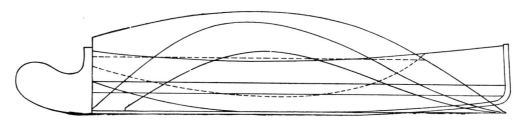

BOSTON RACING CAT EM–ELL–EYE, 19 FT.

# IV. THE CATBOAT COOT

## *PLATE VI*

### TWENTY FEET LONG ON WATER-LINE

THE COOT is a typical "South Bay" catboat of the better sort. She was built at Patchogue, on the south side of Long Island, N. Y., and serves as a representative of a numerous and popular class which resemble her more or less closely. She is able and fairly smart in smooth water, and will live through very coarse weather, though unsuited in model and rig for efficient service in rough water. She will not turn to windward against a sea like a heavier keel boat, but shows the lack of weatherly powers common to all beamy craft of light displacement. In squally winds considerable skill and alertness is required to prevent a capsize, unless the area of canvas be moderate. This fact is, or should be, enough to condemn the construction of the type wherever there is enough water for greater draft and depth of body. Outside weight has not at the time of writing been tried on small, shoal boats of such great beam, but experience on larger yachts seems to point to the practicability of increasing stability and safety by a metal keel of proper mould without loss in speed and without necessarily increasing the maximum draft. The centreboard would be retained and dropped through a slot in the exterior casting.

What is gained in the handiness of the cat rig for short river work is more than lost in the absence of adaptability of the sail plan to the various requirements of regular cruising. For anything more than "afternoon sailing" the COOT would be much better rigged as a sloop, even for singlehand work.

| | | | |
|---|---|---|---|
| Length over all | 23 | ft. | |
| Length on water-line | 20 | " | |
| Beam extreme | 9 | " | |
| Draft extreme | 2 | " | |
| Least freeboard | 1 | " 2 | in. |
| Length of centreboard | 7 | " 6 | " |
| Centreboard pin from end *L W L* | 7 | " | |
| Breadth of centreboard | 2 | " 10 | " |
| Draft with centreboard | 5 | " 6 | " |
| Centre of mast from end *L W L* | 2 | " 2 | " |
| Mast over all | 28 | " | |
| Mast, deck to halliard eye | 23 | " | |
| Diameter in partners | | 7 | " |
| Diameter at halliard eye | | 4½ | " |

PLATE VI

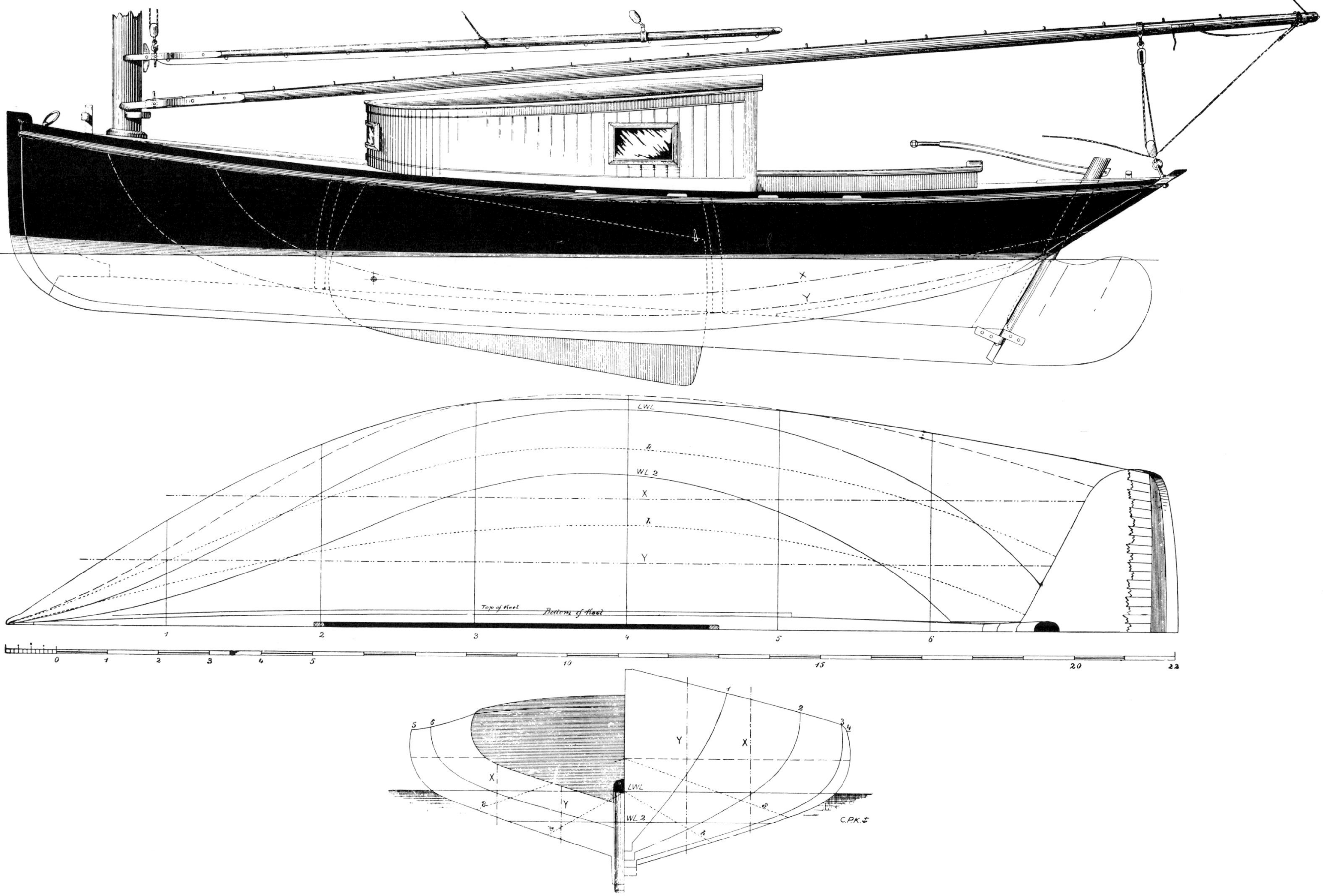

Top of Keel

Pattern of Keel

LWL

WL 2

X

h

Y

C.P.K.I

LWL

WL 2

X

Y

SOUTH BAY CAT-BOAT COOT

Boom over all................................ 24 ft.
Diameter.................................... 3¼ in.
Gaff over all............................... 12 " 6 "
Diameter................................... 2¼ "
Hoist of sail.............................. 20 "
Area of cruising sail...................... 390 sq. ft.
Displacement............................... 5,000 lbs.
Ballast.................................... 1,000 lbs.

Amount of ballast will vary with the cruising stuff aboard and trim, but the weight of hull is much greater in proportion to ballast than in boats of

THE COOT UNDER SAIL

the opposite type, as the COOT takes a great deal of wood in the topsides and deck, and must also be of heavier scantling than boats of the medium or narrow type. While the ballast of a well-built and able catboat will seldom exceed 25 or 30 per cent. of the displacement, some small cutters have as much as 55 per cent. in the shape of ballast. The COOT is exceptionally strong, and in cruising trim made a singlehand voyage of 1,500 miles in midwinter from New York to Beaufort, N. C., and return, with 700 lbs. of iron and 200 lbs. of stores and equipment, but would have been abler with 300 lbs. more.

The building specifications are as follows: Keel of oak, 8 × 8 in. amid-ships with taper to 6 in. at ends. Stem and post of oak, sided 6 in. Frames of oak and hackmatack, 2 in. sided and 1¾ in. moulded at heel, spaced about 16 in. between centres forward of trunk, the rest 14 in. From the trunk aft all are double. Clamps of yellow pine 6 × 1¼ in. Breasthook forward of oak 6 × 3 in. Mast chock under deck of oak 3 in. thick. Beams of oak 1¾ in. square. Cabin house and cockpit framing piece of pine 3 × 1½ in. Garboards and three sheer strakes of 1⅛ in. oak. Side planking of 1 in. cedar; counter of 1½ in. plank; decks 2 × 1 in. white pine; ceiling ¾ in. pine; cockpit coaming 8 × 1 in.; kingplank 2 in. thick. Siding of centreboard trunk 2 in., with headposts of oak 2 × 1¾ in. Waist ¾ in. thick and chafing ribband outside 1¼ × 1¾ in. Centreboard is 1¼ in. thick; rudderhead 3½ in. with blade 3 in. thick and tapering aft. to 1½ in. House beams are 2 × 1¼ in. and the supporting columns 1¾ in. square at base. Siding of house is of 1 in. matched stuff, and roof ¾ in. thick, covered with canvas painted. There are two hanging

knees a side, one at center of cabin house, the other at after bulkhead, under the deck half beams, to stiffen the structure. As built, the COOT was only supplied with a temporary or "sun cabin," consisting of the roof and canvas side curtains, which could be brailed up during pleasant weather.

To alter to a standing cabin was simple enough. Matched pine boarding 1 in. thick was set up all round, outside the coaming, on the bottom and the frame band on top, being held to them by galvanized boat nails and finished off with a panel strip along the deck and roof. This strip was ⅜ in. stuff, beaded and bent round the cabin in two lengths, meeting forward amidships. To facilitate bending to the quarter turns forward a few cross cuts were made half through the strips, and to meet the increased width at top a large chafing batten was substituted, after giving the roof an additional covering of canvas. To avoid soaking up a useless amount of paint, this canvas was dampened with water before applying the brush, thus enabling the paint to run freely. Without this precaution double the quantity would hardly have sufficed; as it was, it required nearly a pint and a half of Pierce's marine pigment for the COOT's top, applied in cold weather. One pint might serve on a warm day. The area covered is 38 sq. ft. Lights were cut in each side of the cabin for

8 × 12 in. double thick glass, which was held in place on the outside by rabbeted pieces forming a frame about the glass. A third light, 6 × 8, was cut through ahead, and also one 6 × 8 in each of the doors. The latter opened into the cockpit, being 22 in. wide and 40 in. high, each closing on a vertical centre jam 6 in. wide, run from roof to cockpit floor. There was also a sill 6 in. deep. The doors were not paneled, but of boards 1 in. thick, battened together on the interior. A bolt inside across the centre jam secured the port entrance, and a clasp, staple and padlock the starboard side, the fastenings being coach bolts with the nuts screwed up on the inside.

In place of the usual transom lockers each side, the cabin of the Coot was left bare and arranged for a long cruise in a special way. All the space forward of the cabin was lightly floored over, and a board 8 in. deep, run

Cabin Doors

across just forward of the centreboard, turned the whole bow into a shelf-like locker. In this were stowed a portmanteau containing long togs and fixings for shore use, and also a waterproof canvas bag holding spare underclothing and a suit of "store clothes." Besides the market basket, a roll of oilcloth and a rubber haversack with sea clothing were packed in the same place. Then there was still any quantity of room left. In the wings of the boat, that is along the sides under the deck, 30 in. out from the centreboard trunk, a board 10 in. deep was run fore and aft each side, turning the wings into long, gutter-like receptacles. On starboard side the forward portion was devoted to cooking utensils, the centre to canned goods and provision which would not spoil, while books and papers were packed aft, the division being made by wooden partitions. On port side the forward half was given up to charts, drawing and writing materials, and the after half reserved for shoes, oilskins and general use. In the stern a large locker was reached by a door in the cockpit. Here the boatswain had his department. Tools, paints, gear, swabs and kerosene, with scores of minor articles, found plenty of space and to spare. This left the wings in the cockpit empty, to be drawn upon as the future might advise. As it was the lockers were only half filled. Bread, spices and perishable goods were stored in two tin cake boxes, 18 × 12 in., kept on the cabin floor near the galley. For cooking there was an oil stove with cast-iron bottom and three wicks 5 in. broad. This was set upon a low shelf across the floor at forward end of the house. It is not advisable to have wicks broader than 3 ½ in. as they are under better control than long ones in turning up or down, and an even flame is assured. In place of trimming the broad wicks they should be allowed to burn to a crisp, which can then be scratched off even with the top of the burner. The slot for filling was covered with an iron flap, working horizontally on a pin, and as the oil sloshed about it would escape through the cracks. A thin piece of rubber introduced underneath the flap made a tight joint.

For a berth the space on port side between trunk and wing locker was utilized. The berth consisted of a platform 6 ft. 6 in. long and 28 in. wide,

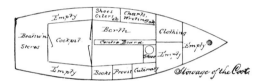

being hinged along the center to admit of folding. The platform rested on legs fitting the cabin floor, which brought it 12 in. above the floor at the trunk. Oilcloth was laid on top to preserve the mattress from damp air rising from the bilge.

Ground tackle consisted of a 25 lb. anchor with 20 fms. ¾ in. manilla line, and a Chester folding anchor of 30 lbs., with 30 fms. line.

As a guide to fitting out for long cruising the annexed table of the Coot's stores and equipments and their approximate cost will be found useful:

### 1. Shore Clothing and Toilet.

| | | | |
|---|---|---|---|
| Suit of clothes. | Razor. | Thin socks. | Tooth powder. |
| Pair of shoes. | Razor strop. | Underclothing. | Towels. |
| Felt hat. | Shaving brush. | White shirts. | Scissors. |
| Neckties. | Looking glass. | Collars. | Needles and silk. |
| Umbrella. | Blacking brush. | Cuffs. | Buttons, etc. |
| Gloves. | Hair brush. | Handkerchiefs. | Pins. |
| Soap. | Tooth brush. | Collar and cuff buttons. | Whisp broom. |
| Shaving soap. | | | |

### 2. Yachting Togs.

| | | | |
|---|---|---|---|
| Two pair trousers. | Leather slippers. | Southwester. | Woollen drawers. |
| Two Jerseys. | Leggings. | Rubber sea boots. | Woollen undershirts. |
| Two neckerchiefs. | Worsted cap. | Insoles for same. | Thick socks. |
| Buckskin gloves. | Cloth cap. | Rubber gauntlets. | Cheap handkerchiefs. |
| Pea jacket. | Old vest. | Suit overalls. | Jack-knife. |
| Canvas shoes. | Oilskin coat. | | |

### 3. Cooking Gear.

| | | | | | | | |
|---|---|---|---|---|---|---|---|
| Oil stove | $4 00 | Pan | $ 55 | Kettle | $1 00 | Water breaker | $1 00 |
| Oil | 50 | Coffee pot | 25 | Tin cans | 25 | Cake boxes | 1 20 |
| Wick | 30 | Ladle | 10 | Dipper | 10 | Knife tray | 20 |
| Stew pot | 1 00 | Griddle | 90 | Market basket | 1 00 | | |

# Small Yachts

### 4. CABIN TABLE.

| | | | | | | | |
|---|---|---|---|---|---|---|---|
| 3 cups | 20 | 3 tumblers | 15 | 3 forks | 60 | Can opener | 25 |
| 3 saucers | 20 | 1 pitcher | 15 | 3 tablespoons | 45 | Corkscrew | 25 |
| 3 plates | 25 | 3 knives | 60 | 3 teaspoons | 25 | Dish towels | 30 |
| 3 dishes | 30 | | | | | | |

### 5. CABIN FURNITURE.

| | | | | | | | |
|---|---|---|---|---|---|---|---|
| Cabin lamp | 3 50 | Blanket | 3 50 | Photos, pictures | — | Oilcloth | 1 50 |
| Clock | 2 50 | Brackets | 25 | Chintz curtains | 50 | Screw hooks | 35 |
| Mattress | 3 50 | Wire baskets | 50 | Camp chair | 1 25 | Picture tacks | 25 |
| Pillow | 75 | Mats | 2 00 | Footstool | 1 00 | Oilcloth covers | 1 00 |

### 6. NAVIGATION.

| | | | | | | | |
|---|---|---|---|---|---|---|---|
| Compass | 6 00 | Thermometer | 25 | Charts, each | 50 | Log book | 25 |
| Barometer | 6 00 | Binoculars | — | Frame | 50 | Flare up | 35 |
| Anchor light | 2 00 | Lead and line | 60 | Parallel ruler | 50 | Burgee | 2 00 |
| Lantern | 1 00 | Fog horn | 40 | Dividers | 50 | | |

### 7. BOATSWAIN'S STORES.

| | | | | | | | |
|---|---|---|---|---|---|---|---|
| Bucket | 25 | Anchor, 30 lbs | 1 80 | Manilla, 25 fms | 1 50 | Cotton | 10 |
| Scrub brush | 10 | Skiff | 15 00 | Manilla, 20 fms | 1 20 | Old canvas | — |
| Salt-water soap | 25 | Oars, 6ft | 1 10 | Spare rope | — | Leather | — |
| Swabs | 30 | Rowlocks | 45 | Ball marlin | 25 | Shackle, slush | — |
| Broom | 15 | Luff tackle | 1 50 | Palm and needles | 30 | Eyebolts | — |
| Anchor, 25 lbs | 1 50 | Sponge | 10 | Twine and wax | 25 | Thimbles, etc | — |

### 8. CARPENTER'S CHEST.

| | | | | | | | |
|---|---|---|---|---|---|---|---|
| Hatchet | 50 | Drawknife | 40 | Saw | 75 | Putty | — |
| Scraper | 30 | Screwdriver | 30 | Vise | 60 | Nails | — |
| Sandpaper | 10 | Chisel | 35 | Brace and bits | 1 15 | Screws | — |
| Rasp | 20 | Gimlets | 10 | Compass saw | 30 | Tacks | — |

### 9. MEDICINE CHEST.

| | | | |
|---|---|---|---|
| Quinine. | Opium pills. | Glycerine. | Liniment. |
| Cathartic pills. | Sticking plaster. | | |

### 10. SKETCHING AND WRITING MATERIALS.  11. LIBRARY.  12. STORES.  13. PHOTOGRAPHY.

As it is next to impossible to keep a small boat dry inside, such articles as would be damaged were enveloped in pliable oilcloth. The charts were cut up into sections and the one in use inserted for the time being in a common glass-covered picture frame. This enabled it to be set up in the cockpit and preserved it from the wet.

The construction of the COOT will be understood from Plate VII. The first frame is merely nailed to the keel at the heel. The second and third are boxed in with a tenon and connected by wood floors. The third frame is without a floor. All abaft that are double, those aft of the centreboard trunk having long and short-arm floors crossing the keel and deadwood upon which they are jogged down. In wake of the centreboard trunk the frames step into mortises, the tenons being secured by wedges driven in underneath, as shown in the section of the trunk. The more customary plan is explained by a separate sketch, one timber having a dovetail tenon and the other cut square to give proper bearing for a wedge driven on the side. The rabbet in the keel is peculiar, being cut from the bottom up to the seat for the garboards. The trunk has bedpieces bolted down to the keel, the side planking of the trunk being riveted at the ends to the head posts and the seams caulked. The bow framing of the boat is stiffened by a long breasthook, the arms of which reach aft to the fore end of the house. The eyes are filled in solid with a 3 in. oak chock underneath the deck and a 2 in. king plank is laid over the beams. This gives 5 in. of bearing to the mast wedges. The gear bitts are rove down through all and pinned underneath. The mast has an iron band and a stout tenon at the heel, and its rake is regulated by a wedge bearing against the butt end of the stem. The cabin and cockpit coaming is shaped in the usual way, by a stout fore-and-aft carlin and half-beams crossing from clamp to the carlin. All beams are cut down partially into the clamps, carlin and breasthook. The counter is closed in by nailing 1½ in. plank across, the upper piece being jogged out to receive the ends of the three oak sheer strakes. The rest of the side and bottom plank simply butts against the plank of the counter.

There is a light band around the masthead, another on the gaff, the mainsheet band on the boom, the traveller and rudder hangings. Beyond this the boat has no ironwork of any kind. Halliard blocks aloft hook to ½ in. eyebolts, passing through the mast with nuts on forward side. Topping-lift hooks to an eye in the masthead band. The manner in which the mainsheet band is wrought is shown in Plate VII. The traveller is ¾ in. round iron, ends rove through the counter and set up with nuts. Sail of 10 oz. duck, 7 in. bights. ⅜ in. roping. Blocks 3½ in. and gear ⅝ in. diameter. The pump is a log 3 in. square, bored out and set up against the centreboard trunk. The plunger is a round stick with leather cup attached to lower end. This cup collapses on the downward and expands on the upward stroke, making a simple and efficient pump, the bilge water emptying through a hole into the centreboard trunk. A leather funnel on top of pump log keeps the water from running over.

## DIMENSIONS OF SOME NEW JERSEY CATBOATS

FIFTEEN-FOOT BOAT —Beam, 5 ft.; depth amidships, 20 in.; draft, 16 in.; centreboard, 5 ft. long; racing sail, 14 ft. 6 in. hoist; 14 ft. head and 24 ft. 6 in. foot. For cruising the sail is about two-thirds of these dimensions.

TWENTY-FOOT BOAT —Length on deck, 24 ft.; water-line, 20 ft.; beam, 10 ft.; depth, 30 in.; draft, 18 to 24 in.; centreboard, 6½ ft. long; hoist of sail, 20 ft.; head, 14½ ft.; foot, 26 ft. This sail is for all-round purposes.

TWENTY-FIVE-FOOT BOAT —Length over all, 29 ft.; water-line, 25 ft.; beam,

PLATE VII

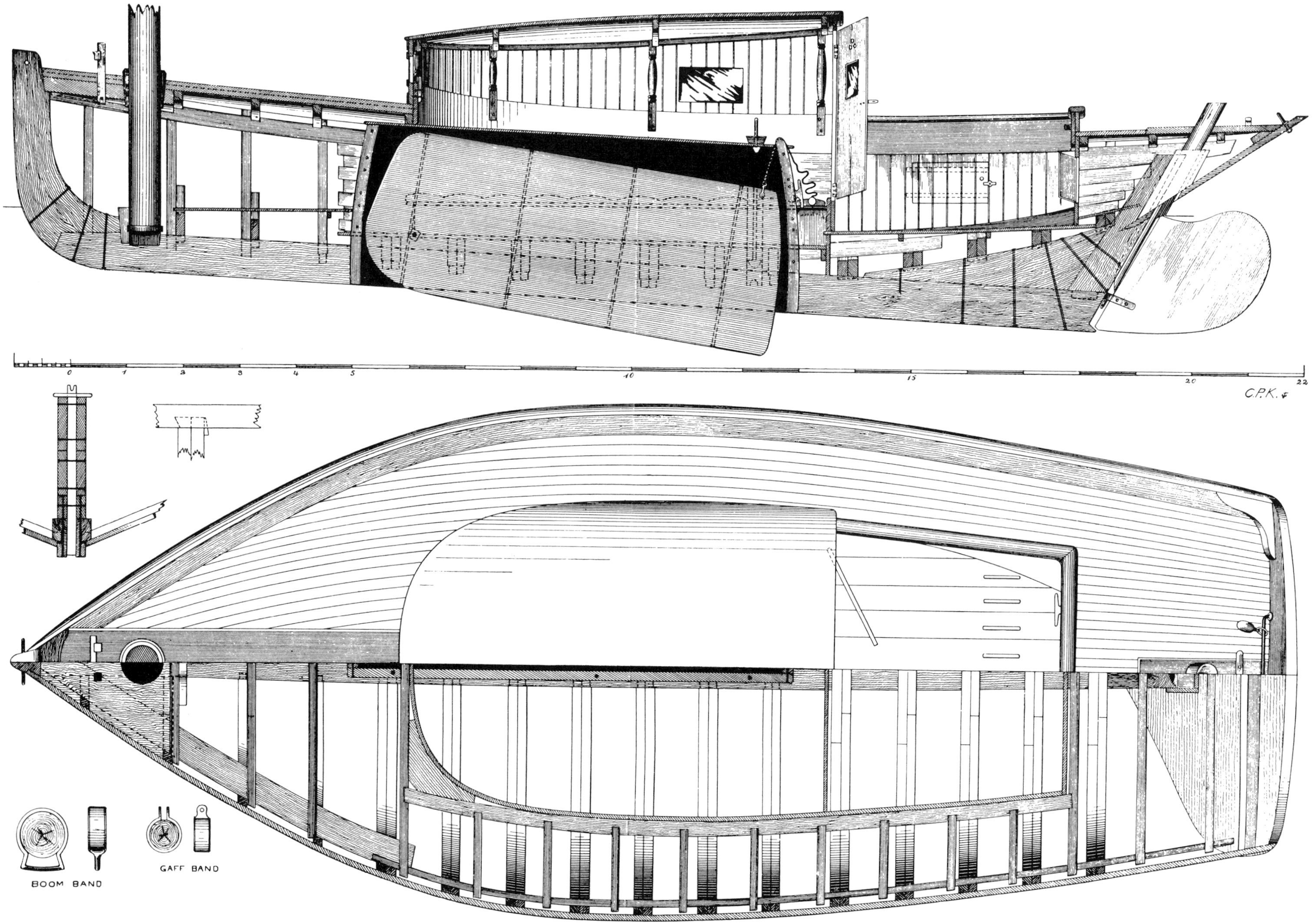
0
1
2
3
4
5
10
15
20
22
C.P.K.
BOOM BAND
GAFF BAND

COOT—INTERIOR AND CONSTRUCTION

11 ft.; depth, 32 in.; draft, 24 in.; centreboard, 8 ft. long. Sail made of 8 oz. duck; hoist, 24 ft.; foot, 31 ft.; head, 19½ ft.

THIRTY-FOOT BOAT —Length over all, 35 ft.; water-line, 30 ft.; beam, 13 ft.; depth, 40 in.; draft, 36 in.; centreboard, 9 ft. 6 in. long; sail has 27 ft. hoist, 19 ft. 6 in. head and 36 ft. foot.

This list is compiled from Tom's River and Shrewsbury River practice. Jersey catboats are of very light draft, have little deadrise, easy bilge and low side. They are for river service only.

## V. THE CHAS. COHILL

### *PLATE VIII*

#### SEVENTEEN FEET SIX INCHES LONG OVER ALL

THE racing catboats of the Delaware River differ from those of New York waters in being finer in the after end and sharper in the floor. The Cohill is one of the most successful of her class. She was built by Capt. Robert G. Wilkins, of Philadelphia, for Mr. Chas. Cohill. The measurement for racing was taken over all, hence the peculiar stem and transom by which extra length on water-line was obtained. The centreboard is well aft to counterbalance the enormous mainsail with its 27 ft. boom and 16 ft. gaff. A skag, extension deadwood and large rudder are supplied for the same purpose. The 32 ft. mast is stayed to a short boomkin over the stem, and has one shroud each side set up to an eyebolt in an outrigger. Sail area 95 yds. of canvas. Boats of this class are of course sailed with shifting ballast, and a numerous crew who lay out to windward by holding on to lines with toggles in the end. One man at the helm, another at the sheet and a third at the peak are required in a breeze to keep the boat from capsizing. A racing boat may be said to be constantly more or less on the verge of capsizing, and nothing but the incessant vigilance and dexterity of the crew will save her from going over. In case of an upset, a frequent occurrence, the sandbags slip off and the crew crawl over and cling to the bottom until rescued by the help which is usually near at hand on a crowded river. The Cohill carries eight men, each handling a 35 lb. sandbag.

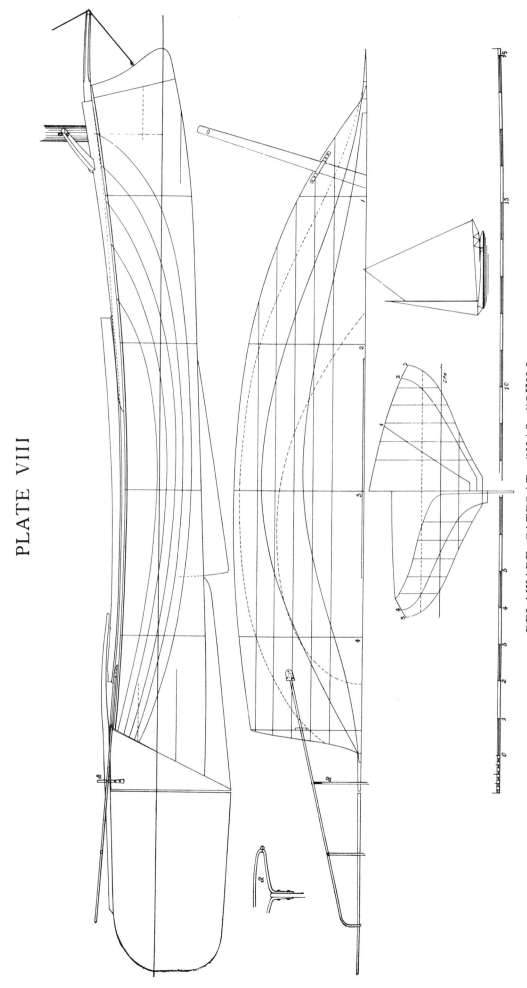

PLATE VIII

DELAWARE CATBOAT—CHAS. COHILL

# II

# KEEL CATBOATS

## I. THE CAPRICE

### *PLATE IX*

SEVENTEEN FEET SIX INCHES LOAD-LINE

BESIDES the quality of being uncapsizable, a boat's exemption from possible fatal disaster is associated with another important requisite. The family boat should be "unsinkable." It will be easily understood that, though impossible to capsize, a boat may nevertheless be knocked down by the wind, lee rail under, and, if fitted with large open cockpit and cabin doors, even coamings under. The water would pour into the lee bilge and prevent the boat righting in spite of good design in other respects. She would be liable to fill and sink. To obviate the danger of being swamped, it is necessary either to so arrange cockpit and cabin doors that no water shall pass below, or else to resort to air tanks inside the boat. The first precaution is by far the simplest, and covers the demands of safety, except in case of collision or staving a hole in the bottom. The cockpit must be kept shoal, the sill of the cabin doors about at deck height, and the companion hatch should be narrow. The shoal cockpit, say 9 in. deep with a washstreak of 6 in., surmounted by a broad cap 5 in. wide, will be found a decided improvement upon deep wells needing seats around the sides. The rail serves as a seat, or, when protection is needed, the floor itself, either for sitting or reclining, with the rail as a support to the back or shoulders.

The effort of climbing out of a deep cockpit on deck to tend gear, etc., is thereby done away with. The high cabin sill involves merely lifting the feet over when going below. Narrowing the companion cuts off the light and ventilation below in theory more than in practice. If it does curtail those essentials, other means can easily be drawn upon. Look upon wide barn doors leading to the cabin as a direct challenge to Providence, and in defiance of common sense, all for the sake of gratifying sensual luxury incompatible with the primary

PLATE IX

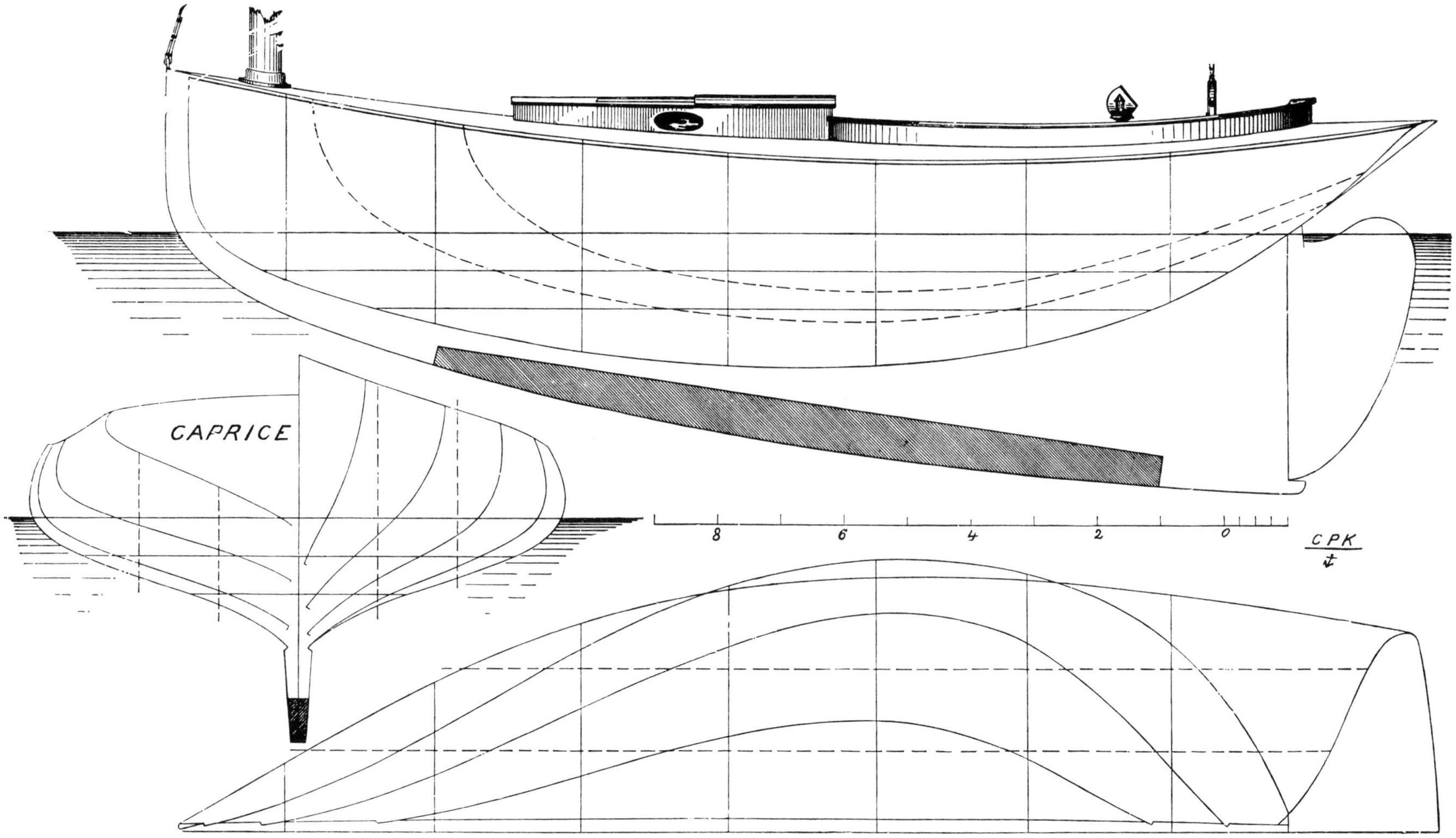

$\dfrac{CPK}{\dot{\iota}}$

CAPRICE

KEEL CAT-BOAT CAPRICE

objects of the sport. Precautions of this kind have the advantage over inside tanks, inasmuch as stowage is not interfered with in the least, but rather increased.

If it be deemed desirable to provide fully against sinking under any circumstances, the only effectual provision is to lock up enough air to float the displacement with crew and stores on board. One way is to bulkhead off the required space in the bow, the run, and at the sides, so as to interfere the least with cabin and lockers. Bulkheads should be built of stout matched boards, and stiffened with cross-braces of scantling. When constructed with reasonable care they can be relied upon in the hour of extremity. Another plan, where small spaces are to be utilized here and there in the boat, is to stow away sealed powder cans, or fit small zinc cases of the required shape. Copper can be trusted more than zinc, tin or sheet-iron, and all should be under occasional inspection. Theoretically, the space thus to be inclosed is ascertained from these figures: One cubic foot of air floated by salt water will support 64 pounds, and 35 cubic feet will support 1 long ton. If 3 long tons represent the displacement of a boat with a crew and stores, 105 cubic feet of air would be required to float the mass. But the wooden sides and fittings of the yacht will in themselves float quite a fraction of the weight, and the sheer or weather bilge never quite fill, the air confined in such portions of the boat contributing to buoyancy when swamped. Hence a material reduction in the sealed space is permissible, the exact amount to be determined in each individual case. In boats of light displacement in proportion to wood and fittings, 50 per cent., or even less may be enough, and in boats heavily ballasted 60 to 70 per cent. In boats of extremely light displacement and rig, such as the sharpie, the hull will float itself and ballast without artificial assistance. Such boats are only exceptional, and there are few, if any, regular yachts, which, in racing trim, would not sink upon being filled. In general, those least liable to sink when swamped, are, on the other hand, all the more easily capsized for the want of enough weight low down. Unless the buoyancy of the hull is pretty accurately known, a margin on the safe side should be preserved, as boats supposed to be perfectly safe would naturally be put to harder service and take greater risks than others whose treachery is continually uppermost in the skipper's mind.

Under-rigging of course renders disaster less immediate, but few care to stultify the sailing qualities of their boats, and a short rig, moreover, has its drawbacks from a sailing standpoint as well.

As coming very near to the foregoing in point of provisions for safety, the CAPRICE is an interesting study.

The deep drag at the heel of the CAPRICE is a valuable provision where draft need not be stinted. It prevents the excessive weather helm experienced in catboats generally for the lack of head sail, and it also renders running before a sea safe and comparatively pleasant work, while in heavy weather the draft adds to the boat's ability and close-winded qualities. The CAPRICE was built by Wood Brothers, of East Boston, in 1881, for service between Boston and Marblehead and in adjacent waters, and a trial of two years has proven the principles of her construction perfectly adapted to the wants of her owner.

| | |
|---|---|
| Length over all | 20 ft. |
| Length on load-line | 17 " 6 in. |
| Greatest beam moulded | 8 " 5 " |
| Depth planksheer to rabbet on M. S. | 3 " 2 " |
| Greatest draft | 4 " |
| Least freeboard | 13 " |
| Area immersed M. S. with keel | 9.63 sq. ft. |
| Area load-line | 91.50 " " |
| Area longitudinal section, no rudder | 49.00 " " |
| Ratio of same to area M. S. | 5.1 |
| Displacement | 5,750 lbs. |
| Displacement per inch at load-line | 488 " |
| Ballast, inside lead | 1,000 " |
| Ballast, iron on keel | 856 " |
| Ratio of ballast to displacement | 32 per cent |
| M. S. from forward end of *L W L* | 11 ft. |
| Centre lateral resistance from do | 11 " |
| Centre of effort of sail from do | 10 " 4 in. |
| Centre of buoyancy from do | 10 " 9 " |
| Sail area | 415 sq. ft. |
| Proportion to square of load-line | 136 per cent |
| Area of wetted surface, no rudder | 154 sq. ft. |
| Sail per square foot of wetted surface | 2.63 " " |
| Centre of mast from stem | 18 in. |
| Mast, deck to hounds | 24 ft. |
| Diameter at deck | 6½ in. |
| Diameter at hounds | 5 in. |
| Main boom over all | 23 ft. |
| Diameter in slings | 4 in. |
| Diameter at end | 2½ in. |
| Gaff over all | 15 ft. |
| Diameter, oval section | 3½ x 2¼ in. |
| Hoist of mainsail | 20 ft. |
| Foot of do | 22 " |
| Head of do | 14 " |
| Leech of do | 31 " |

The Sail Plan of CAPRICE will be found on Plate X.

# PLATE X

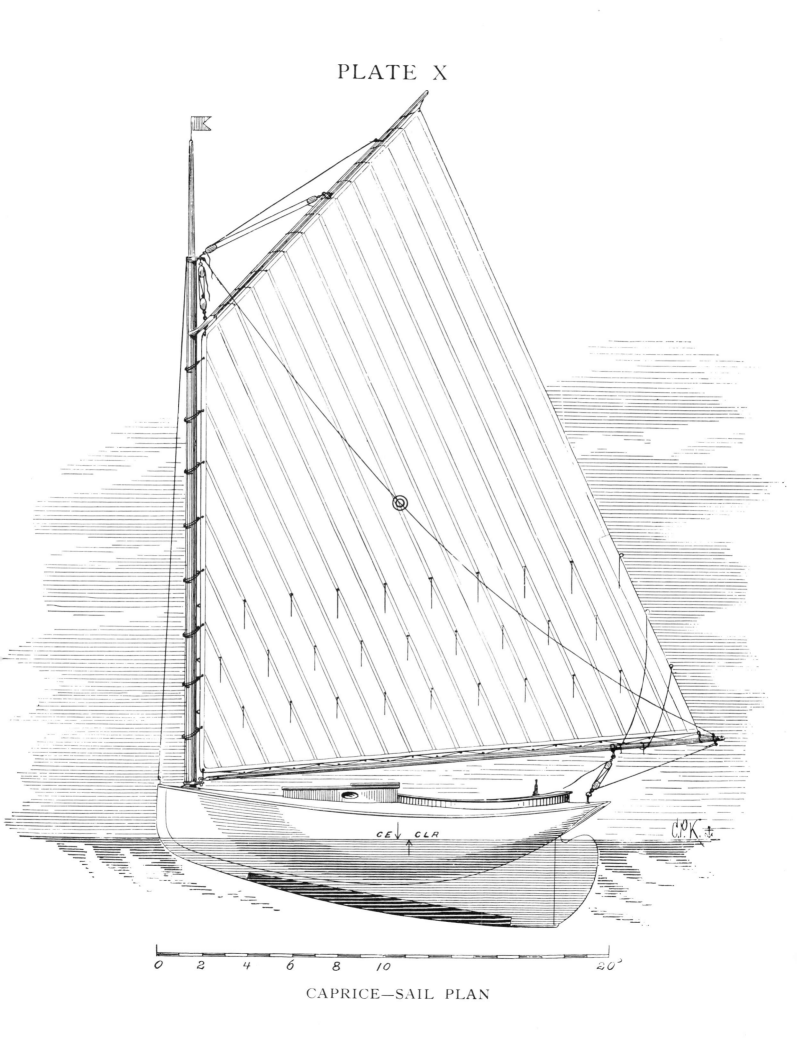

CAPRICE—SAIL PLAN

The building specifications of the CAPRICE are as follows: Keel, best white oak, 5 in. thick, tapering to 3 in. forward and 4 in. aft. Stem 3 in. sided and sternpost 4 in. Floor timbers are 2½ in. sided, 2¾ in. moulded at keel and 2¼ in. at head. Frames 2¾ in. at heel and 1¾ in. at head, spaced 14 in. Planking of hard pine 1 in. thick without butts; deck plank 2 x 1¼ in., sprung to sheer. The outside iron keel weighs 856 lbs. and is 4 in. wide on top, tapering to 2 in. at fore end and 2½ in. aft. It is bolted up with ¾ galvanized bolts with large nuts on top of keel and floor timbers. The floor timbers are bolted with ⅝ galvanized iron and the planks fastened with 2½ nails plugged.

## II. THE DODGE No. 2

### *PLATE XI*

ELEVEN FEET ELEVEN INCHES LOAD-LINE

THE first DODGE was built in England as a tender to a schooner yacht, and in test of certain convictions. She was hoisted to davits, and to that end had for ballast a number of shot bags which could be passed up beforehand. The design exhibits many novelties in form, build and rig. It would be advisable to fit the cockpit with hatches, on the canoe plan, to prevent shipping seas from a passing steamer's swell or in choppy water. The boat is, however, very buoyant and lifts quickly, having a fine after-body and good free-board. She was designed by Mr. John Harvey, M. I. N. A., and shows the fairness for which all his productions are noted; also many of the ideas prevalent in other yachts from the same source. The plans are to outside of all. The hull has the usual keel, stem, apron, post and deadwood knee with horns for the counter. The keel is crossed by wooden floor knees, as shown in the Sheer. The sides are of two thin cedar skins, the outer one overlapping the seams of the inner, both being riveted together. No frames are required, the temporary moulds being removed before decking in.

The gear leads to the cockpit. It comprises halliard and peak in one, rove as in Plate XII, the main sheet, reef tackle fall and boom tricing line.

The horns on the boom extend some distance forward the mast. If a tripping line is taken from the fore end of these horns, passed through a block slung at the hounds of the rigging, and from thence through a leading block or bullseye at the deck on one side of the mast, and from there made fast to a cleat on the side of the boom, the tripping line acts as a purchase to keep the

PLATE XI

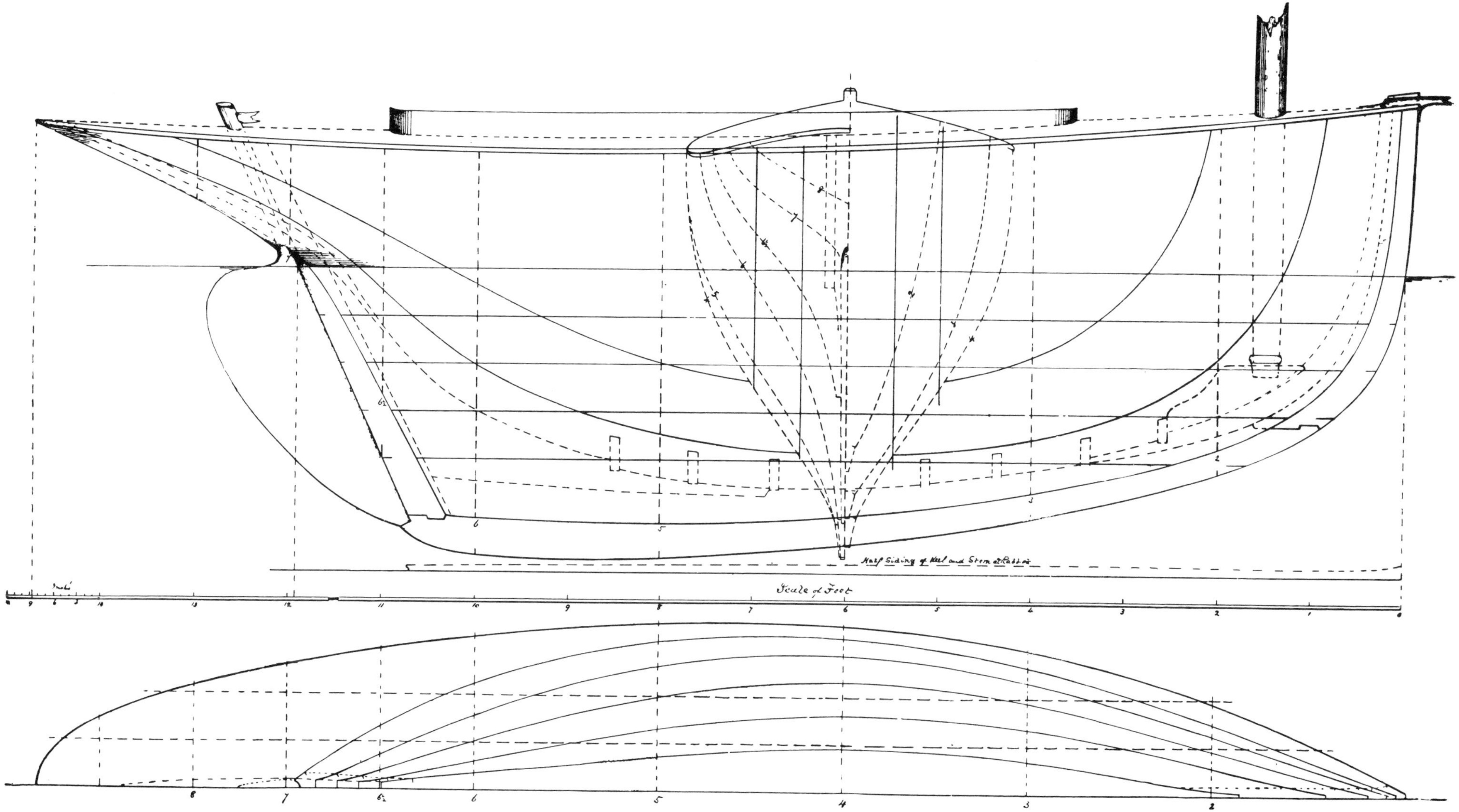

KEEL CAT-BOAT DODGE

Scale of Feet

PLATE XII

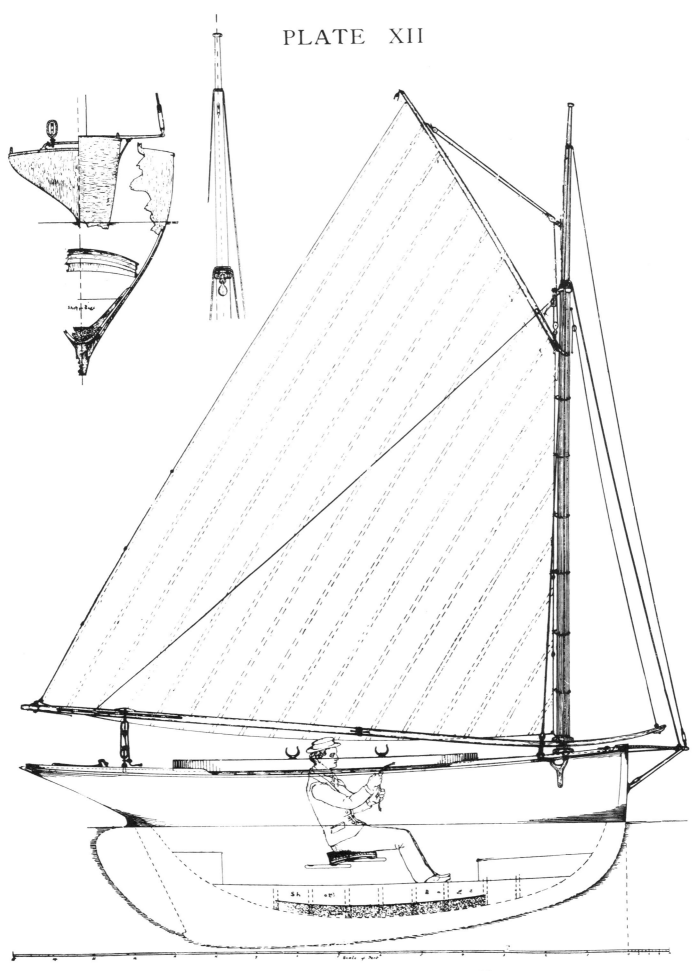

CAT-BOAT DODGE—SAIL PLAN

boom down at the outer end when the main sheet is slacked for the purpose of running before the wind.

This tripping line is always useful. Going to windward it keeps the sail flat and steady at its work, and when running before the wind it keeps the boom down in its place, so that the whole spread of canvas is exposed to the wind. The time, however, when the tricing line is of the greatest service is when little craft are gibed when blowing hard in a seaway. "Goosewinging" is an ugly predicament which the line renders impossible.

For steering, tiller ropes lead from a yoke forward to a footboard, canoe fashion, leaving the crew with both hands free. An oscillating seat low down accommodates the skipper, and this can be slid fore-and-aft to trim with a passenger on board.

DODGE No. 2 has half her ballast in small lumps of cast lead, the rest in shot bags, which are not for shifting purposes, however. The total weight of ballast is a little more than half a ton. The mast is stayed to a boomkin forward and to outriggers abreast, which, with details of build, are made clear by the plates.

It should be added that the first DODGE in England was most severely tried in Lake Windemere racing and in rough work about the coast, and that she demonstrated herself a boat of remarkable hard weather qualities, small and inconsequential as she appears. For light winds, a yard topsail is hoisted to a sheave under the pole shoulder.

| | | |
|---|---|---|
| Length over all | 14 ft. 9 in. | |
| Length on water-line | 11 " 11 " | |
| Greatest beam | 3 " 6 " | |
| Beam at water-line | 3 " 4 " | |
| Extreme draft | 3 " | |
| Depth at side, No. 5 | 3 " 11 " | |
| Least freeboard | 1 " 3 " | |
| Displacement | 1¼ ton | |
| Ballast inside | ½ " | |
| Mast from stem | 1 ft. 7 in. | |
| Mast, deck to hounds | 11 " 8 " | |
| Mast, deck to shoulder | 15 " 2 " | |
| Diameter at deck | 4 " | |
| Boom over all | 12 " 10 " | |
| Diameter in slings | 2¾ " | |
| Gaff over all | 7 " 4 " | |
| Diameter of gaff | 1¾ " | |
| Luff of sail | 9 " 8 " | |
| Leech of sail | 17 " 6 " | |
| Area of sail | 115 sq. ft. | |
| Topsail yard | 13 ft. 6 " | |

## RIGS OF KEEL CATBOATS

| Water-line | Beam | Hoist | Foot | Head |
|---|---|---|---|---|
| 10 ft. 8 in. | 4 ft. 10 in. | 11 ft. 0 in. | 12 ft. 0 in. | 6 ft. 0 in. |
| 11 " 11 " | 3 " 6 " | 9 " 8 " | 12 " 6 " | 7 " 2 " |
| 17 " 6 " | 8 " 7 " | 20 " | 22 " | 14 " |
| 18 " 6 " | 8 " 6 " | 20 " 8 " | 22 " 8 " | 12 " 4 " |
| 19 " 9 " | 8 " 7 " | 21 " | 27 " 6 " | 14 " 6 " |
| 20 " 5 " | 8 " 7 " | 21 " 6 " | 25 " 9 " | 12 " 6 " |
| 21 " | 9 " | 21 " | 27 " | 16 " |

# III

# LIGHT DRAFT
# CENTREBOARD SLOOPS

## 1. THE CRUISER

### PLATE XIII

#### TWENTY FEET EIGHT INCHES LONG ON LOAD-LINE

SHIFTING ballast has been the prime mover in the production of broad, shoal boats. The greater leverage of ballast piled up to windward than could be got from restricted depth, enables the enormous spread of canvas common in the type of "open jib and mainsails," of which the CRUISER is an exemplification. All desiderata are subordinated in her to the one requisite of speed upon length, so long as dexterity can be depended upon to keep the contrivance on its legs. Boats of this kind are not specially speedy in their form when sailed with fixed ballast and limited crew, as the area of canvas has to be cut down very materially. To their extravagant rigs, and the desperate chances taken when driving in a match, their remarkable velocity in smooth water is to be ascribed. In rough water the danger of spilling or washing sand-bags over the side is a contingency still further imperilling safety, but the boats act as preventives in themselves, as they pound and splutter in an exasperating way, rendering them so unfit for hard service that they are scarcely ever put to severe test. Their sphere of usefulness is confined to short bursts in sheltered surroundings, and excellence is attended with great first cost and the drawback of shipping large crews. But their undoubted superiority in speed for racing, under comparison by length, over all other types in smooth water, earns for them consideration where nothing else is sought.

The CRUISER, although built in 1868 by C. A. Willis, of Port Washington, Long Island, is still a crack in her class, and in the hands of Mr. A. B. Alley,

31

PLATE XIII

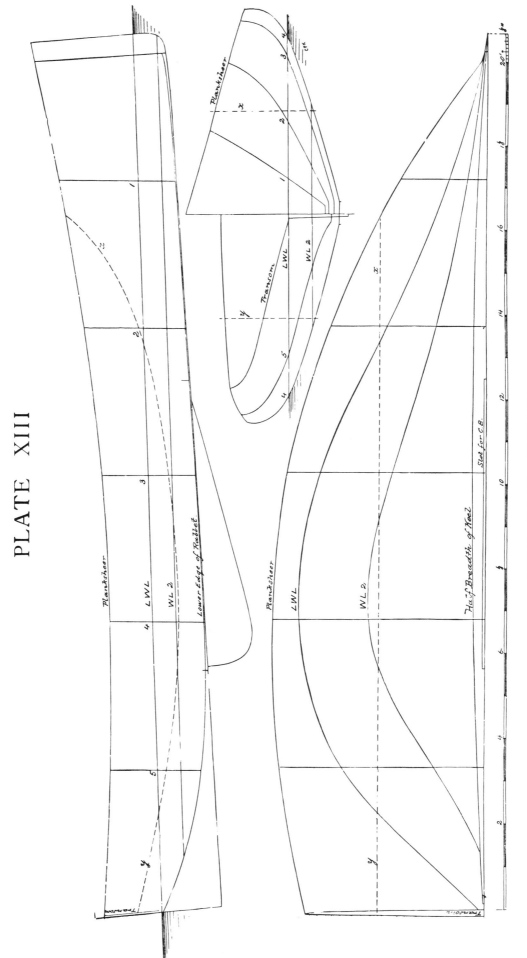

OPEN BOAT CRUISER

was shipped to Boston in 1884, where she disposed of the fuller bodied Eastern boats, which were of heavier build with something sacrificed to comfortable cruising adaptability. The lines in Plate XIII. are to outside of plank.

| | | | |
|---|---|---|---|
| Length over all | 20 | ft. | 8 in. |
| Length on water-line | 20 | " | 8 " |
| Beam extreme | 9 | " | 8 " |
| Beam on water-line | 8 | " | 6 " |
| Breadth across transom | 8 | " | 4 " |
| Depth at side. No. 4 | 2 | " | 2 " |
| Least freeboard | 1 | " | |
| Sheer forward | 1 | " | 4 " |
| Sheer aft | | | 5 " |
| Draft without board | 1 | " | 4 " |
| Draft with board | 6 | " | |
| Length of board | 6 | " | 8 " |
| Pin from stem | 8 | " | 6 " |
| Breadth across after end | 3 | " | 6 " |
| Area racing mainsail | 527 | sq. | ft. |
| Area racing jib | 272 | " | " |

The large rig is seen on Plate XIV, which will also explain the lead of the gear and construction of outrigger over the stern. With the big sails 25 sandbags of 50 lbs. each are stacked in the weather gangway outside the cockpit and shifted across with all possible agility upon going in stays. The mast can be shifted forward to a step 20 in. from the stem and the jib dispensed with, the CRUISER being transformed into cat rig. Most of her racing as a sloop is done under a smaller mainsail shown by the dotted lines in Plate XIV, when she sails with fixed bottom ballast and a crew of five, the latter planting themselves on the weather rail. In light air matches the ballast is sent ashore with all movables, such as the bottom boards, the crew being sufficient weight for so small a boat. The mast is 6½ in. at deck, the diameter being held up to the hounds, above which the spar tapers to 3 in. at peak strap. In Plate XIV the Centre of Effort has been located from the areas of mainsail and jib upon the principle of combining two bodies, explained with Fig. 34 in the chapter on Computations. This centre is 19 in. forward of the Centre of Lateral Resistance, an extraordinary balance necessary to meet the change of form upon heeling. As a cat, the centre of sails is 7 in. forward. CRUISER works well with two reefs down in mainsail and full jib, two reefs and no jib, or with full mainsail and reefed jib, proving the great latitude permissible in the practical balance of shoal, easy-bilged boats, carrying considerable weather helm consequent upon form, pretty much regardless of theoretical balance of sail.

Two iron travelers span the tiller across the quarters. To the top of the forward one a cleat is attached, about which a turn may be caught with the mainsheet. On the wind, the sheet is jumped into a snatch block on the boom and the fall diligently attended by hand as the boat needs to " beg " or luff out to puffs to prevent a capsize.

PLATE XIV

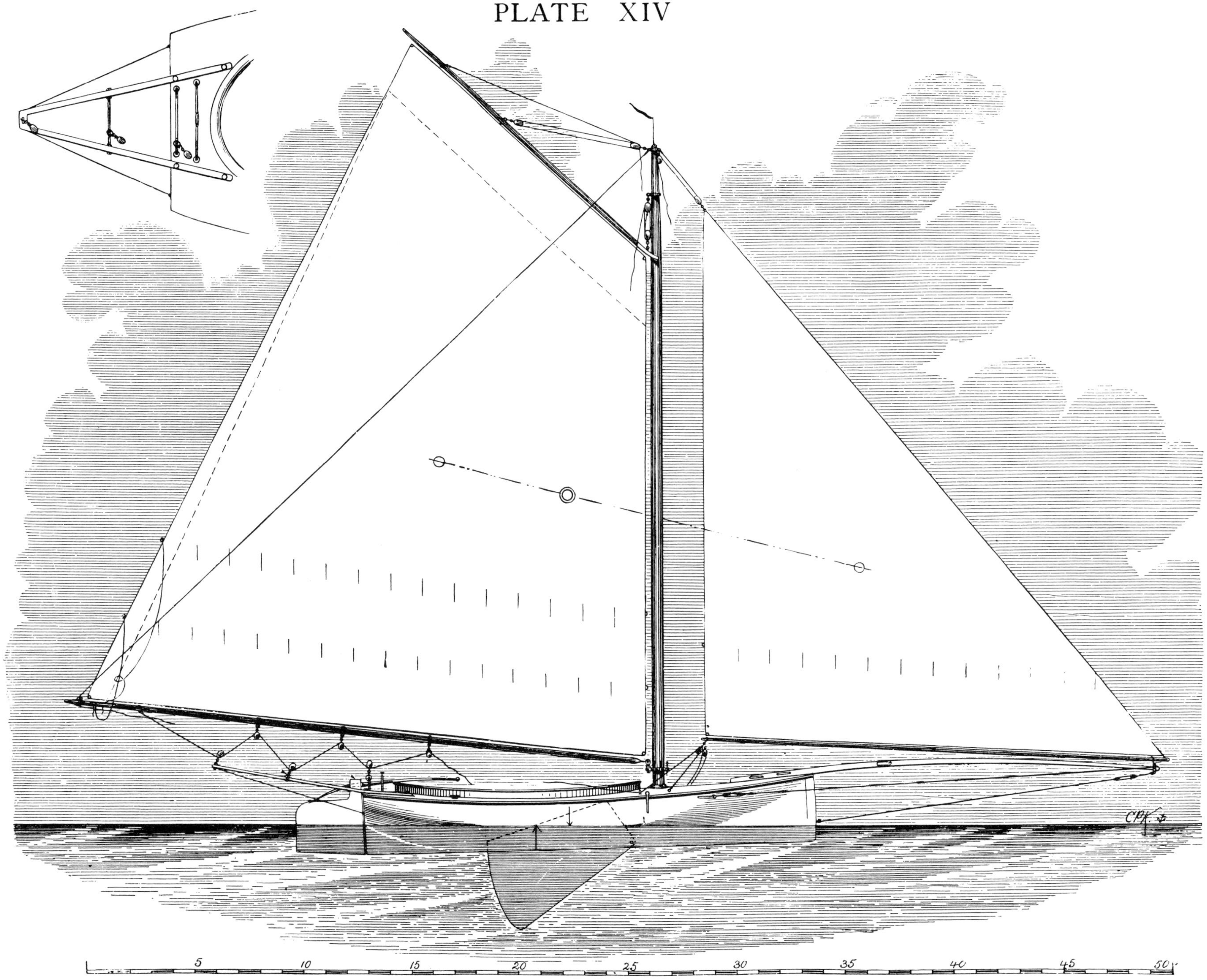

THE CRUISER—SAIL PLAN

The jib is set on its own luff, there being no headstay.    Rigging is set up by turnbuckles, which facilitates shifting to cat.    The tiller is rove through the rudder-head and clutches the blade to ease the torsion.

### SPARS AND SHORT RIG

| | | | | |
|---|---|---|---|---|
| Mast from end *L W L* | 7 | ft. | 4 | in. |
| Mast, heel to truck | 28 | " | 8 | " |
| Mast, deck to hounds | 24 | " | 3 | " |
| Diameter at deck | | | 6 | " |
| Boom over all | 25 | " | | |
| Diameter in slings | | | 4½ | " |
| Gaff over all | 15 | " | | |
| Diameter of gaff | | | 2¾ | " |
| Bowsprit outboard | 14 | " | 6 | " |
| Jibboom | 21 | " | 6 | " |
| Hoist of mainsail | 19 | " | 6 | " |
| Jib on luff | 32 | " | | |
| Jib on leech | 22 | " | 6 | " |

### SPARS AND LARGE RIG

| | | | | |
|---|---|---|---|---|
| Mast from end, *L W L* | 7 | ft. | 4 | in. |
| Mast, heel to truck | 31 | " | | |
| Mast, deck to hounds | 26 | " | 8 | " |
| Diameter at deck | | | 6½ | " |
| Boom, over all | 27 | " | | |
| Diameter in slings | | | 4¾ | " |
| Gaff over all | 15 | " | | |
| Diameter of gaff | | | 2¾ | " |
| Bowsprit outboard | 16 | " | | |
| Jibboom | 21 | " | 6 | " |
| Hoist of mainsail | 22 | " | 6 | " |
| Jib on luff | 32 | " | | |
| Jib on leech | 23 | " | 6 | " |

## II.  THE  TRIDENT

### *PLATE XV*

#### TWENTY-ONE FEET EIGHT INCHES LONG ON LOAD-LINE

AN abler and roomier style of open boat, sailed with fixed ballast, is produced in Plate XV, from a working drawing by Mr. David Kirby, of Rye, N. Y. The TRIDENT was built by him in 1884 for Mr. Geo. A. Adee, on original ideas which have ruled all the output of the Rye yard in progressive improvement, and which met with signal success in many "sandbaggers" as well as in

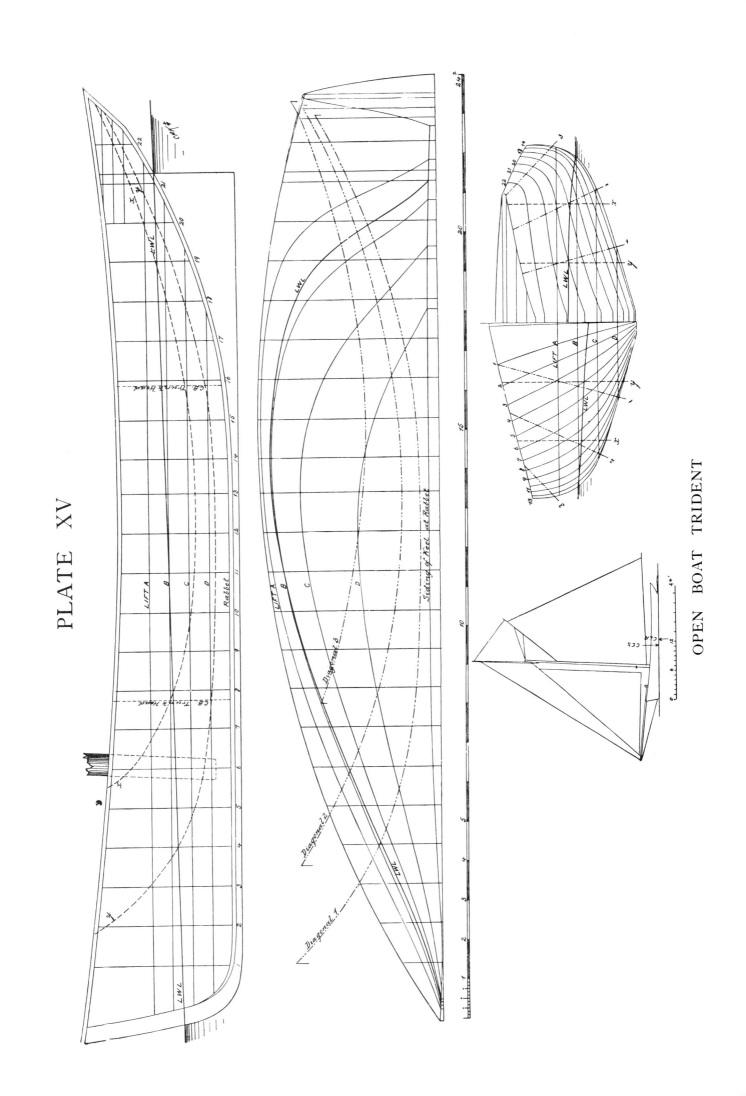

PLATE XV

OPEN BOAT TRIDENT

# *Light Draft Centreboard Sloops*

the large sloops, ARROW, ADDIE V. and others. The builder has decided preference for all the weight a boat's form will stand, and opens with very long entrance, clearing from below on a raking midship section.

The TRIDENT has these features to a marked degree and is reported an able and weatherly boat, sufficiently light in draft and flat in floor to enter shoal creeks and anchorages, and lie on the mud at low water.

| | | | | | |
|---|---|---|---|---|---|
| Length over all | 24 | ft. | | | |
| Length on water-line | 21 | " | 8 | in. | |
| Beam, moulded | 9 | " | 1 | " | |
| Beam at water-line | 8 | " | 6 | " | |
| Breadth across counter | 6 | " | 6 | " | |
| Depth at side, No. 14 | 2 | " | 10 | " | |
| Least freeboard | 1 | " | 3 | " | |
| Draft without board | 2 | " | | | |
| Draft with board | 6 | " | | | |
| Length of board | 7 | " | | | |
| Pin from stem | 9 | " | | | |
| Sheer forward | 1 | " | 5 | " | |
| Sheer aft | | | 6 | " | |
| Mast from end *L W L* | 6 | " | 8 | " | |
| Rake to one foot | | | ¾ | " | |
| Mast, deck to hounds | 23 | " | | | |
| Diameter at deck | | | 6 | " | |
| Mast head | 2 | " | 2 | " | |
| Topmast above cap | 11 | " | | | |
| Boom over all | 23 | " | | | |
| Gaff over all | 14 | " | | | |
| Bowsprit stem to stay | 11 | " | 6 | " | |
| Hoist of mainsail | 18 | " | | | |
| Leech of mainsail | 30 | " | | | |
| Luff of jib | 26 | " | | | |
| Foot of jib | 17 | " | | | |
| Area mainsail | 375 | sq. ft. | | | |
| Area jib | 170 | " " | | | |

TRIDENT's frame is 1½ in. sided, and 2¼ in. moulded at heel, and 1¾ in. at head; double from keel to turn of bilge. Space, 12 in. between centres. Deck framing, 1¼ in. sided; 2 in. moulded. The centreboard is 4 ft. 1 in. deep at fore end, and 4 ft. 7 in. across after end. Ballast, 2,240 lbs. iron cast to fit the floor.

## III. THE SCHEMER

*PLATE I*

THIRTY-SIX FEET TEN INCHES LONG ON LOAD-LINE.

THE SCHEMER is surpassed in speed by very few sloops of her water-line length. As a racing boat, she has a brilliant record. In the fall of 1881 she was matched against the imported Scotch cutter MADGE (Plate LXXI), and was defeated, though she would have reduced the margin of the cutter's victory considerably but for want of the most perfect equipment. She was built in 1871 by J. P. Wilkins, Jersey City, for Mr. J. C. Hall, of Brooklyn, and slightly altered in 1873. Her peculiarities are a long, hollow floor, quick bilge, the turn being below water, a plumb side, and a flat along the midships. Afloat she is a sightly vessel. Her rig is by John M. Sawyer, of New York.

| | | | | |
|---|---|---|---|---|
| Length over all | 39 | ft. | 8 | in. |
| Length on water-line | 36 | " | 10 | " |
| Greatest beam | 14 | " | | |
| Beam at water-line | 13 | " | 8 | " |
| Breadth across transom | 10 | " | | |
| Height at side, No. 4 | 4 | " | 2 | " |
| Least freeboard | 1 | " | 8 | " |
| Sheer forward | 2 | " | | |
| Sheer aft | | | 10 | " |
| Draft without board | 3 | " | | |
| Draft with board | 9 | " | | |
| Length of board | 10 | " | 9 | " |
| Pin from stem | 13 | " | | |
| Ballast | 4.5 | tons | | |
| Mast from stem | 11 | ft. | | |
| Mast to jibstay | 30 | " | 4 | in. |
| Mast, deck to hounds | 36 | " | | |
| Mast head | 4 | " | 6 | " |
| Topmast cap to shoulder | 18 | " | 6 | " |
| Boom over all | 43 | " | | |
| Gaff over all | 23 | " | | |
| Mainsail, hoist | 28 | " | 6 | " |
| Mainsail, foot | 41 | " | | |
| Mainsail, head | 21 | " | 6 | " |
| Mainsail, leech | 49 | " | | |
| Mainsail, clew to knock | 48 | " | 6 | " |
| Mainsail, tack to head | 47 | " | | |
| Jib on luff | 41 | " | | |
| Jib on foot | 30 | " | 6 | " |
| Jib on leech | 30 | " | | |
| Hank topsail on luff | 17 | " | | |
| Hank topsail on leech | 17 | " | | |
| Topmast stay | 63 | " | | |

# PLATE I

## SHEER PLAN

## HALF-BREADTH PLAN

## BODY PLAN

THE
SLOOP YACHT
# SCHEMER

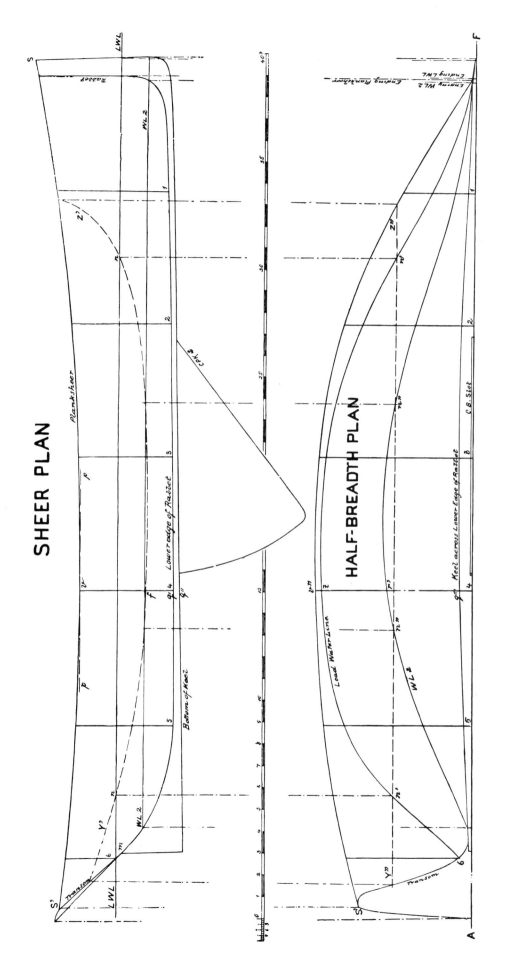
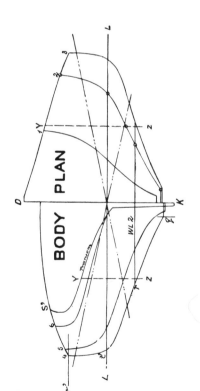

## IV. A SKIPJACK

*PLATE XVI*

TWENTY-SIX FEET SIX INCHES LONG ON LOAD-LINE

THE "skipjack" is in the main a light-draft sloop, having a sharp knuckle to the bilge at which the floor heads and top timbers meet without intervention of futtocks. In performance she assimilates the sloop, but is given more to pounding. Some skipjacks have shown a very fair turn of speed. In build they are a trifle cheaper if closed in with wide plank, but correspondingly inferior in point of duration. Plate **XVI** is from a boat by Mr. Thomas Clapham, Roslyn, Long Island. She has neither external keel nor skag, deadwood, aft. A false bow is fastened up below the hull proper for 7 ft. from the stem. This consists of a solid piece of timber, hewed to a sharp bevel, and is intended to lessen the pounding. The rudder is of the balance sharpie pattern. The rig is a yawl, peculiar in some details, which the plate will explain.

| | | | | |
|---|---|---|---|---|
| Length over all | 30 | ft. | | |
| Length on water-line | 26 | " | 6 | in. |
| Beam extreme | 13 | " | | |
| Beam on water-line | 10 | " | 4 | " |
| Breadth across counter | 8 | " | 3 | " |
| Draft without board | 1 | " | 3 | " |
| Draft with board | 6 | " | | |
| Depth at side, No. 12 | 3 | " | | |
| Least freeboard | 1 | " | 5 | " |
| Sheer forward | 1 | " | 4 | " |
| Sheer aft | | | 3 | " |
| Length of board | 9 | " | | |
| Pin from stem | 9 | " | 6 | " |
| Mast, deck to hounds | 21 | " | | |
| Mast, deck to truck | 30 | " | | |
| Boom over all | 19 | " | | |
| Gaff over all | 12 | " | | |
| Bowsprit out-board | 9 | " | 4 | " |
| Jibboom | 15 | " | 4 | " |
| Mizzenmast, deck to head | 13 | " | | |
| Mizzenboom | 10 | " | | |
| Mizzenyard | 11 | " | | |
| Hoist of mainsail | 17 | " | | |
| Area mainsail | 288 | sq. | ft. | |
| Area jib | 132 | " | " | |
| Area mizzen | 80 | " | " | |

# PLATE XVI

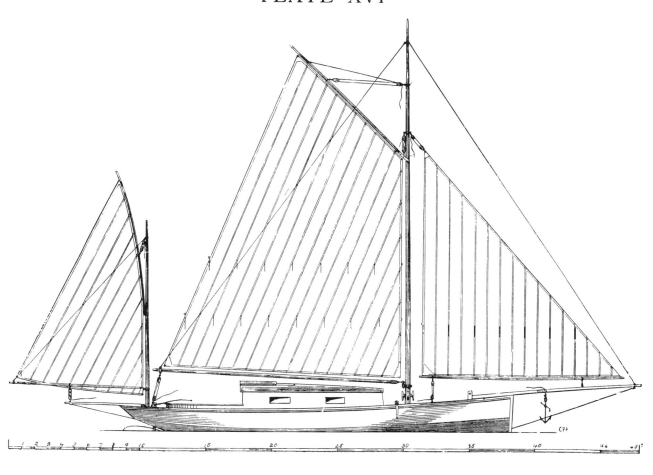

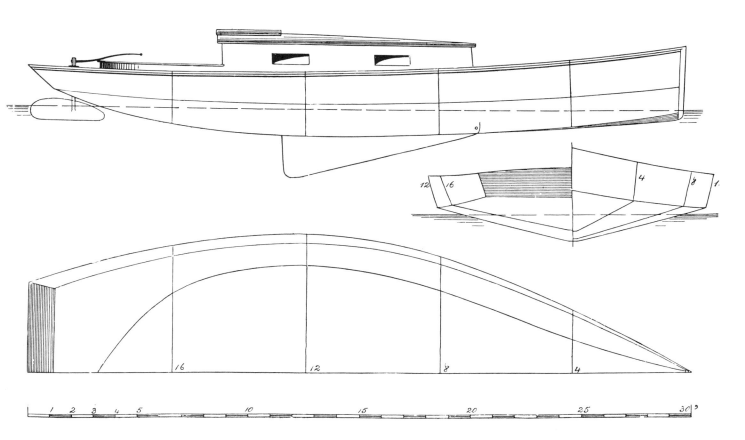

## A SKIPJACK

## V. A GERMAN LIGHT-DRAFT

### *PLATE XVII*

#### FORTY FEET LONG ON WATER-LINE

YACHTING in Germany has developed rapidly in late years, and designing has reached a high state of perfection among the leaders of the profession. German yachts, like those of France, have had their origin mainly in English and American practice, the former supplying the standards for sea-going purposes and the latter the features for smooth-water sailing. The narrow cutters of Von Saefkow, such as the Anna and Lolly, are equal in their planning to anything English, and in centreboard light-drafts the Germans are little behind the best examples we have in America. Many yachts of foreign construction have from time to time been imported into Germany, so that the relative performances of all kinds are well understood. For coast cruising the English cutter of moderate beam is decidedly preferred, but for river service and the interior the American centreboard is extensively adopted. Recently, of course, the light-drafts have undergone all the modern improvements in the way of increased depth, lead keels, long overhangs, etc., which have received recognition in America since we became familiar with the good points of the modern English racer.

In Plate XVII the plans of a German light-draft of recent construction are given. They show that the characteristics which should govern good design are thoroughly understood, and that in regard to fairness of volume, fine entrance, clean run and high bilge belonging to boats of that type, the Germans can fairly claim to lead the English. This same superiority in centreboards over English practice is quite general throughout the German fleet. The boat in question was built at the yard of H. Heidtmann at Hamburg, a yard which has made a specialty of the centreboard for two generations, and has achieved international fame, putting up numerous craft for exportation. Length on deck, 47 ft. 6 in.; on load-line, 40 ft.; beam at load-line, 12 ft.; draft, 3 ft. 4 in. Owing to moderate beam and displacement on the length, the boat requires only a small rig, and is altogether an economical craft in build and keep.

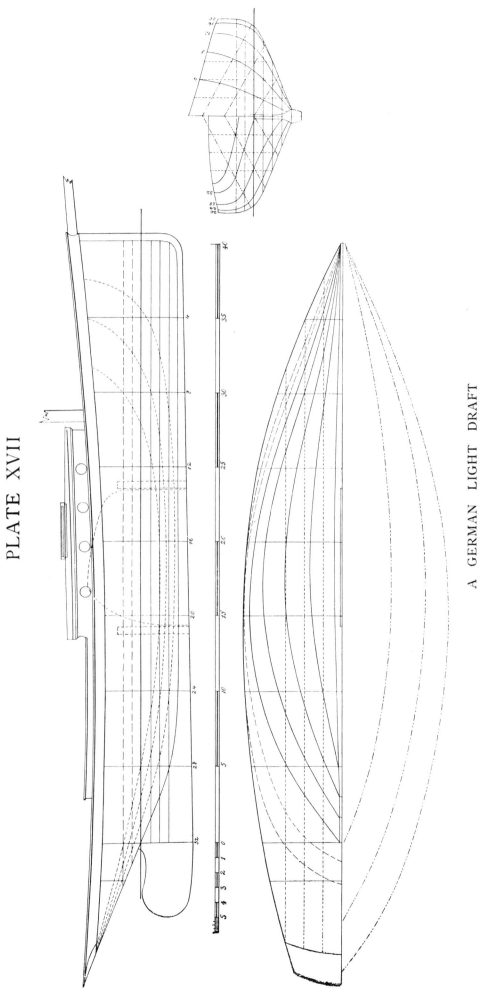

PLATE XVII

A GERMAN LIGHT DRAFT

# IV

# DEEP CENTREBOARD SLOOPS

## I. THE GLEAM

### *PLATE XVIII*

#### TWENTY-THREE FEET LONG ON LOAD-LINE

DEPTH contributes in a small boat so greatly to the accommodations, that, in a cabin yacht, all the law allows should be expected. Attempts have been made to retain the beam of a shoal vessel and add to depth as much as experience seems to counsel. The limit in displacement is soon reached beyond which a boat will lose in performance at a rapid rate, unless beam be modified to suit. Extreme depth and displacement have undoubtedly been reached on the beam of the GLEAM (Plate XVIII), and more weight would demand compensating relief in reduction of breadth. Even as it is, boats of the GLEAM's class can only be driven by exceedingly large rigs. Whether it is true economy to combine a hull poorly adapted to high speed with the enormous rig the form is able to carry without capsizing, or whether the same size is not better disposed upon dimensions from which speed can be coaxed with less rig, is a question for individuals to answer according to their own ideas as to what constitutes accommodation and economic handling.

The GLEAM has a good record in light weather, but seems to fall short in strong winds and a chop, the weight of her spars causing her to labor and her beam refusing to be driven at high speed except under full sail. The yacht gives the impression of being short, with a tendency to choke instead of going through clean, and from the time the canvas is snugged down, the GLEAM falls short of her light weather attainments.

She is of more than ordinary shapeliness, with claims to style in her whole make up. Her lines will prove of special interest to those who have to moor in shoal water, or cannot avail themselves of more depth for particular reasons. The

# PLATE XVIII

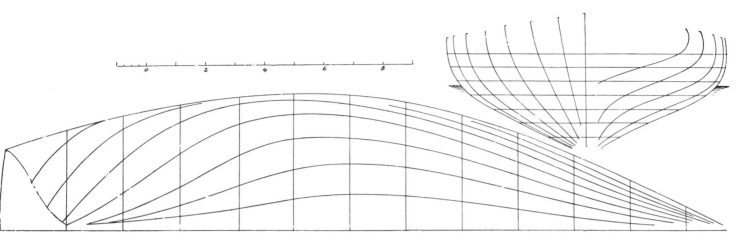

THE C. B. SLOOP GLEAM

# Small Yachts

GLEAM was built by John Mumm, of South Brooklyn, for Mr. N. D. Lawton, to designs of his own in 1883. More difficult dimensions could scarcely exist, yet, in spite of their exceptional proportions, the GLEAM exhibits unrivaled clean-cut fairness of body. This extreme fairness, coupled with enormous light weather rig, is the real secret of her success. In view of the varied results of trial races during the past few years, it is more than ever convincing that far too much stress is laid upon mere type by itself when the question of speed is agitated, and that the clue to success should be sought in the most favorable selection of bulk and general symmetry of hull, let the cardinal dimensions be what they may. We have all seen square races won by out and out cutters, by half-breeds, with and without keel, and with a little of both, by orthodox light drafts of a past epoch, and by all kinds of go-betweens.

Extensive and close observation will, in the long run, justify the view that all types within certain not well defined limits can be made to reach equally high rates of speed, though some will excel under certain conditions, and others again under an opposite state of affairs. But it will ever be a losing game to pit against perfection of one type anything of another possessed of less sweetness of form. In more detail, though, there seems to be evidence enough at hand that the deep, narrow keel has the call in light and baffling wind, and in any kind of weather accompanied by a sea, while the centreboard sloop's especial opportunity will be found in smooth water and good whole sail breezes.

As our plans will explain, GLEAM is entitled to the claim of being handsome. In her depth, high side and comparatively liberal displacement, and in the absence of flare can be traced commendable properties.

| | | | |
|---|---|---|---|
| Length over all | 25 ft. | 10 in. | |
| Length on *L W L* | 23 " | | |
| Beam on *L W L* | 9 " | | |
| Beam extreme | 9 " | 6 " | |
| Depth, top of deck to keel | 4 " | 9 " | |
| Draft without board | 3 " | 3 " | |
| Least freeboard to planksheer | 1 " | 9 " | |
| Displacement | 12,000 lbs. | | |
| Ballast inside | 4,500 " | | |
| Ballast on keel | 1,700 " | | |
| Area lower sail | 788 sq. ft. | | |
| Mast, deck to hounds | 29 ft. | | |
| Boom over all | 26 " | | |
| Gaff over all | 16 " | | |
| Bowsprit outboard | 15 " | | |
| Topmast over all | 16 " | | |
| Hoist of mainsail | 23 " | | |
| Jib on luff | 31 " | | |
| Jib on foot | 20 " | | |

# PLATE XIX

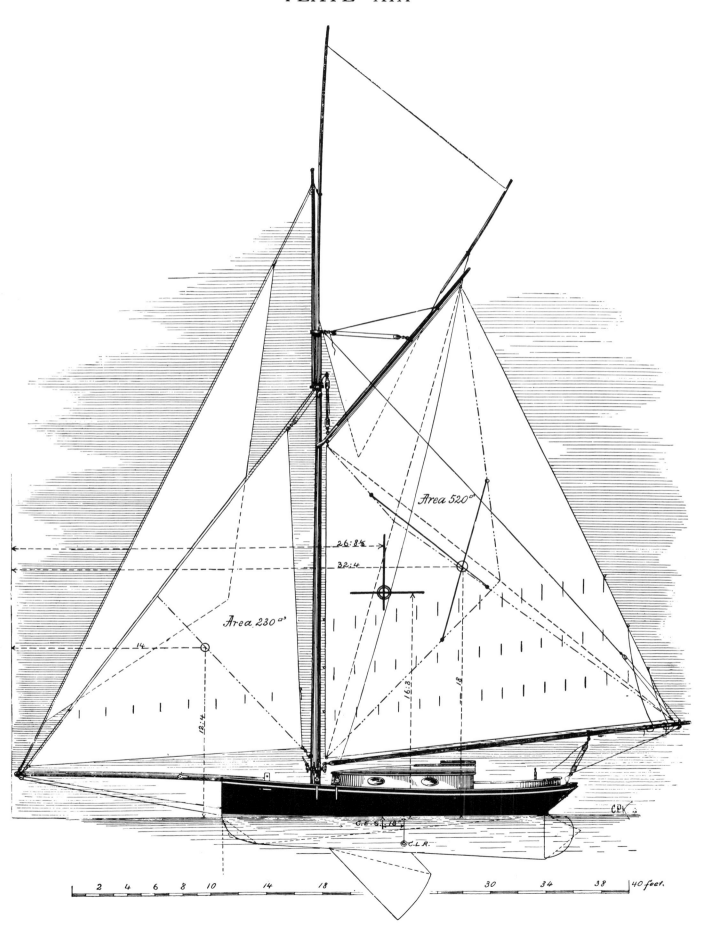

Area 520ᵈ

26:8½

32:14

Area 230ᵈ

14

12:4

16:3

18

C.E.S. 18.

C.L.R.

CPK

2    4    6    8    10        14        18                    30        34        38    |40 feet.

GLEAM—SAIL PLAN

The keel is of white oak, 8 x 8 in. amidships, frames 3½ x 2 at heel, 3 x 2 at head, oak. Extra frame on bilge, 2 x 3, of hackmatack. Deck framing, 3 x 3 and 2 x 3, oak. Bed pieces for centreboard trunk, 7 x 4 in., oak. Stem, post and rudder of oak, with locust stock. Plank, 1⅛ yellow pine, no butts above water-line. Deck stuff, 1¼ white pine, square, no butts. Trimmings, hatches and rail in mahogany. Cabin roof is of three layers thin boards, with canvas between. Sails of 10 oz. duck, double bighted, also storm jib. Club topsail of 8 oz. duck. The bowsprit is a bright spar, run out nearly horizontal. Decks and interior of bright finish. The cockpit floor is 1 ft. above water-line, and the centreboard trunk is kept low in the cabin, the top being " sealed " and caulked.

The sail plan (Plate XIX) has the Centre of Effort calculated by the moments of jib and mainsail referred to a perpendicular at bowsprit end and the load-line, the figures and scale being noted so that the student can follow the computation.

The Centre of Lateral Resistance was determined with enough approximation for practice by triangulation and reference of moments to fore side of stem for fore-and-aft position and to load-line for depth. An 18 in. arm between the two centres prevents too strong weather helm. The sails are by John M. Sawyer, of New York.

Plate XVIII shows no outside ballast, the keel weight having been added in the spring of 1884.

## II.  THE  MIDGE

### *PLATE XX*

#### TWENTY-SIX FEET SIX INCHES LONG ON LOAD-LINE

A SECOND specimen of good design in this class, the MIDGE (Plate XX), was built in 1876 by Alonzo Smith, of Islip, Long Island, for Mr. G. C. Barnette, from drawings by the latter. The Body points to an easy vessel and the Half Breadth shows a finer after-end than customary. As was to be expected, the MIDGE turned out rather better in lumpy water than the average sloop, and owing to snug skin surface, proved also fast and close-winded in light weather, under comparatively small rig. She is, on the whole, a very acceptable embodiment of sloop principles within moderation. The accommodations below are rather scant, however, especially in the forecastle, where the headroom is not 3 ft. 6 in. Owing to fair draft, the board is shorter than usual:

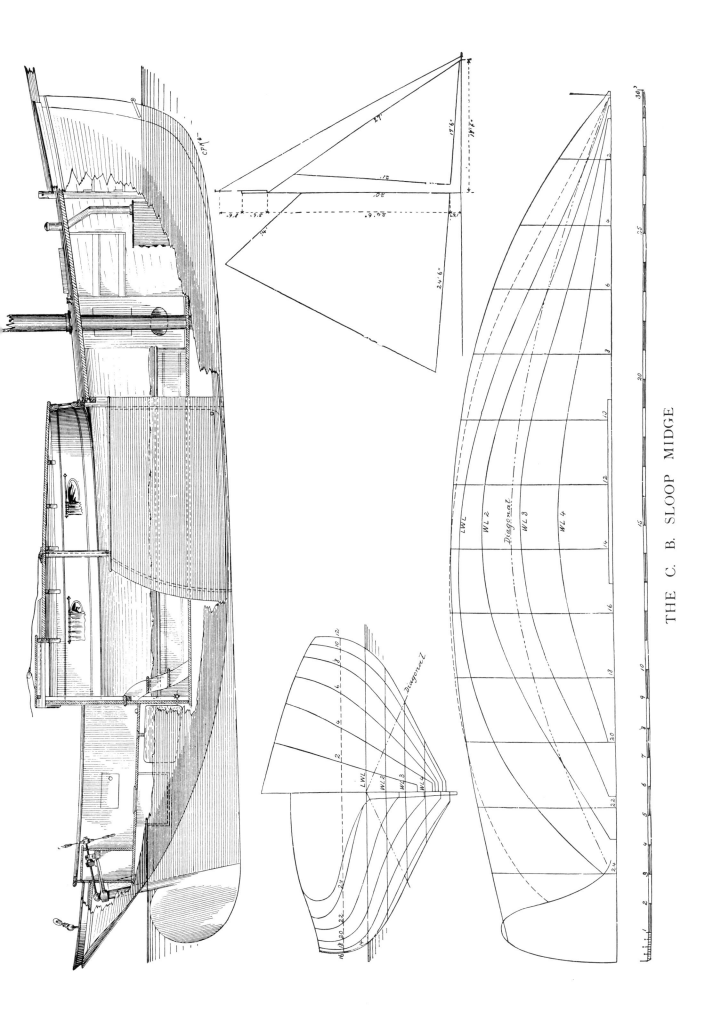

THE C. B. SLOOP MIDGE

| | | | | |
|---|---|---|---|---|
| Length over all | 30 ft. | | |
| Length on water-line | 26 " | 6 in. |
| Greatest beam | 11 " | |
| Beam at water-line | 10 " | 4 " |
| Breadth across counter | 7 " | 4 " |
| Depth at side, No. 16 | 4 " | 4 " |
| Least freeboard | 1 " | 8 " |
| Draft without board | 3 " | 2 " |
| Draft with board | 7 " | 9 " |
| Sheer forward | 1 " | 10 " |
| Sheer aft | | 7 " |
| Length of board | 6 " | 3 " |
| Pin from stem | 10 " | 6 " |
| Breadth after-end. | 4 " | |
| Mast from end *L W L* | 7 " | |
| Mast, deck to hounds | 26 " | |
| Mast head | 3 " | 6 " |
| Topmast, cap to shoulder | 8 " | 6 " |
| Mast to jibstay | 18 " | 6 " |
| Boom over all | 25 " | 3 " |
| Gaff over all | 14 " | 6 " |
| Hoist of mainsail | 20 " | |
| Jib on foot | 17 " | 6 " |
| Jib on luff | 27 " | |
| Area mainsail | 460 sq. ft. | |
| Area jib | 180 sq. ft. | |

The MIDGE has since appeared as a keel boat under the name RECKLESS.

CHESAPEAKE BUCKEYE

# V

# LIGHT DRAFT KEEL YACHTS

## I. THE MIGNONETTE

### *PLATE XXI*

#### TWENTY FEET TEN INCHES LONG ON LOAD-LINE

THE Mignonette was built in 1884 by Wallin & Gorman, of South Brooklyn, for Dr. E. G. Loring, New York, from a model by Keating, of Marblehead, Mass. She is the product of ingrafting beam enough upon the cutter type to realize the objects for which she is intended—for cruising about the coast between this and Mount Desert, in all weather. Long experience in small boat and yacht sailing along the coast and experiments with various styles and rigs have led up to the construction of the Mignonette, and there is little doubt that she suits her purposes famously. With a 1,500 lbs. shoe hung low and a small well, the Mignonette is, without question, uncapsizable, and also "unfillable" in the event of a serious knock down. A judicious apportionment of beam and depth permits 4 ft. 8 in. under a low house of 12 in. height, with a floor of 30 in. This, with two berths of 24 in. width (shown too low in the plans) by 7 ft., lockers, shelving, racks, etc., give exceedingly liberal accommodations on the length of 20 ft. 10 in. The cockpit is peculiar. The floor of the well is 12 in. below level of deck and 6 by 3½ ft., with 14 in. of deck all round utilized for seats, the mahogany combing being set back from the well that distance. In this way the volume of water which could be shipped is reduced to a harmless amount, and the cabin doorsill is almost at deck height to prevent a sea finding its way below. The overhang supplies a good lead to mainsheet, and increases useful deck area. The rig is that of a full cutter, chosen after experiment with many other kinds. The division of sail puts the yacht within easy control of one hand, who finds himself at all times prepared for anything that may come along. The Mignonette, for example, strikes into strong wind.

PLATE XXI

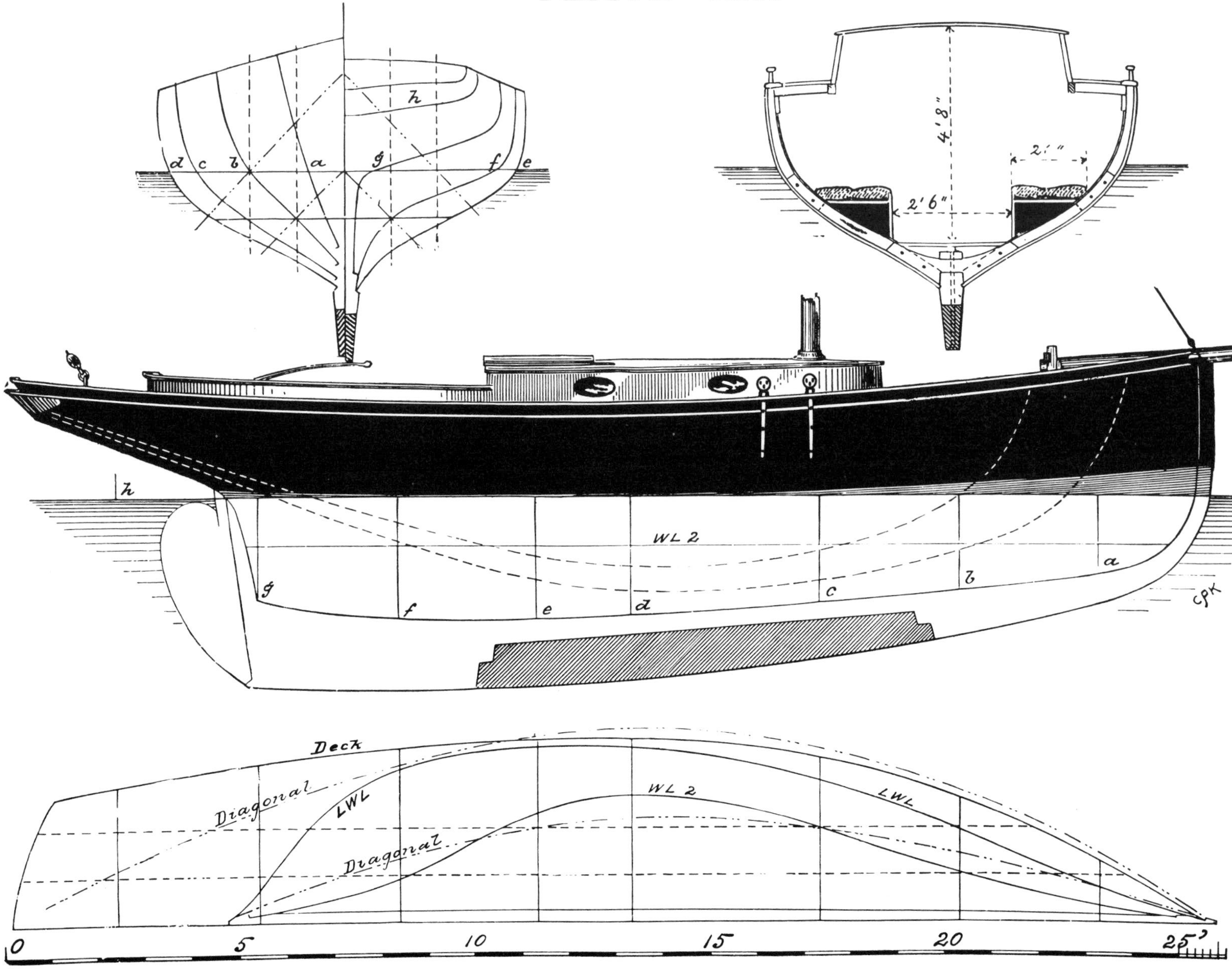

2' 6"

2' 1"

"8, 7"

WL 2

a

2

c

d

z

e

f

g

h

e

f

h

g

a

2

c

d

Deck

LWL

Diagonal

WL 2

LWL

WL 2

Diagonal 2

0    5    10    15    20    25'

LIGHT-DRAFT CUTTER MIGNONETTE

# Light Draft Keel Yachts

She lowers foresail in a jiffy, and has taken off nearly one-fourth the sail plan, equivalent to a double reef in mainsail, at a tithe of the trouble and time. Should a squall overtake her, mainsail and jib can be let go by the run, and the boat can still ply to windward under foresail alone. To enable her to do so to some good, the foresail is " lugged " three feet abaft the mast. The owner states that by keeping foreside of mast clear of pins, and jointing the boom band by a bolt passing down flush through lugs, dovetailing hinge fashion, in place of setting up with screw and nut, he finds no trouble in lighting over the sheet when heaving about in stays, and that he finds the long foot foresail a fine pulling sail, a sort of continuation of the mainsail forward the mast, sheets being led to trim very flat. Under all circumstances just the right balance can be preserved through five successive modifications of the sail plan. Thus : All plain lower sail ; mainsail and jib ; reefed mainsail and small jib, or full foresail ; close reefed mainsail and reefed foresail or small jib ; and fifth, under foresail only. You can always reef at leisure by keeping on your course with foresail, making more sail as convenient. You can work out of a harbor under foresail and set the rest when clear. The mainboom is but 19 feet long. The jib is small and easily trimmed. It is run out to bowsprit end on a traveler, and when not wanted is quickly got rid of by a pull on the inhaul and lowering away. In a sea it saves laying out on a light spar to furl, and likewise takes the weight and bunt of the sail out of harm's way. A little dexterity is required in handling the jib lest it get away from you during the operation, and this a little practice speedily teaches. This method also enables you to run jib out or in to a suitable distance to balance the rest of the sail.

The principal specifications of the MIGNONETTE are as follows : Keel, 6 x 8 ; stem, sided 3½ ; post, 10 in. moulded, all of oak, including deadwood. Frames, oak, 1½ x 3 at heels and 1½ x 1¾ at head, double, rivetted together, boxed into keel, with hackmatack floors bolted through keel. Clamps of oak, 1 x 3½, full length of boat, as is also all other plank. Deck frame of oak, 1½ x 2¼, rivetted to clamps, with knees to side. Top streaks of oak, 1 x 3½, with two wales of Georgia pine, rest of 1 in. cedar. Planksheer of oak, 1½ x 3½, whole length ; deck of white pine, bright, 1¼ square. Ceiling, ½ in. thick, narrow and beaded. Mahogany fittings. Four sidelights to house and two 5-in. brass ports in forward end. All ironwork of best galvanized Norway iron ; lignum vitæ deadeyes, iron strapped, two shrouds each side. Spars of spruce, three coats of varnish. Patent bouched iron strap, lignum vitæ blocks. Builder furnished yacht complete with all rigging, gear, anchors, chain, hawser, sails of 10 oz. doublebighted cotton duck. Ballast, 2,300 lbs. inside and 1,500 lbs. on keel.

The manner of keying the locust bitts to the deck to do away with crowding the eyes below is shown in Plate XXII. A wood knee will in addition be worked on the forward side on deck to further stiffen them.

# PLATE XXII

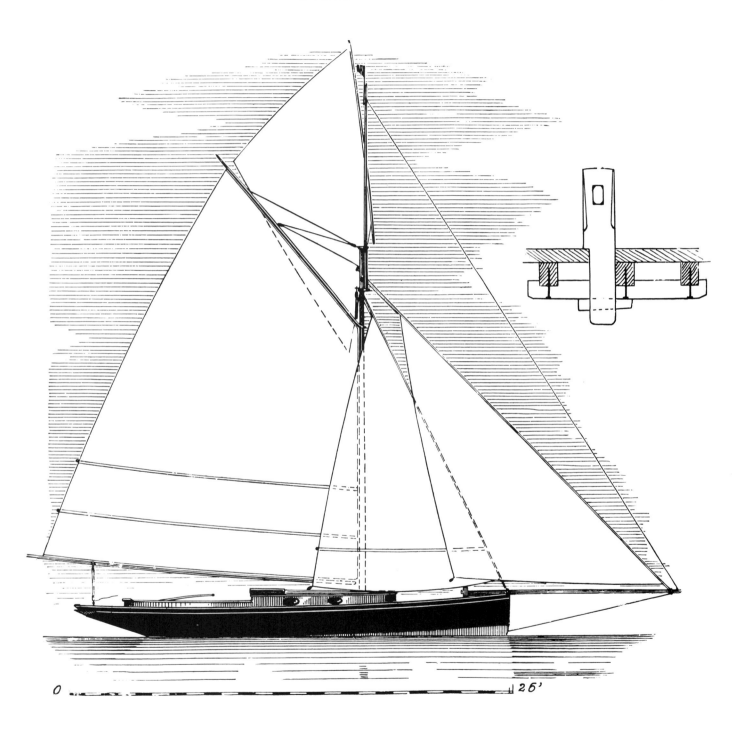

0 ⊢ ‑ ‑ ‑ ‑ ‑ ‑ ‑ ‑ ‑ ‑ ‑ ‑ ‑ ‑ ‑ ‑ ‑ ‑ ⊣ 25'

MIGNONETTE—SAIL PLAN

# Light Draft Keel Yachts

The sections shown in the plans are not building frames, but the sections by which the boat was laid down. The elements are as under:

| | |
|---|---|
| Length on deck | 25 ft. 10 in. |
| Length load-line | 20 " 10 " |
| Greatest beam moulded | 7 " 9 " |
| Beam on load-line | 7 " 3 " |
| Depth $MS$ planksheer to rabbet | 4 " 2 " |
| Greatest draft | 4 " |
| Least freeboard top planksheer | 1 " 9 " |
| Area immersed $MS$ with keel | 11.46 sq. ft. |
| Area load-line plane | 105.35 " " |
| Area longitudinal section, with rudder | 71.5 " " |
| Ratio sq. root $MS$ to $LWL$ | 3.39 |
| Ratio $MS$ to same | 6.24 |
| Area wetted surface with rudder | 203 sq. ft. |
| Displacement | 8,350 lbs. |
| Displacement in short tons | 4.175 tons |
| Same per inch at load-line | 562 lbs. |
| Wet surface per short ton displacement | 46.2 sq. ft. |
| Ballast, inside | 2,350 lbs. |
| Ballast on keel | 1,500 " |
| Ratio ballast to displacement | 46 per cent |
| $MS$ from end $LWL$ | 12 ft. 4 in. |
| Centre lateral resistance from $LWL$ | 12 " 4 " |
| Centre of effort of sails from $LWL$ | 11 " 8 " |
| Area three lower sails | 460 sq. ft. |
| Ratio to square of load-line | 106 per cent. |
| Sail per sq. ft. wet surface | 2.28 sq. ft. |
| Sail per ton of displacement | 110.2 " " |
| Area mainsail | 279 " " |
| Area lug foresail | 91 " " |
| Area large jib | 93 " " |
| Hoist of mainsail | 15 ft. |
| Foresail on foot | 11 ft. 3 in. |
| Jib on foot | 12 " |
| Mast from end $LWL$ | 8 " 6 " |
| Mast from deck to hounds | 19 " |
| Boom over all | 19 " |
| Gaff over all | 12 " |
| Bowsprit end $LWL$ to stay | 9 ft. 6 in. |

## II.  A SMALL CRUISER

*PLATE XXIII*

SEVENTEEN FEET LONG ON LOAD-LINE

THIS boat was designed in 1881 for single hand sailing in the Sound and the more open waters about Newport and New Bedford.  She has been reported as very satisfactory in her qualities and well suited to knocking about, being quite roomy and safe :

| | | | | | |
|---|---|---|---|---|---|
| Length over all | 20 | ft. | 5 | in. | |
| Length on deck | 20 | " | | | |
| Length on *L W L* | 17 | " | | | |
| Beam extreme | 7 | " | | | |
| Beam on *L W L* | 6 | " | | | |
| Beam moulded | 5 | " | 10½ | " | |
| Depth at side, amidships deck to rabbet | 3 | " | 5 | " | |
| Draft extreme | 3 | " | 3 | " | |
| Draft 2 ft. from forward | 1 | " | 9 | " | |
| Draft aft | 2 | " | 11 | " | |
| Depth keel amidships | 1 | " | 3 | " | |
| Rake of sternpost | 18 | deg. | | | |
| Length of cockpit | 4 | ft. | 3 | in. | |
| Width of cockpit | 4 | " | | | |
| Depth of cockpit | 1 | " | 4 | " | |
| Length of cabin | 7 | " | | | |
| Height in cabin | 3 | " | 10 | " | |
| Side of trunk | | | 8 | " | |
| Least freeboard to deck | 1 | " | 4 | " | |
| Overhang aft | 3 | " | 4 | " | |
| Displacement | 2 | tons | | | |
| Displacement per inch *L W L* | 354 | lbs. | | | |
| Coefficient of displacement | 0.31 | | | | |
| Area midship section | 7.65 | sq. ft. | | | |
| Area *L W L* plane | 66.33 | " | " | | |
| Area longitudinal section | 49 | " | " | | |
| Area wetted surface | 117 | " | " | | |
| Canvas per sq. ft. do | 3 | " | " | | |
| Centre of buoyancy from fwd. perp | 9 | ft. | 6 | in. | |
| Centre of buoyancy below *L W L* | | | 9 | in. | |
| Centre lateral resistance from f. p | 9 | ft. | 11½ | in. | |
| Centre of effort of sails from f. p | 9 | " | 4¼ | " | |
| Centre of effort of sails above *L W L* | 10 | " | 6½ | " | |
| Ballast inside | 500 | lbs. | | | |

56

# Light Draft Keel Yachts

| | | | |
|---|---|---|---|
| Ballast on keel | 1,000 lbs. | | |
| Mast from end *L W L* | 5 ft. | | |
| Mast, deck to hounds | 16 " | | |
| Mast pole | 10 " | | |
| Mast diameter at partners | 4¾ in. | | |
| Mast rake | 0 | | |
| Boom | 9½ ft. | | |
| Boom diameter | | 3¾ in. | |
| Gaff | 12½ ft. | | |
| Gaff diameter | | 2¾ " | |
| Bowsprit outboard | 8 ft. | 3 " | |
| Bowsprit diameter at stem | | 3½ " | |
| Steeve of do | | 3 " | |
| Topsail yard | 14 ft. | | |
| Topsail yard, diameter | | 2¼ " | |
| Topsail club | 8 ft. | | |
| Luff of mainsail | 13 " | 6 " | |
| Foot of mainsail | 19 " | | |
| Head of mainsail | 12 " | | |
| Leech of mainsail | 23 " | 8 " | |
| Tack to peak | 23 " | 8 " | |
| Knock to clew | 22 " | 6 " | |
| Foot of jib | 13 " | | |
| Luff of jib | 18 " | 4 " | |
| Leech of jib | 13 " | 4 " | |
| Area mainsail | 261 sq. ft. | | |
| Area jib | 87 " " | | |
| Area topsail | 80 " " | | |

The problem was to compose a safe, comfortable, weatherly, handsome and fast boat about a given amount of accommodation. The latter was to consist of a couple of berths, a small cockpit and stowage for a week's cruise or more. The design was to be, so far as qualities were concerned, a ship on a small scale—not a makeshift, or an extemporized affair—and she was to be handled in all weathers by a single person with a reasonable amount of labor.

Seven feet of cabin and about four or five for cockpit, with enough more for ends, furnished a length of 17 ft. for the design. A little experimenting with midship sections gave 6 ft. on the load-line as the least beam for a two-foot floor, eighteen inch berths and sitting room under a "house." With more beam the depth would have had to have been decreased, or the displacement would have become too large and the boat too much of a tub. The least depth amidships convenient for "sitting height," and the beam adopted, was found to be two feet, measured from load-line down to rabbet. With the three chief dimensions settled upon, the boat was gradually sketched in in such a way as to

57

# PLATE XXIII

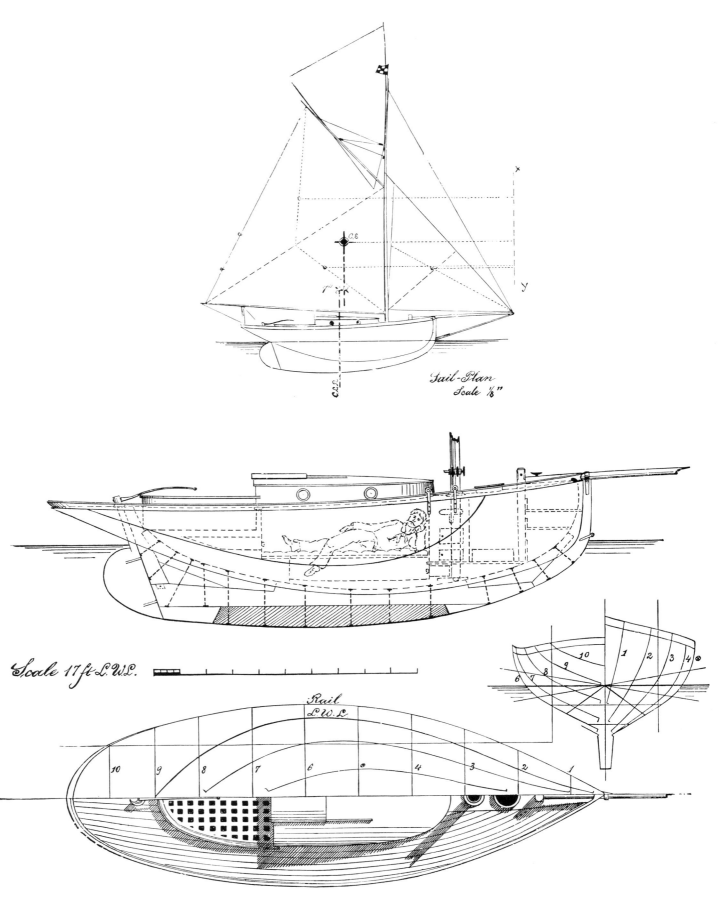

Sail-Plan
Scale 1/8"

Scale 17 ft L.W.L.

Rail
L.W.L.

A SINGLE-HAND CRUISER

combine fairness of body, easy lines, the most accommodations, the cheapest form of construction and sightliness.

The round up aft to the rabbet line was governed by reasons of fairness and economy, and forward with the desire partly of making both ends match in displacement in the ratio of the lengths of fore and after body, partly of aiding the handiness of the yacht and of making her more weatherly, without too large a longitudinal section, by transferring the gripe cut off into rocker to the keel amidships, thereby bringing the ballast lower down as well. The heel was rounded up, and the post raked for similar purposes, a small effective longitudinal area always being preferable to a large and less effective one, as a reduction in area means a reduction in skin friction, and greater speed in light winds where friction is the main source of resistance. The ends of the lower water-lines forward become more obtuse in consequence, but it should be borne in mind that the lower lines are always out of proportion sharp compared to those above. When a sailing yacht attains her maximum speed under canvas, the lower body contributes to resistance little more than friction, its " wave-making " propensity being so much less than that of the much wider body above. In thus cutting away useless deadwood, for deep-throated floors are little else, the speed is favorably affected, and a keel-boat can be made to work like a cat. The freeboard was made ample, without being more than necessary to lift the boat out well so as to keep her as dry as possible. The sheer is moderate and will show less in relief than in the plans. Her nose has been kept high, not by undue sheer, but by keeping the least freeboard well aft and giving relief to the eye by a bowsprit nearly horizontal. The cabin house has been proportioned for appearances, sufficient room below and as much clear deck as we could gain. The cockpit is small and shoal, and the sill of the cabin door is carried up flush with the deck, a single adjustable panel taking the place of doors. If a sea washes fore and aft unexpectedly, the cockpit may fill without drenching the skipper's duds down below. Steers with a tiller, as she is too small for the more expensive wheel, and a good keel is so easy to steer compared with a centreboard that a tiller is all that is required; besides, some prefer to " feel" their boats. For rig, the sloop, with pole mast, has been adopted as the least expensive and simplest for so small a boat. The mast was stepped well forward to reduce the size of the jib and to sail as a cat when boxing about, and a little weather helm is no objection. A storm jib, say 8 ft. on the foot and 14 ft. on the luff, No. 6 canvas, can be set on its own luff by hooking into an eyebolt or temporary rope strap $4\frac{1}{2}$ ft. out on the bowsprit. The mainsail has two rows of reefs, 3 ft. 9 in. apart, with which the canvas can be snugged down for a stiff gale. Should the cruiser be caught out of reach of a harbor, in the very worst of it he can extemporize a storm trysail out of his storm jib. The lower sails may be of 8 oz. duck, the topsail of stout drilling. The latter has been made large for light weather, but a simple working jib-header may be all that some would want. The relation of the various areas and centres to one another can be gathered from the table published. The centre of buoyancy with the boat inclined was found to be in the same longitudinal position as when plumb, so that we may conclude a proper distribution of volume "between wind and water" has been obtained, the flare forward and quarter aft balancing fairly, doing away with "rooting" or "squatting." The coefficient of displacement, representing the proportion to which the solid circumscribed about the three dimensions of the underwater body has been cut away, is moderate, the skin has been kept at a minimum, the bow is fine and easy, the run clear and the boat very stiff for sail without being hard at the bilge. With a lighter frame, etc., from two to four hundred pounds could be saved for additional ballast, and nearly the whole amount put on the keel. In that case a foot more hoist and boom, a foot more gaff and bowsprit would not be out of proportion. With hatches down there is no doubt but that the little boat will right when knocked on her beam ends. The emersed, immersed and diagonal lines are of a very satisfactory nature as shown in the accompanying cut, all of them corresponding closely in their features and proving the design to be a unity in conception throughout, not a patchwork of bow, middle body and stern, or underwater and above water bodies having no relation to one another. The frames, every other one only being represented, likewise show "the same boat" all the way through, and are the cheapest to get out.

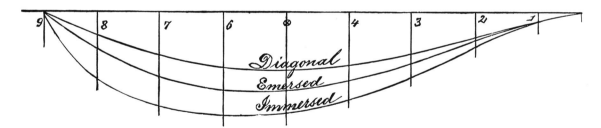

The scantling was made heavy for strength and rough usage. Oak keel, stem, post, garboards and sheer strake, yellow pine deadwood, knees and beams, cedar plank, hackmatack frames, white pine deck, spruce spars. The keel is 7 in. on top, 4 in. on bottom of iron amidships, tapered at ends and moulded as shown in the sheer plan. Stem and post 3 in. sided; frames, single, sawed, each 2½ x 2½ at heel, and spaced 12 in. between centres; beams, 1¾ x 1¼, spaced 15 in.; mast beams to have hanging and lodge knees; deck plank, 1 x 2 in.; side plank, ¾ in.; ceiling, ⅜ in.; bilge strakes, 1 in.; clamps, 1¼ in.; house of 1 in. oak, varnished; waist, ¾ in.; transoms and lockers, ½ and ¾ in.; decks kept bright or paid with spar varnish. Bitts of oak or locusts, 4 x 6 at deck. From 1,000 to 1,200 lbs. iron cast to a mould to carry the taper of the keel down and fore and aft. Cored holes for say 1 in. bolts, galvanized iron.

These bolts are set up on top with nut and washer. Part of the inside ballast may consist of a long casting to go over the floors a couple of inches thick and six inches wide. Fill underneath with hard wood chocks between the floors and run the keel bolts up through all. Deadwood bolted with ½ in. galvanized iron, both ends headed, as shown in the plans. Main throat, peak, sheet, jib halliards and sheets of 1¼ in. manilla. Topsail gear of ¾ in. manilla. Shrouds 1 in. wire, and bobstay ⅝ in. round iron. Anchors 40 and 25 lbs., with 25 fms. ¼ in. best chain and a coil of whale line.

## III. THE CARMITA

### PLATE XXIV

#### TWENTY FEET SIX INCHES LONG ON LOAD-LINE

THE CARMITA was modeled by J. H. Keating, of Marblehead, Mass., and launched in 1882 for Mr. C. H. W. Foster. Mr. Keating had previously built the LOLA, a boat of larger displacement and draft than usual, and after careful study of her behavior concluded the innovations upon former practice were in the right direction. As far as safety is concerned, she cannot capsize, having 1,150 lbs. iron on the keel and 1,500 lbs. at good depth inside, and to prevent sinking in case of collision or being stove, she carries 330 gallons of sealed air tanks, stowed where most convenient. Her working has been found most satisfactory in all conditions of wind and sea. As a flyer in light weather, she has particularly distinguished herself. She is a living denial of the idea that light weight and draft are necessary for speed in light winds.

Heavy boats are the most satisfactory to those doing much "drifting," and in a season of light winds passed aboard a big displacement, the owner emancipates himself from much of the tedious disappointment. The CARMITA behaves splendidly in a heavy sea, fetching where she points in the face of a gale. She has been knocked down again and again by vicious squalls, but came up smilingly every time without begging. When knocked down, she always holds her way, and remains under control of the man at the helm. She handles tip top, steers without griping, and works without fail under any sail. She beat dead to windward under foresail only for a mile and a half off Marblehead Point in a stiff blow and never missed stays in the short boards she made.

The lines and details of CARMITA are not produced as the only shape through which good results can be expected, but as an illustration of type. In point of principle the CARMITA can be cited as an excellent example. It is quite possible

# PLATE XXIV

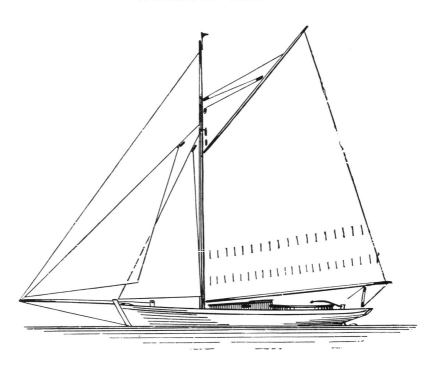

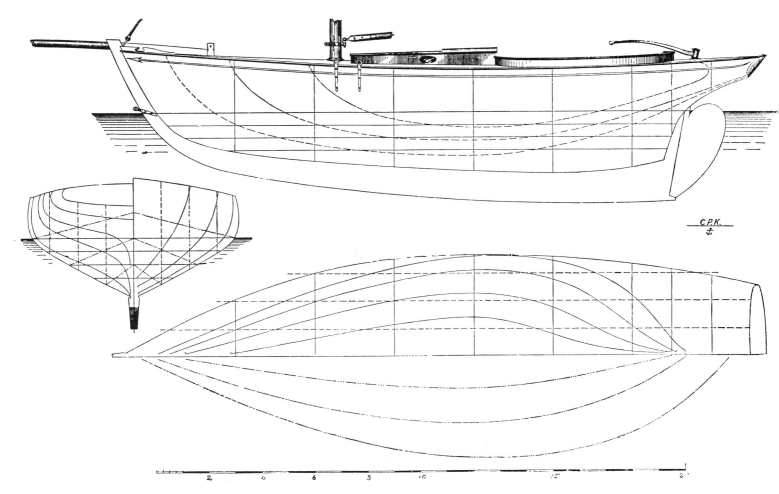

C.P.K.

LIGHT-DRAFT CUTTER CARMITA

that her lines admit of a "refining" process, and that variations in her proportions can be attempted without courting failure. Stem and counter might easily be made to assume any sweep indicated by taste or fancy :

| | |
|---|---|
| Length over all | 24 ft. 8 in. |
| Length on load-line | 20 " 6 " |
| Greatest beam moulded | 7 " 11 " |
| Depth planksheer to rabbet on *M S* | 3 " 11 " |
| Greatest draft | 3 " 7 " |
| Least freeboard | 1 " 7 " |
| Area immersed *M S* with keel | 10.25 sq. ft. |
| Ratio sq. root *M S* to *L W L* | 3.20 |
| Area load-line | 101.20 " " |
| Area longitudinal section, with rudder | 62 " " |
| Ratio of same to area of *M S* | 6.05 |
| Displacement | 7,735 lbs. |
| Displacement per inch at load-line | 540 lbs. |
| Wet surface per short ton displacement | 47.6 sq. ft. |
| Ballast inside | 2,650 lbs. |
| Ballast on keel | 1,150 " |
| Ratio of ballast to displacement | 48 per cent |
| *M S* from forward end of *L W L* | 12 ft. 6 in. |
| Centre of lateral resistance from end *L W L* | 11 " 4 " |
| Centre of effort of sails from end *L W L* | 11 " 4 " |
| Centre of buoyancy from end *L W L* | 11 " 6 " |
| Sail area, three lower sails | 430 sq. ft. |
| Ratio to square of load-line | 102 per cent |
| Area of wetted surface, with rudder | 184 sq. ft. |
| Sail per sq. foot of wetted surface | 2.33 sq. ft. |
| Sail per short ton displacement | 111.2 sq. ft. |
| Centre of mast from end *L W L* | 7 ft. 4 in. |
| Mast, deck to hounds | 17 " 6 " |
| Mainboom over all | 18 " |
| Gaff over all | 16 " |
| Bowsprit outboard | 9 " |
| Hoist of mainsail | 15 " |
| Foot of foresail | 8 " |
| Foot of jib | 10 " 6 in. |
| Airtight safety tanks | 53 cub. ft. |
| Floating capacity of same | 3,000 lbs. |

## IV.  THE DART

*PLATE XXV*

FOURTEEN FEET LONG ON LOAD-LINE

A SMALL boat on a given length is deficient in sail-carrying power, as the weight operating at the ends of the righting lever corresponds to the small displacement.  If the beam be restricted, the lever itself will be short and stability a minimum.  To do such forms justice, the ballast must be hung as low as possible, so that the length of righting lever may be favorably affected.

At first glance it seems like a mistake to build with small displacement and beam at all, but certain aims are thereby accomplished.  It is to be borne in mind, that though large displacement stands sponsor to the greatest ability, it is also associated with expense in first cost and in maintenance, because " more boat " on the length, and this is what we often wish to escape, without foregoing " uncapsizability " and the speed of a liberal rig.  A certain load-line length is wanted, and upon that as *small* a boat as consistent with general efficiency and safety. What is lacking in such a plan in displacement and beam can be made up to a fair extent by resorting to *low* weight.  Without that provision the yacht would be a disappointment to windward for lack of enough sail.  Running free, kites could be displayed and want of stability would not be felt.  But the test of design lies in its weatherly powers.  Any kind of affair can get down wind sooner or later, but it is by no means certain that a poorly devised composition can be turned up against breeze and sea.  A boat should, above all things, be smart and able in climbing a-weather.  Footing with lifted sheets is to the cruiser really a second consideration.

The DART, built in 1885 by Thomas Webber, of New Rochelle, N. Y., for Dr. A. H. Buck, of New York, represents a solution to economy in displacement stretched fore-and-aft to obtain the results of length, and hung with weight low down for reasons already explained.  Instead of disposing the displacement in a broad, shoal form, the governing ideas in the DART seem more preferable for cruising.  From easy beam speed can be expected which could only be got from the " flounder " type with very large rig, and a crew to shift ballast, with the likelihood of capsizing, and without the " drieness " in lumpy water or the stowage below decks of the DART.  This boat is in reality a shining sister of the Mersey canoe family; that is, a more yacht-like adaptation of the same underlying principles.  Or she can be regarded as a more advantageous expression of the elements which would be prominent in a 14 ft. sharpie of the keel class.  To somewhat greater proportional beam, the DART adds a lower centre of weight, with more sail area for driving, and total absence of pounding.  She

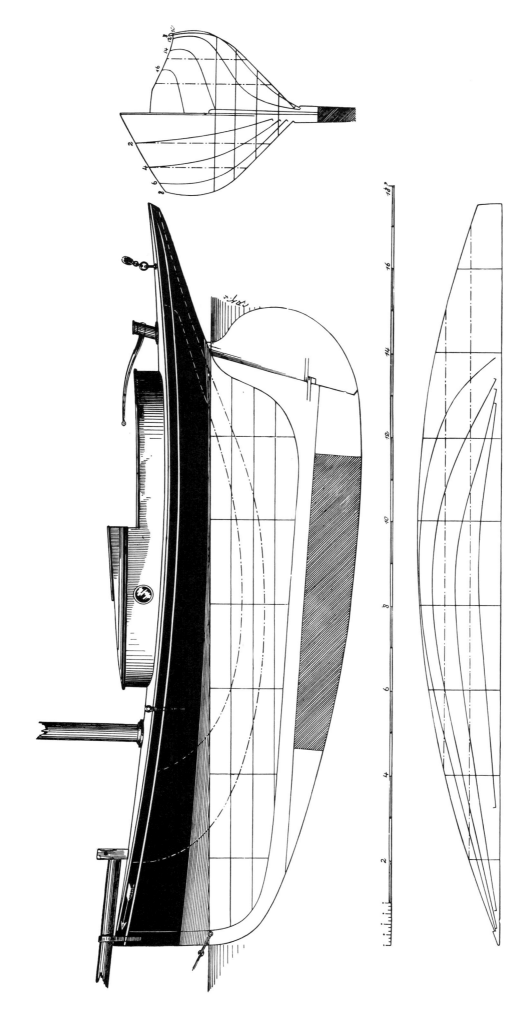

PLATE XXV

THE DART

may also claim greater steadiness on her helm, more momentum in a sea and in fickle airs, with reliability in stays and more " accommodation," if the tiny cuddy forward is to be one of the items submitted to comparison. *Per contra*, her draft will be greater than that of a keel sharpie or Mersey canoe ; but as it is only 3 ft. 6 in., this is not worth taking account of in practice, unless the DART is to moor on a flat which nearly dries out at low water, leaving the boat on her bilge at 60° inclination. From this position she would, no doubt, right without filling, if the washboard about the cockpit be sufficiently high. Still, to settle on the mud in that way would be awkward to any one on board at the time. What is more serious, however, the boat, after grounding, would work her keel into the soft bottom, and, as the water left her, she would be liable to fall over suddenly to a gust of wind and damage might result. Large yachts avail themselves of " legs " when grounding ; but in a crewless boat they could not be depended upon, and are a nuisance in any case. For mooring on flats the DART would have this serious drawback from which boats of less rise to floor and less external keel would not suffer. First cost per foot of load-line would be rather greater, but, quality for quality, the excess should be limited to getting out a balk keel instead of the " alligator" plank common in ordinary open boats and to difference in ballast. Frame, siding, deck, rig and equipment need count up no more in the DART than in any other style.

The beam of the DART's underwater body is well aft and the entrance long and fine. This would indicate a lifting of the quarters with a tendency to plunge by the head in a sea. But a high bow, concentrated weight and narrow quarters serve as a preventive. She is made " unsinkable" by about 16 cubic feet of zinc tanks stowed as most convenient.

| | |
|---|---|
| Length over all | 18 ft. |
| Length on water-line | 14 " |
| Beam moulded | 4 " |
| Beam moulded at *L W L* | 3 " 8 in. |
| Depth at side, No. 6 | 3 " |
| Least freeboard | 1 " |
| Sheer forward | 1 " 3 in. |
| Sheer aft | 6 " |
| Greatest draft | 3 " 6 " |
| Displacement, approx | 3,000 lbs. |
| Ballast on keel | 1,018 " |

There is 3 ft. 4 in. headroom under the house and a cockpit 5 ft. 3 in. long. The rig plan of the DART is as follows : Mast from stem, 5 ft. ; mast, deck to hounds, 13 ft. 6 in. ; deck to shoulder of pole topmast, 18 ft. Bowsprit, stem to jibstay, 7 ft.; with 1 ft. pole beyond. Mainsail on foot, 13 ft.; hoist, 11 ft.; head, 8 ft. ; leech, 17 ft. 6 in.; knock to clew, 15 ft. 8 in. Jib on foot, 11 ft.

6 in.; on leech, 11 ft. 6 in.; on stay, 16 ft. 6 in.   Yard topsail, 13 ft. 9 in. on luff; 9 on foot; 7 ft. on leech.

The keel is of white oak, 7 in moulded, 5-in. sided amidships.  Frame of oak and hackmatack, 1¼ x 1¾ in.  Plank, ¾-in. white cedar; wales, ¾-in. yellow pine; deck, ⅞ in. square, bent to sheer, with yellow pine waterways and mast partners.  Cabin-house and cockpit of 2½ x ⅞ white pine, with mahogany cappings.  Hatch and fittings of mahogany.  The cockpit coaming is carried round the rudder head, and does not stop short, as shown in the Plate.  The DART makes a handsome appearance afloat.

## V.  THE NUCKEL

### PLATE II

#### SEVENTEEN FEET LONG ON LOAD-LINE

A WELL tested boat of moderate displacement, easy form and low weight is the NUCKEL.

She was designed in 1881, by Marine Engineer Saefkow, Imperial German Navy, and built of oak at Kiel, on the Baltic, as a test model to a larger yacht it was proposed to construct upon the lines.  Below water the planking was flush or carvel, but above the load-line a system of "ribband carvel" was adopted to make a light, tight job.  The ribbands lapped the seams fore and aft and were through riveted from outside.

The originality of the design is striking.  Flare forward has been almost wiped out by the tumble home to the stem and ease guaranteed by roundish frames and water-lines as full as the beam will allow together with concentration of keel weight.  The sheer outline is exceptional.  It was adopted to preserve some straight to keel for hauling out and to get the ballast as low down as possible on a determined draft.  The straight and depth of keel also act as correctives to the wide yawing to which the rake of post and peculiar forefoot would lend their aid.  Useless skin surface in deadwood is saved and put by preference into extra depth of keel.

The NUCKEL holds a steady course, and is able in a sea, keeping her way well in rough water.  She has been heeled to 50°, and as might be expected, flies back to a vertical.  The cockpit can be partially closed by folding boards along the coaming, so that no water will pour in, even if knocked down to 75°.  In the short, steep jump of the Baltic, the NUCKEL has often buckled

PLATE II

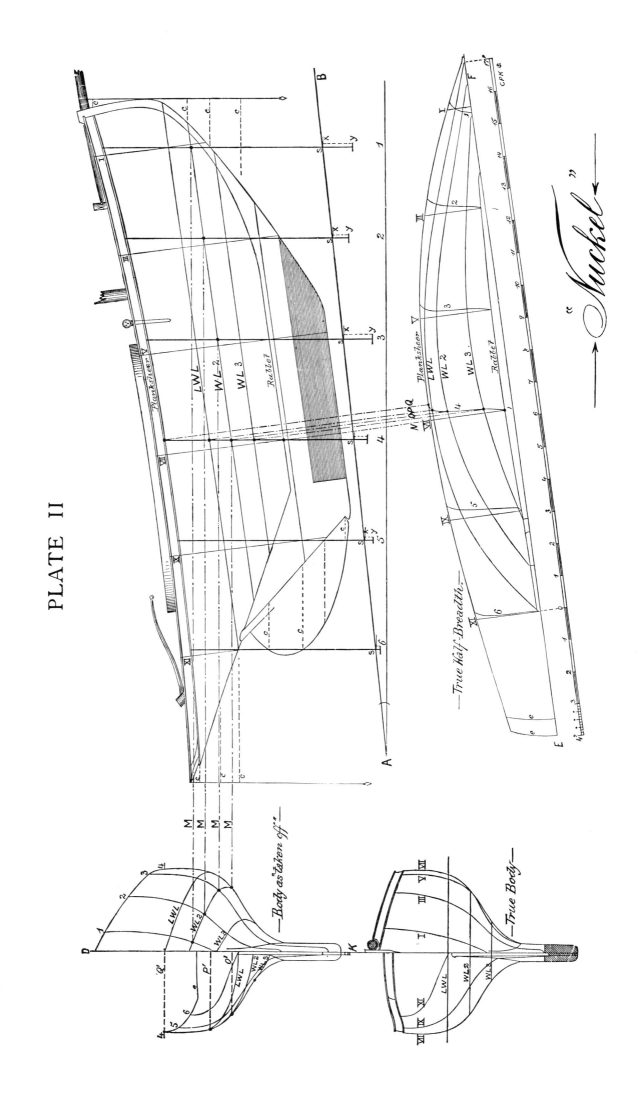

"Nuckel"

down to tough work. When blowing too hard to show mainsail, the jib tack is secured to the stem head, which brings the clew about to the after end of the cockpit, the jib then serving as a trysail, under which the boat turns to windward handily. The NUCKEL is as quick in stays as any centreboard boat, with the further advantage of holding her way. Two hands can stow away forward,

THE NUCKEL—SAIL PLAN

though a low cabin trunk would add to their comfort. The boat is famous as a dry craft, for speed in light winds and in strong blows with heavy sea. Her weakest point is in moderate wind and smooth water. The jib hoists on its own luff and the mainsail is loose on the foot.

| | | | |
|---|---|---|---|
| Length over all | 21 ft. | | |
| Length on water-line | 17 " | | |
| Greatest beam | 5 " | | |
| Beam on water-line | 4 " | 10 in. | |
| Breadth across counter | 2 " | 10 " | |
| Depth at side, No. 4 | 3 " | 6 " | |
| Least freeboard | 1 " | 5 " | |
| Extreme draft | 3 " | 11 " | |
| Sheer forward | | 9 " | |
| Sheer aft | | 3 " | |

| | | |
|---|---|---|
| Displacement | 1.75 | ton |
| Lead on keel | 1 | " |
| Lead inside | 0.02 | " |
| Mast from end *L W L* | 5 ft. | 8 in. |
| Mast, deck to hounds | 17 " | |
| Mast, deck to truck | 22 " | 9 " |
| Boom over all | 17 " | |
| Gaff over all | 12 " | 3 " |
| Bowsprit outboard | 9 " | |
| Area mainsail | 194 sq. ft. | |
| Area jib No. 1 | 92 " | " |
| Area jib No. 2 | 65 " | " |
| Topsail yard | 17 ft. | |

## VI.  THE ALICE

### *PLATE XXVI*

#### TWENTY-ONE FEET SIX INCHES ON LOAD-LINE

THIS sloop was built in 1885 by F. C. Smith, of New Bedford, for Mr. D. W. Tryon, of New York, who intends to cruise in Eastern waters and desired room for stowing artists' materials below, so the yacht might serve as his studio during summer, and also light draft to enter creeks and harbors not on the chart as regular anchorage.

| | | |
|---|---|---|
| Length on deck | 24 ft. | |
| Length on water-line | 21 " | 6 in. |
| Beam extreme | 10 " | |
| Beam on water-line | 9 " | |
| Extreme draft | 3 " | 6 in. |
| Mast from stem | 7 " | |
| Mast, deck to truck | 33 " | |
| Mast, deck to hounds | 24 " | |
| Bowsprit outboard | 13 " | |
| Hoist of mainsail | 19 " | |
| Boom over all | 27 " | |
| Gaff over all | 17 " | |

The rig is that of a pole-mast sloop, with a small storm jib to set flying in bad weather. Her cockpit is 5½ ft. long and 7 ft. wide, with tight deck and scuppers, while a house 10 x 7 ft. gives over 4 ft. height in cabin. There will be two berths or lockers, ice-box, water-tank, oil-stove, pantries and shelves

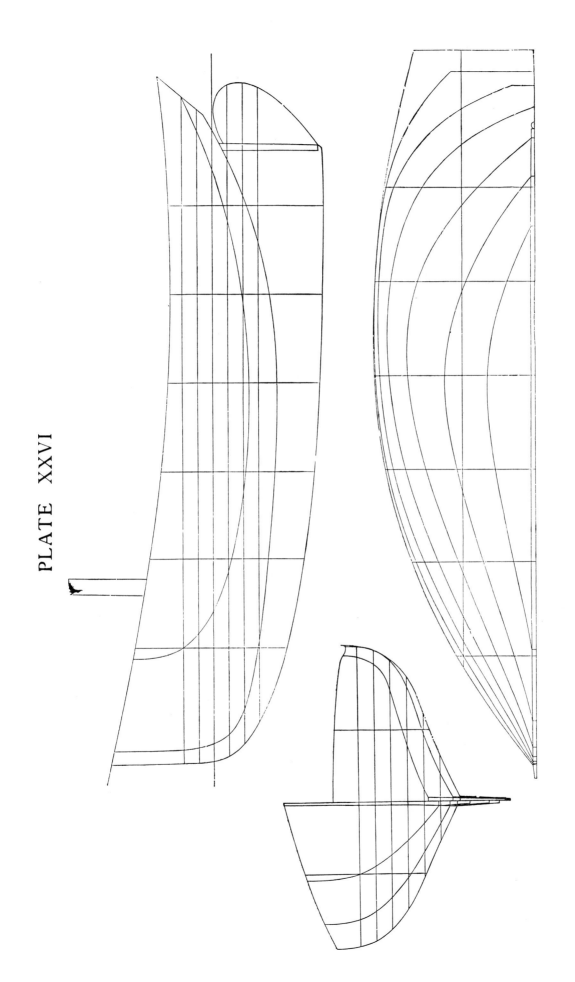

PLATE XXVI

THE KEEL SLOOP ALICE

for stores and utensils, and she will be comfortably fitted for living aboard. In model the ALICE is similar to the usual type of centreboard boats in use about New Bedford; but the board has been dispensed with, and a keel 21 in. deep added, making the total draft 3 ft. 6 in. Ballast is about two tons of iron inside.

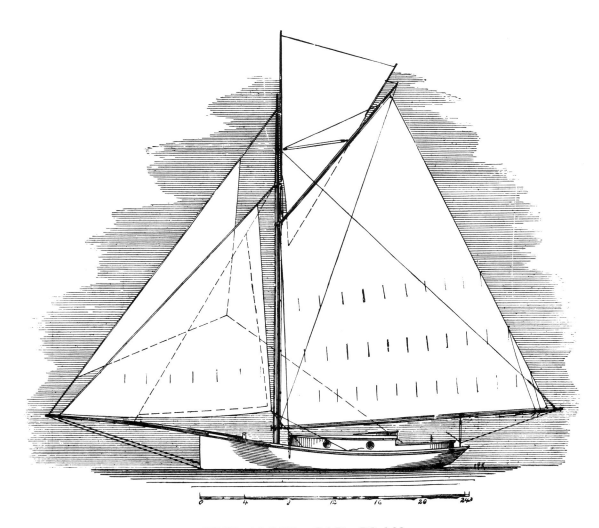

THE ALICE—SAIL PLAN

## VII. THE LARK

*PLATE XXVII*

SEVENTEEN FEET SIX INCHES LONG ON WATER-LINE

A VERY good example of what can be done on small dimensions in the way of a *bona fide* cruising yacht is furnished in the plans of the keel sloop LARK. She is in all respects a complete little vessel of good speed and considerable ability. Her maximum draft is 2 ft. 11 in. This might with advantage be increased to 3 ft., or even to 3 ft. 2 in., by deepening the keel through the addition of 300 lbs. outside weight. With this the boat would be better able to carry the rig, which seems too liberal for regular cruising. The topmast is lofty, but can be housed when not in use. No fid is required, the heel of the topmast resting in the heel-rope when up. The cabin is roomy owing to absence of centreboard trunk, and will berth two hands. The LARK was built by H. C. Ford, of Bordentown, N. J., in 1886. Like small keel boats in general, she excels in light winds and works like a top.

| | | |
|---|---|---|
| Length over all | 21 ft. | 4½ in. |
| Length on water-line | 17 " | 6 " |
| Beam moulded at deck | 7 " | |
| Beam moulded at *L W L* | 6 " | 2 " |
| Breadth across transom | 3 " | 6 " |
| Greatest draft | 2 " | 11 " |
| Least freeboard | 1 " | 3 " |
| Sheer forward | 1 " | 1½ " |
| Sheer aft | | 3½ " |
| Rake of sternpost | 40 deg. | |
| Displacement | 4,600 lbs. | |
| Iron on keel | 1,200 " | |
| Ballast inside | 1,000 " | |
| Mast from stem | 5 ft. | 8 in. |
| Mast, deck to hounds | 17 " | 6 " |
| Diameter in partners | | 5½ " |
| Masthead | 3 " | 6 " |
| Topmast over all | 16 " | 6 " |
| Diameter in cap | | 3¼ " |
| Bowsprit outboard | 10 " | 6 " |
| Diameter at stem | | 3½ " |
| Boom over all | 21 " | 6 " |
| Diameter | | 4 " |

PLATE XXVII

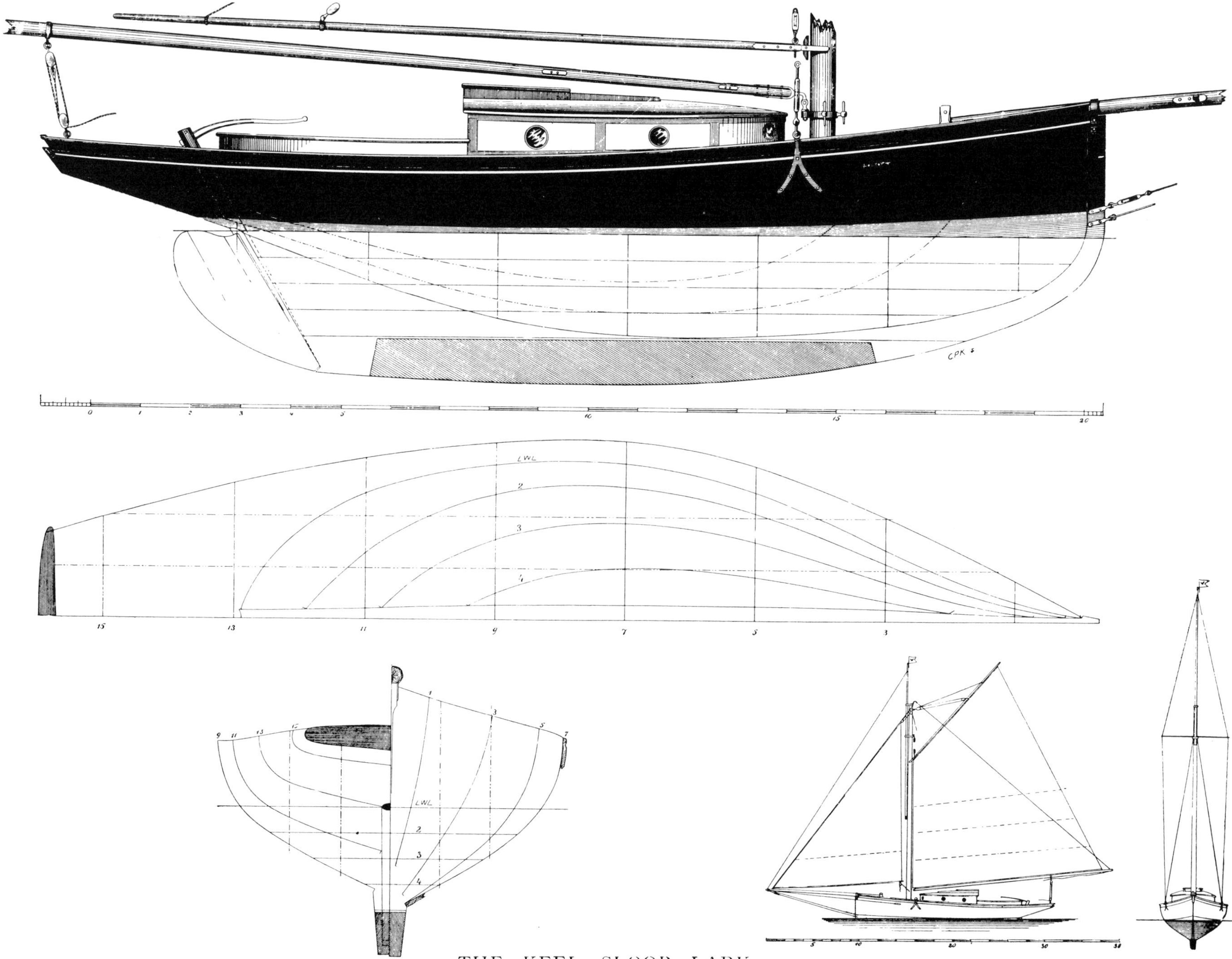

THE KEEL SLOOP LARK

```
Gaff over all..............................  14 ft.
Diameter...................................         2½ in.
Area mainsail.............................. 300 sq. ft.
Area jib................................... 110  "   "
Area clubtopsail........................... 110  "   "
Area lower sail to square L W L............ 1.34
```

The building specifications are as follows: Keel of white oak, 6 × 8 in.; stem and sternpost of oak, sided 4 in.; frame of white oak, double, 3 × 4 at heel and 2½ × 3 at head. These frames are boxed into the keel and through riveted. The iron ballast is bolted up with 1 in. bolts set up with nuts inside. Clamps of oak 1 × 4 in., sprung to sheer in one length; ceiling of Norway pine ½ × 3 in.; deck beams of yellow pine 2 × 4 in., with taper at ends; breasthook of oak; knees of hackmatack; side plank 1 in. Georgia pine with oak garboards and sheer strakes. Plank sheer 1 × 3 in. oak, sprung to side line; mast partners or king plank of oak, 1½ × 15 in., running from stem to cabin house and oak chocks underneath between the mast beams, so as to give good bearing to the mast wedges. Deck of white pine 1 × 3 in., covered with canvas and painted to keep it tight in all weather; waist 1 × 3 in. oak with caprail 1 × 2 in., oval section. Cabin house of 1 × 18 in. oak boards, sprung to shape and paneled on the outside with ½ in. pine. Six brass air ports in the house. Cockpit furnished in walnut and chestnut staving with cherry cap 1 × 2½ in., oval section. Cockpit floor covered with canvas and painted. Hatches and fittings of hard wood; interior of cabin in hard oil finish with cherry trimmings. Rudderhead 3 in. diameter, blade of 1½ in. oak. Lower sails of 8 oz. yacht duck, close bighted; topsail of 6¼ oz. drill.

## VIII. THE GIPSY

### *PLATE XXVIII*

#### TWENTY-THREE FEET LONG ON WATER-LINE

THE Gipsy was built in 1885 by Daniel C. Bernard, South Brooklyn, for Mr. Theo. C. Hall, of Newburgh, N. Y. The plans were made by Mr. J. A. Wylie with a view to producing a comfortable and roomy yacht of economic construction. By the use of the keel the cabin was kept clear of an obstructing centreboard trunk. Having considerable beam, inside ballast is sufficient for keeping the boat up to her work. The performance of the Gipsy in light and heavy weather has given excellent satisfaction.

PLATE XXVIII

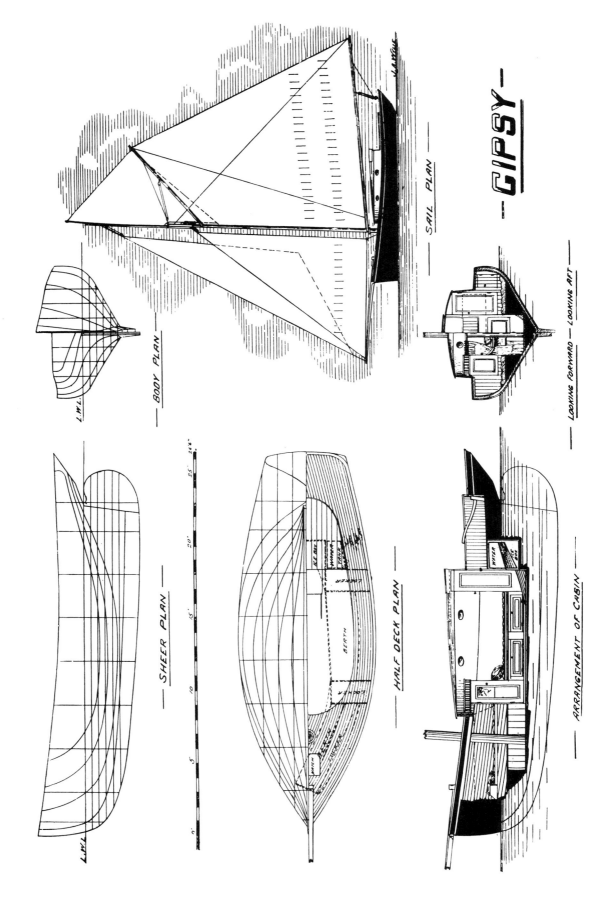

— BODY PLAN —

L.W.L.

— SAIL PLAN —

— GIPSY —

— LOOKING FORWARD — LOOKING AFT —

— SHEER PLAN —

— HALF DECK PLAN —

— ARRANGEMENT OF CABIN —

THE KEEL SLOOP GIPSY

## Light Draft Keel Yachts

| | | | | |
|---|---|---|---|---|
| Length on deck............................ | 26 ft. | 6 | | in. |
| Length on water-line...................... | 23 " | | | |
| Beam extreme............................. | 9 " | | | |
| Breadth across transom.................... | 5 " | 4 | | " |
| Greatest draft............................ | 4 " | | | |
| Least freeboard........................... | 1 " | 8 | | " |
| Sheer forward............................. | 1 " | 8 | | " |
| Sheer aft................................. | | 4 | | " |
| Displacement ............................. | 11,500 lbs. | | | |
| Ballast, inside iron ...................... | 5,000 " | | | |
| Mast from stem........................... | 7 ft. | | | |
| Mast, deck to hounds...................... | 25 " | | | |
| Diameter in partners...................... | | | 6 | in. |
| Boom over all ............................ | 27 " | | | |
| Diameter.................................. | | | 4½ | " |
| Gaff over all.............................. | 14 " | 2 | | " |
| Diameter ................................. | | | 2½ | " |
| Bowsprit outboard......................... | 12 " | | | |
| Topmast, cap to truck..................... | 11 " | | | |
| Luff of mainsail........................... | 22 " | | | |
| Jib on luff ............................... | 29 " | | | |
| Jib on foot............................... | 16 " | | | |
| Area lower sail ........................... | 728 sq. ft. | | | |
| Ratio lower sail to square of load-line........ | 1.38 | | | |

Keel of white oak 14 × 6 in. amidships.    Stem and post of oak, sided 4 in.    The frames are steam bent, 12 in. between centres, 2½ × 2 in. at heel and 2 × 1¾ in. at head.    Floors of hackmatack of natural crook cross the keel, the arms laying hold of the timbers.    Bilge strakes of 1 × 4 in. white pine; clamps, 1 × 4 in. yellow pine; deck beams, 2 × 2¼ in.; ceiling of ½ in. white pine.    Plank of 1¼ in. cedar with wales of 1¼ in. Georgia pine, worked in single lengths; deck stuff, 1¼ in. square white pine.    Fittings, such as companion slide, doors, cockpit rail, etc., are in cherry.    The accommodations are very liberal and pleasing.    The forecastle has a transom locker along the port side and a swing berth above for the paid hand.    The cabin, finished in white pine and hard oil with cherry trimmings, is 10 ft. long.    The floor measures 3 ft. between the sofas, and the headroom 5 ft.    Lockers, 18 in. wide, rise from floor to roof at the after end, so that oilers and clothes can be hung up full length.    The wing space or the run each side of the cockpit is reached from a door in the after cabin bulkhead.    The cockpit floor being carried out to the boat's side and caulked, these lockers are watertight.    They serve for stowing awning stanchions, boathooks, brooms, etc.    The sofa berths are 6 ft. 3 in. long with locker room underneath, accessible through doors in the fronts.    Other lockers at the forward end of the sofas serve for pantry, linen, glass and wine. Cooking is done over oil stoves in the forecastle. Under the cockpit, and opening into the cabin by means of a sliding door, is the ice-box, 2 ft. square, with water tanks each side of it. These are connected by a pipe, and can be drawn off by a faucet under the companion ladder. They hold thirty-five gallons.

## IX. THE YAWL SYLVIA

### PLATE XXIX

TWENTY FEET LONG ON WATER-LINE

ONE of the best attempts at a compromise between cutter and sloop hull is represented by the SYLVIA. This yacht was designed by Mr. Henry K. Wicksteed, C. E., of Port Arthur, Lake Superior. In point of beauty, excellent proportions and unity of purpose throughout the SYLVIA is very striking. The ease and fairness of her bow and buttocks and diagonals on the displacement of three tons are specially commendable, and insure speed and good behavior in rough water. As an "all round" vessel the SYLVIA meets every requirement, besides economy in first cost. Perhaps it would be advisable to retain 500 lbs. of ballast inside for purposes of trim and lightening off when aground. As to the control of a jib set flying or on a stay, it is much a matter for individual preference, although a standing jibstay would give support to the bowsprit end, and lessen the danger of carrying away that spar. For greater certainty in shifting over headsheets the jibs should be cut with less overlap than shown in the Sail Plan. The mizzen may also have more peak to the yard, which would give a flatter set on the wind.

| | |
|---|---|
| Length over all | 24 ft. 6 in. |
| Length on water-line | 20 " |
| Beam extreme | 6 " |
| Beam on water-line | 5 " 9½ " |
| Draft extreme | 3 " 6 " |
| Draft at heel | 2 " 8½ " |
| Depth of keel amidships | 1 " 6 " |
| Least freeboard | 1 " 6 " |
| Displacement | 3 tons |
| Ballast on keel | 3,000 lbs. |
| Area midship section | 8.33 sq. ft. |
| Area load water-line plane | 76.54 " " |

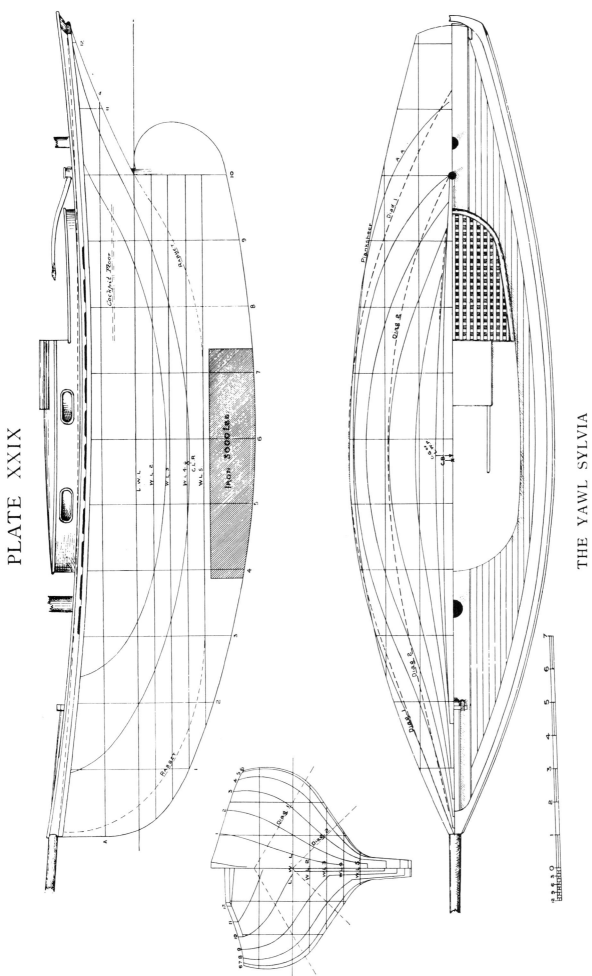

PLATE XXIX

THE YAWL SYLVIA

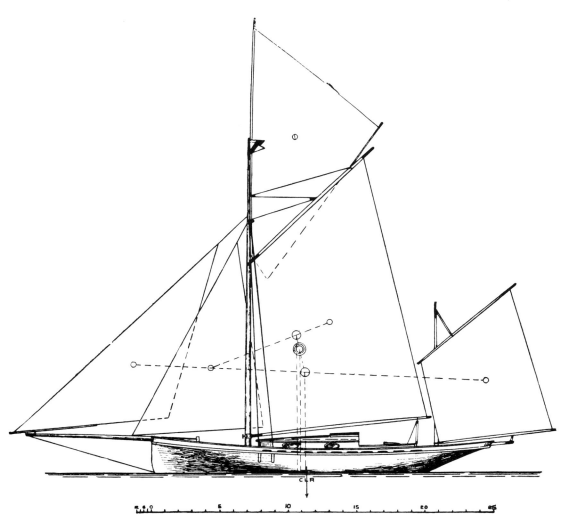

RIG OF THE SYLVIA

| | | | |
|---|---|---:|---|
| Area longitudinal section | 56.13 sq. ft. | | |
| Area wetted surface with rudder | 158 " " | | |
| Centre of buoyancy from end *L W L* | 11 ft. 4 | in. | |
| Centre of buoyancy below *L W L* | 1 " | | |
| *C G* of *L W L* plane from end *L W L* | 11 " 6 | " | |
| Centre of lateral resistance from end *L W L* | 11 " 2½ | " | |
| Centre of effort lower sails from end *L W L* | 10 " 10 | " | |
| Centre of effort above *L W L* | 9 " 2½ | " | |
| Mast from end *L W L* | 7 " | | |
| Rake of mast | 0 | | |
| Diameter in partners | 5½ | " | |
| Mast, deck to hounds | 17 " | | |
| Bowsprit outboard | 9 " | | |
| Hoist of mainsail | 13 " | | |

Boom over all............................. 13 ft.
Gaff over all............................. 12 " 6 in.
Area mainsail............................. 178 sq. ft.
Area foresail............................. 67 " "
Area jib................................. 70 " "
Area mizzen ............................. 67 " "
Area topsail............................. 76 " "
Area lower sail ......................... 382 " "
**Ratio** to square of *L W L*................. 0.955
**Amount** per sq. ft. wetted surface............ 2.42 sq. ft.

The **cockpit** is 4 ft. long and 4 ft. wide. Cabin 7 ft. long with 4 ft. head-room under a 9 in. trunk. The same plans will serve for a boat 21 or 22 ft. water-line, by altering the scale to suit.

A FAIR DAY SINGLE-HANDED

# VI

# DEEP DRAFT KEEL YACHTS

## I. THE NEVA

*PLATE XXX*

TWENTY-FIVE FEET LONG ON LOAD-LINE

THERE flourishes in Eastern waters a very numerous fleet of wholesome big-bodied vessels, closely allied to the genuine cutter in all respects save in the matter of beam. They have the depth, more than the draft, the outside weight and much of the rig and outfit.

In yachts like the NEVA, of Boston, no one need hesitate to take up permanent quarters, to ship for the season, sail where and when he listeth, so far as any danger from trickiness or dubious stability of form is concerned, and in point of room, accommodation, and that "comfort" due to ability in lumpy water, the NEVA class holds out inducements.

The NEVA was built for Mr. George G. Granger, of Boston, in the spring of 1881. In model she is rather more taking than others of the type. A fine easy bow, with high side and no hard flare, swelling into a bold and well proportioned midships, running off in a clear run, make up a whole quite pleasing and more agreeable than the naked dimensions would lead one to expect. She was one of the first of the kind, and many wise shakes of the head did the local sharps indulge in when they saw 1,100 lbs. of iron go underneath the keel in shape of a shoe, and when her owner fixed upon the cutter rig.

Ballast inside at the time of launching was 5,400 pounds, the total displacement being seven tons. With this stowage she proved herself easy and manageable in a sea as well as dry compared to sister boats. In 1882 her owner decided to change to lead and increase the amount outside to 3,050 pounds, with 3,550 pounds stowed in a length of 8 ft. inside. Spars, rig and trim were preserved. In her new form the NEVA was found materially stiffer and no note-

PLATE XXX

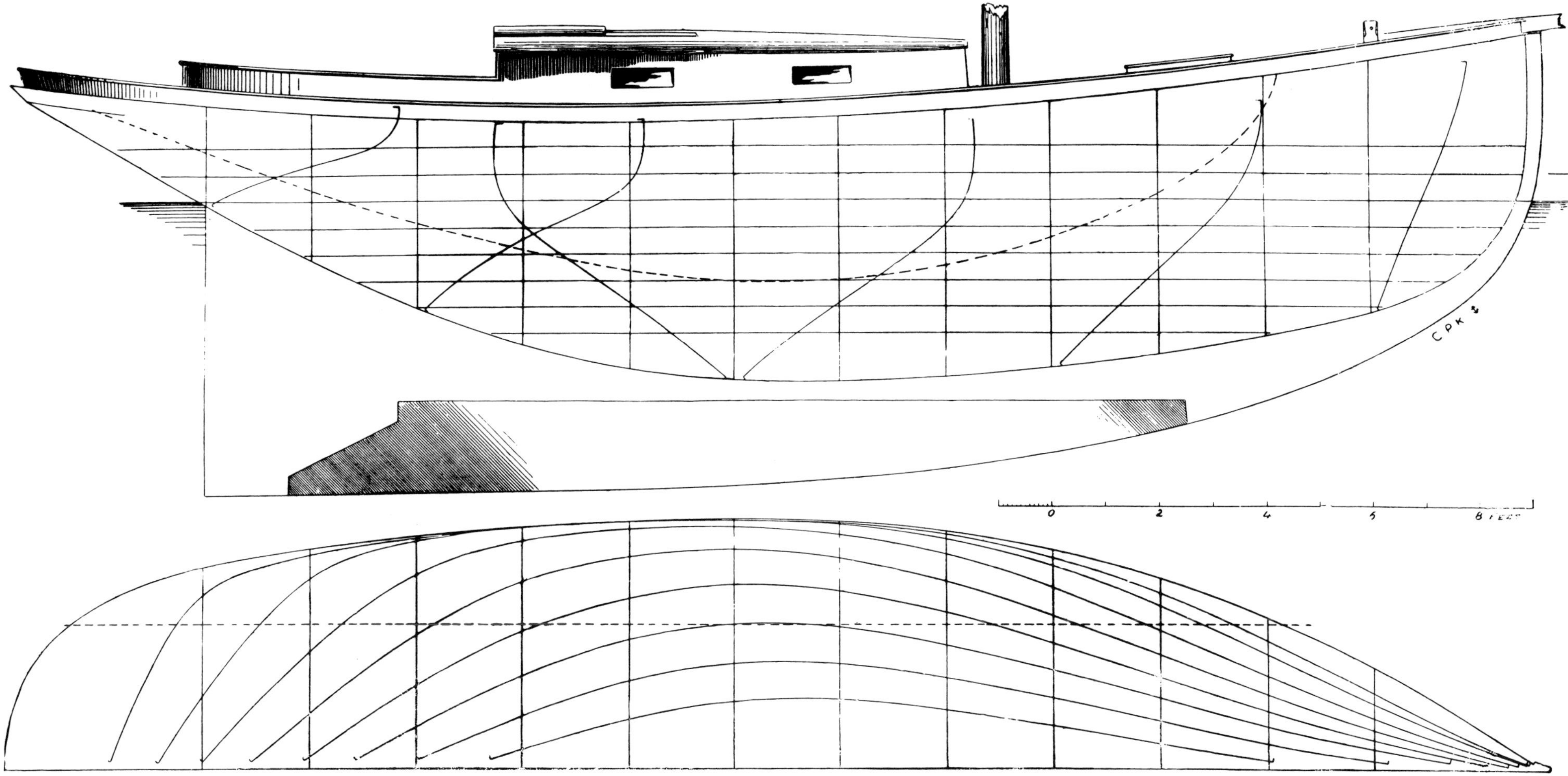

THE BOSTON SLOOP NEVA

worthy difference in her behavior at sea was recorded. The addition outside involved an increase of 3½ in. draught, bringing it up to 5 ft. 5½ in., a figure since exceeded by other Boston yachts of no greater length. NEVA has not been raced, though in strong winds she has made an excellent showing. Her rig is small for racing in light to moderate breezes, as cruising was kept in view when selecting her spar plan, the lower sail area being 725 sq. ft.

The ground tackle consists of two Trotman anchors, 50 and 75 lbs. Cables, 55 fathoms of 2¾ in. manilla, and 40 fathoms of 3¾ in. Standing rigging, 1½ in. galvanized wire; blocks, 4 ins. Bagnall & Loud patent brass-bouched with lignum vitæ shells. Lower sails of 10 oz. duck. Hull and fastenings particularly strong. Keel of oak, 7 in. sided; frames of oak, sided 2½ in., and moulded 3 in. at floor and 2 in. at gunwale; deck beams, 3 x 3½ in.; plank, yellow pine, 1⅛ in. thick; deck and house top, 1¼ in. double, with tarred paper in a layer between.

| | | | |
|---|---|---|---|
| Length over all | 29 ft. | 2 | in. |
| Length on load-line | 25 " | | |
| Beam, moulded | 9 " | | |
| Depth, deck to top of keel | 5 " | | |
| Draft greatest | 5 " | 5½ | in. |
| Least freeboard to planksheer | 1 " | 6 | " |
| Lead keel, depth amidships | 1 " | 7 | " |
| Lead keel, length | 17 " | 6 | " |
| Lead keel, width on top | | 3½ | " |
| Lead keel, width on bottom | | 2 | " |
| Lead keel, weight | 3,050 lbs. | | |
| Lead ballast, inside | 3,550 " | | |
| Total ballast | 6,600 " | | |
| Displacement | 7 tons | | |
| Mast, 10 ft. 6 in. from bow over all | 35 ft. | | |
| Mast, diameter at partners | | 7 | in. |
| Main boom, egg section, 3 x 5 in. | 24 " | | |
| Gaff, egg section, 2½ x 4 in | 15 " | | |
| Topmast, 3½ in. diameter above cap | 9 " | | |
| Length of mast doublings | 4 " | | |
| Bowsprit outboard to stayhole | 9 " | | |
| Hoist of mainsail | 20 " | 6 | in. |
| Foot of mainsail | 23 " | | |
| Head of mainsail | 14 " | 6 | in. |
| Leech of mainsail | 31 " | | |
| Staysail on foot | 12 " | | |
| Staysail on leech | 26 " | | |
| Jib on foot | 11 " | | |
| Jib on leech | 24 " | | |
| Area lower sail | 725 sq. ft. | | |

| Length of cabin trunk | 9 ft. | | |
|---|---|---|---|
| Height of side aft | 1 " | 3 | in. |
| Length of cockpit | 6 " | | |
| Height of rail with cap | 3¾ " | | |

There are two deadlights in forward bulkhead of trunk and a 20 in. circular scuttle to the forecastle. The water tank under the cockpit is piped to draw water in the forecastle from copper tanks holding 50 gallons ; lockers and pantry below are especially convenient in arrangement of detail. Cabin is finished in cherry and pine polished ; the cockpit in cherry. Cabin cushions of hair, covered with Brussels. Cabin table supported by four shifting legs, which can be quickly unscrewed and stowed away. It is made of cherry, with nickel-plated fastenings. The steering gear consists of iron wheel and quadrant, with cog and ratchet to set it. The outfit is complete, her owner being given to extensive cruising. Galley, side lights, Fresnel riding light, liquid compass, etc., and a full line of supplies. The yawl is whaleboat shape, 11 ft. long, and owing to sharp ends can be stowed inboard with less trouble than a square transom.

## II. THE NYSSA

### *PLATE XXXI*

TWENTY-SIX FEET NINE INCHES LONG ON LOAD-LINE

THE NYSSA, built by Wood Brothers, of East Boston, and now the property of Mr. J. L. Wall, of New York, is another excellent example of the modern Boston keel sloop. It will be seen that to good depth she also adds large beam, and requires a correspondingly liberal rig. Boats of this class are very stiff and powerful, and, of course, uncapsizable. In some recent specimens nearly all the weight is hung on the keel. The drag and deep heel is peculiar to the East Boston builders. Where there is enough water this deep heel is an advantage in steadying the boat, and doing away with long bowsprits, as the Centre of Lateral Resistance is well aft.

The extent to which such boats can be modified with benefit by clipping some of the beam and filling below, making an easier form to drive, is indicated in the success of such yachts as VAYU, BEETLE, ORIVA, MAVIS, and many others. Such alterations would in nowise interfere with cabin floor, but add to its width and to the height below as well, so that even in boats of the NYSSA's length a flush deck is not impossible. The typical Boston sloop, evolved since the

# PLATE XXXI

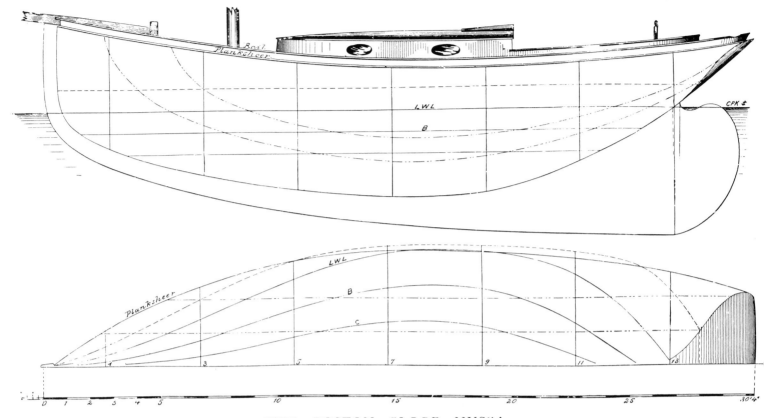

## THE BOSTON SLOOP NYSSA

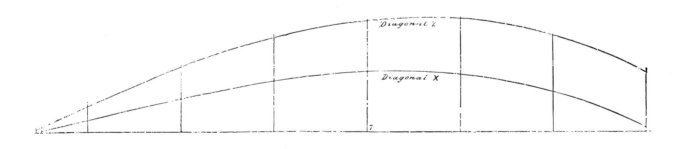

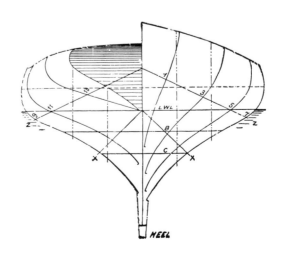

# Deep Draft Keel Yachts

introduction of keel ballast, is slowly approximating the regular cutter with three to four beams.

How far this gradual merging into the cutter will be carried in our waters it is for the future to tell. Under length measurement boats must always remain very large on their load-line; hence we may look for all the depth, displacement and draft which experience will allow, and in addition such beam as is congenial to the other requisites. This tendency has received exemplification in the numerous new yachts built in Boston. When a yacht becomes so deep as to afford head room under the beams, houses and encumbrances on deck will disappear of themselves. The large class of Eastern sloops have deservedly become widely popular in the search for a reliable substitute to take the place of the light drafts and light displacements. But for the prevalence of these deep drafts with their outside weight, general cruising along the Eastern coast would be practically impossible, as it would be fraught with such risks and so many accidents, that few would care to expose themselves to the chances of going to Davy Jones' locker. The annals of the past have recorded many instances of close escapes in Boston sloops, where disaster would have been a certainty in a light draft centreboard.

The NYSSA was well built in the first place, and in 1883 received a thorough overhauling, fresh rig and outfit, under the superintendence of Mr. John Harvey, so that she is one of the most complete and best equipped sloops of her class in New York waters. The keel is 6 in. sided, stem and post 4 in., all of oak. The deadwood is 4 in. thick. Timbers below the bilge are of oak 2½ x 2½, and of natural crook hackmatack from the bilge up, the floors 3-in. oak, and the frames double up to turn of bilge. The planking is yellow pine 1⅛ in. thick; the deck being 1¼ in. white pine laid tapering with the sheer.

| | |
|---|---|
| Length over all | 30 ft. 4 in. |
| Length on load-line | 26 " 9 " |
| Beam moulded on *L W L* | 9 " 10 " |
| Depth, rabbet to planksheer on *M S* | 5 " 11 " |
| Draft at heel | 5 " 7 " |
| Least freeboard | 1 " 11 " |
| Displacement | 10 short tons |
| Ballast on keel | 2,500 lbs. |
| Ballast inside | 6,577 " |
| Hoist of mainsail | 24 ft. |
| Mainboom over all | 30 " |
| Gaff, over all | 20 " |
| Jib on foot | 20 " |
| Bowsprit outboard | 13 " |

The NYSSA has lead ballast, housing topmast, runners and backstays.

## III.  THE COLUMBINE

*PLATE XXXII*

NINETEEN FEET TWO INCHES LONG ON LOAD-LINE

THE COLUMBINE is a handsome, roomy little yacht, built by George Lawley & Son, City Point, South Boston, for Mr. Edward Burgess, from his own drawings.  She is a well shaped boat all through and a good performer, though rather sharp in her roll in a ground swell.  In type she is an average between cutter and sloop.  A slight alteration would be enough to throw her either way. The rig (Plate XXXIII) is that of a pole sloop with broad head mainsail.

| | |
|---|---|
| Length over all | 24 ft. 6 in. |
| Length on water-line | 19 " 2 " |
| Greatest beam | 7 " |
| Beam on water-line | 6 " 9 " |
| Depth at side, No. 6 | 4 " 9 " |
| Least freeboard | 2 " |
| Sheer forward | 11 in. |
| Sheer aft | 3½ " |
| Greatest draft | 4 " 4 " |
| Displacement | 3.75 tons |
| Iron on keel | 3,040 lbs. |
| Mast from end *L W L* | 6 ft. 2 in. |
| Mast, deck to hounds | 19 " 6 " |
| Mast, deck to truck | 25 " 6 " |
| Boom over all | 20 " 6 " |
| Gaff over all | 14 " |
| Peak of gaff | 54 deg. |
| Bowsprit, stem to stay | 8 ft. |
| Area mainsail | 334 sq. ft. |
| Area jib | 110 " " |

The Centre of Lateral Resistance is 10.9 ft. from end of *L W L*, and the Centre of Effort of Sails is plumb over it.  The iron keel measures 21 in. across at widest part and 9 in. across the bottom, with a depth of 2 ft. 9 in. at midships.

KEEL SLOOP COLUMBINE

# PLATE XXXIII

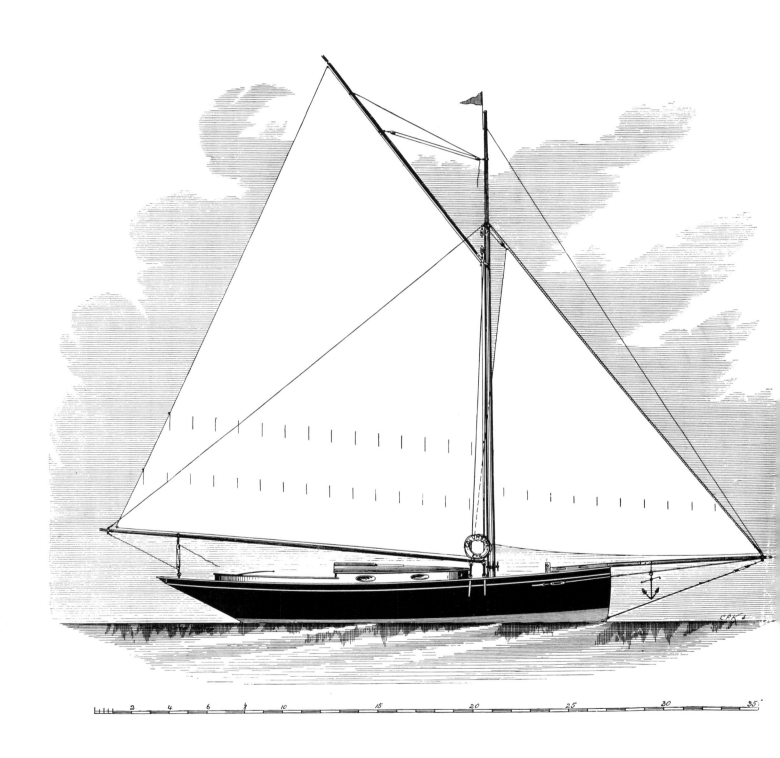

COLUMBINE—SAIL PLAN

## IV. THE CRUISER MERMAID

### *PLATE XXXIV*

#### TWENTY-TWO FEET LONG ON WATER-LINE

FOR open water cruising east of Long Island Sound, Mr. J. Borden, Jr., of Fall River, designed the MERMAID, and launched her in 1886. She was planned to be absolutely safe, to accommodate two adults and three children, and to be as able and speedy as possible without intrenching upon the first-mentioned requisites. The yacht is smart in light winds, and in strong breezes with sea overpowers other types of her length. In moderate wind and smooth water she is not quite equal to the best centreboard sloops, but by no means dull.

| | | |
|---|---|---|
| Length over all | 26 ft. | 6 in. |
| Length on water-line | 22 " | |
| Beam extreme | 8 " | 6 " |
| Breadth across counter | 4 " | |
| Draft, extreme | 4 " | |
| Least freeboard | 1 " | 10 " |
| Sheer forward | 2 " | 2 " |
| Sheer aft | | 4 " |
| Displacement | 6.53 tons | |
| Ballast, iron on keel | 4,850 lbs. | |
| Centre of buoyancy abaft middle of $LWL$ | 1.25 ft. | |
| Centre of buoyancy below $LWL$ | 1.21 " | |
| Area water-line plane | 125 sq. ft. | |
| Area midship section | 18 " " | |
| Area immersed longitudinal section | 87 " " | |
| Area wetted surface | 230 " " | |
| Centre $LWL$ plane abaft middle of $LWL$ | 1.58 ft. | |
| Centre of lateral resistance abaft middle of $LWL$ | 1.65 " | |
| Centre of effort of sails forward $CLR$ | 0.04 " | |

The accommodations have probably never been exceeded in so small a vessel. The sectional plans in Plate XXXV will give a clear idea of the arrangements below. The gangways on deck are from 18 to 27 in. wide, with a cabin trunk 4 ft. across. Cockpit is 6 ft. long, the floor being 1 ft. above the line of flotation and supplied with self-closing scuppers. The seats can be lifted in sections, disclosing locker room for warps, gear, buckets, swabs and tools. The sill of the cabin door is at deck height, so that water shipped in the cockpit will not find its way below. The cabin door is a lid hinged

PLATE XXXIV

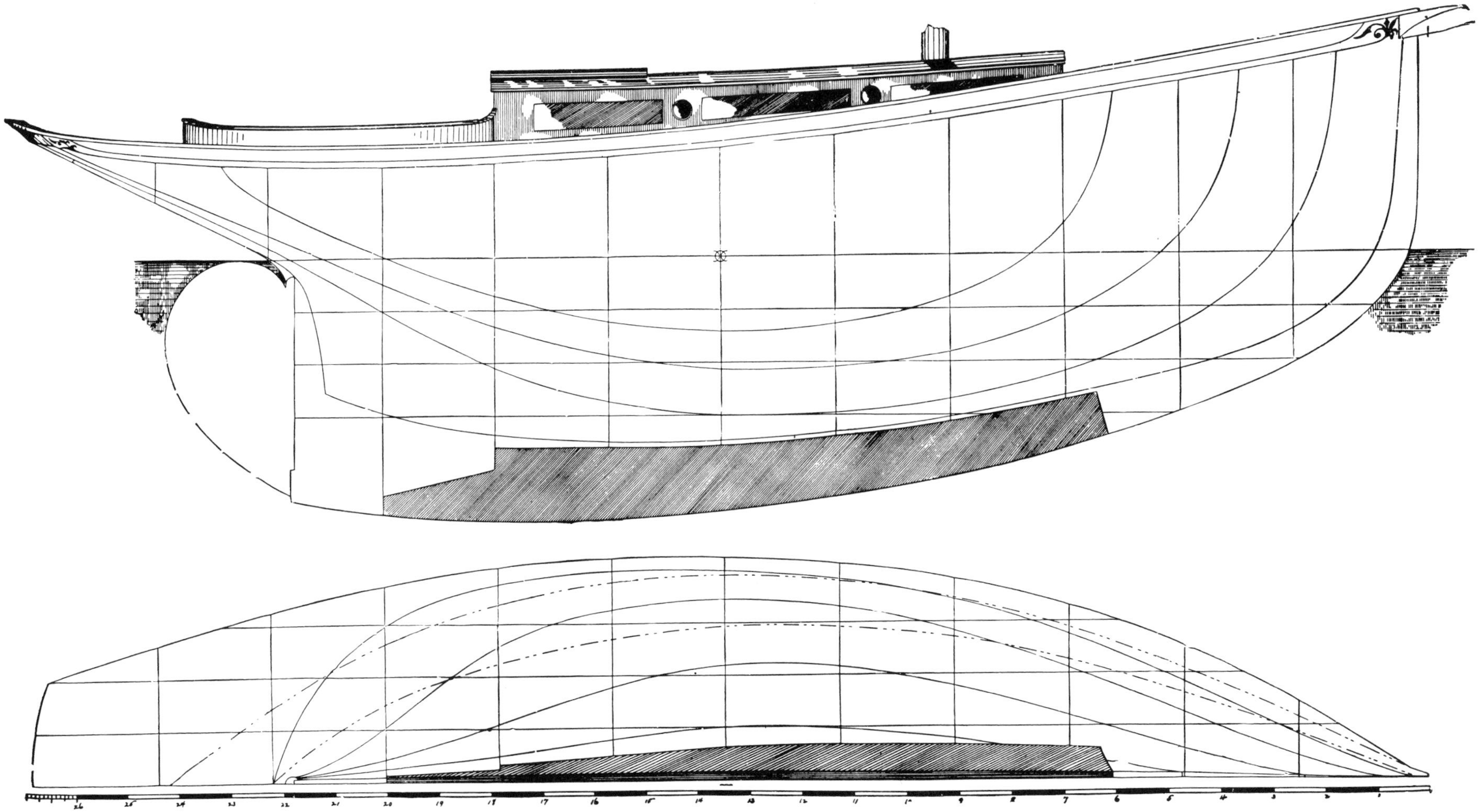

KEEL YACHT MERMAID

PLATE XXXV

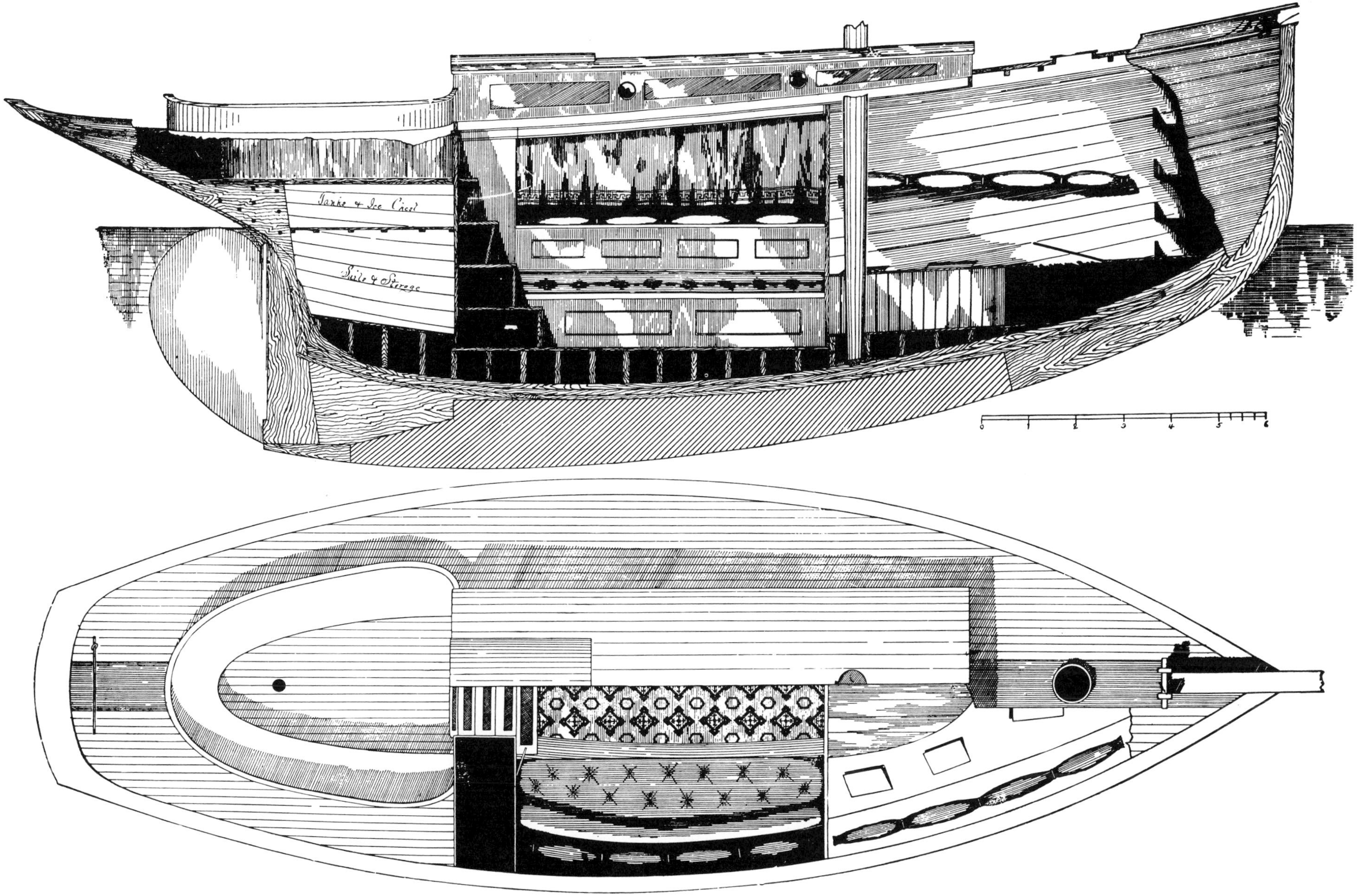

MERMAID—CABIN PLANS

on the bottom and drops down outside of the sill, doing away with swinging doors. It can be closed in an instant by being thrown up with enough force for the spring latch to catch. The cabin is reached by five steps, the upper one forming a grip to the ice drawer, the others being utilized as lockers. There is 5 ft. 10 in. headroom under the carlins and a floor 3 ft. wide. For berthing, canvas bunks are attached to eyebolts in the ceiling above the sofas, the inboard corners being hauled out to suitably located eyebolts in the bulkheads by means of lanyards. These supply two tiers of berths with the sofas, so that four can be slept in the cabin. When not in use the canvas bunks are rolled up fore and aft to the ceiling and hid from view by curtains. Similar arrangements are provided in the forecastle. The cabin is finished in hard woods, the forecastle in cypress. The only paint is the black of the topsides and the bronze on the bottom.

The water tanks are arranged under the cockpit floor in a hollow square, the ice drawer in the middle. An oil tank, filled from the cockpit, is also placed in the run with a pipe leading to the forecastle, thereby avoiding dirt and smell below.

The yacht is cutter rigged, with fixed bowsprit, running jib and laced mainsail. In place of mast hoops, the sail hoists on a Haggerty railway. Mainsail, jib and small topsail of 10 oz. duck; foresail of 8 oz. duck; club-topsail and jibtopsail of heavy drilling and spinnaker of stout sheeting. The sail plan is shown in Plate XXXVI.

DIMENSIONS OF RIG

| | | |
|---|---|---|
| Mast from stem | 10 ft. | 2 in. |
| Mast, deck to hounds | 19 " | |
| Masthead | 5 " | |
| Diameter in partners | | 6 " |
| Topmast, fid to sheave | 16 " | |
| Bowsprit outboard | 12 " | |
| Bowsprit, rabbet to stayhole | 11 " | |
| Boom over all | 23 " | |
| Gaff over all | 17 " | |
| Spinnaker boom | 25 " | |
| Topsail yard | 19 " | |
| Topsail club | 18 " | 6 " |
| Mainsail on luff | 16 " | |
| Mainsail on foot | 22 " | |
| Mainsail on head | 16 " | |
| Mainsail, angle of peak | 55 deg. | |
| Foresail on luff | 18 ft. | |
| Foresail on foot | 10 " | |
| Foresail on leech | 17 " | 6 " |
| Jib on luff | 28 " | |

PLATE XXXVI

MERMAID—SAIL PLAN

Jib on foot.................................. 15 ft.
Jib on leech................................ 20 "
Cringle topsail on luff.......................... 19 " 2 "
Cringle topsail on leech........................ 10 " 8 "
Cringle topsail on foot......................... 15 " 4 "
Yardtopsail on luff........................... 25 " 8 "
Yardtopsail on leech.......................... 14 " 9 "
Yardtopsail on foot........................... 22 "
Jibtopsail on luff............................. 30 "
Jibtopsail on leech........................... 20 "
Jibtopsail on foot............................ 14 " 3 "
Spinnaker on luff............................. 35 " 6 "
Spinnaker on leech........................... 36 " 6 "
Spinnaker on foot............................ 26 "
Area mainsail................................ 386 sq. ft.
Area foresail................................ 87 " "
Area jib.................................... 143 " "
Three lower sails............................. 616 " "
Cringle topsail.............................. 80 " "
Yardtopsail................................. 163 " "
Jibtopsail.................................. 124 " "
Spinnaker. ................................ 462 " "
Area lower sails per sq. ft. wetted surface........ 2.68 " "
Ratio lower sails to square of $L\,W\,L$........... 1.27 " "

# VII

# COMPROMISE KEEL
# AND
# CENTREBOARD YACHTS

## I.  THE GANNET

### *PLATE XXXVII*

TWENTY FEET LONG ON LOAD-LINE

THE yawl GANNET was built by Wallin & Gorman, of South Brooklyn, for Mr. Oliver Adams, Larchmont, in 1883, from designs by Mr. H. W. Eaton, New York.

The GANNET differs from the other examples in being a combination of the keel and centreboard types, and is therefore especially interesting to many who object to the draft of a keel and the smaller beam of a deeper boat. It is very difficult indeed to make a successful combination of two types, as those who have attempted that kind of work know full well. It is easy to produce a centreboard craft and plaster lead underneath, calling her a combination boat, but to devise a cross which shall possess the good qualities of either extreme, and a minimum of their undesirable peculiarities, is a different matter. Such attempts have generally failed, because the originator found it impossible to divorce himself from preconceived preference for one of the two extremes. Thus the predominating features would in one case be those of the usual shoal sloop, with a trifle outside weight and the cat or sloop rig. She would still remain open to all that is urged against the sloop and possess too little of the excellence of the opposite style in the way of an offset, or she would be narrow and deep like the cutter breed, and then completely spoiled by being minus the benefit of a keel and low ballast, a board being substituted, without good reason, only as a claim to representing a combination of the two chief types. The underlying qualities which really ought to receive consideration in place of the mere garb of shape visible to the eye, almost always escape proper attention.

97

# PLATE XXXVII

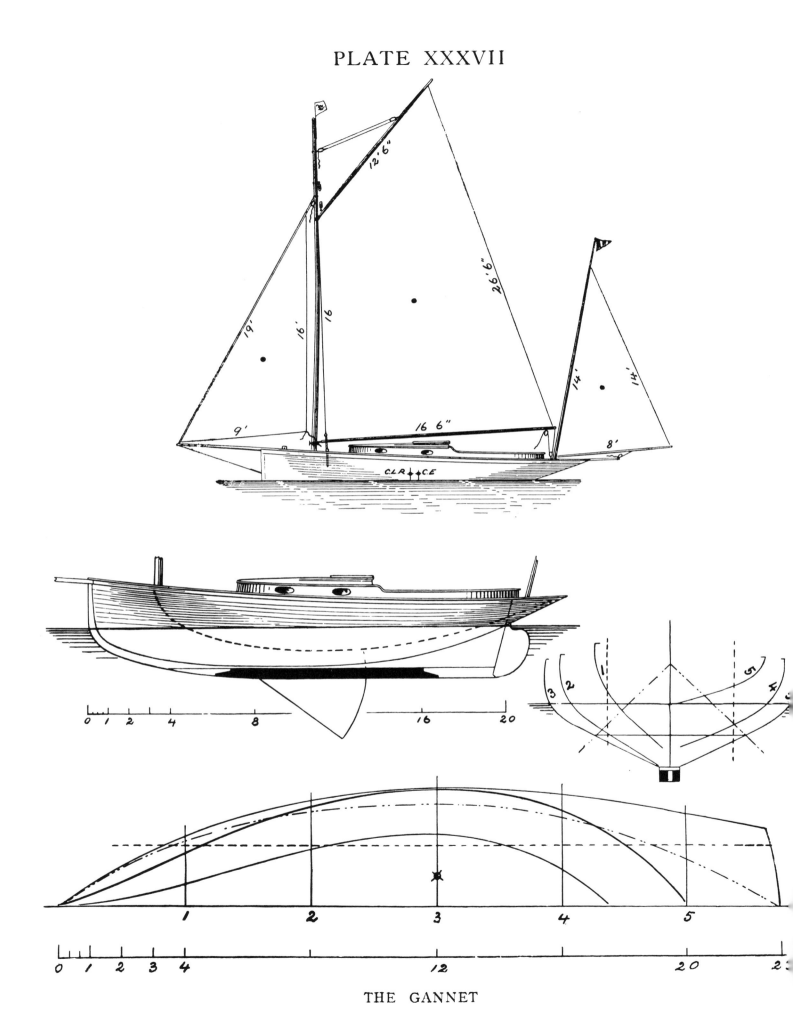

THE GANNET

# Compromise Keel and Centreboard Yachts

In the GANNET, the best performance for all round work in connection with certain definite stipulations, such as safety, room, stiffness, small draft and handy rig, has been studied.

For family sailing, cruising in the Sound, and for the rational enjoyment of life afloat, the GANNET appeals forcibly to those who hold aloof for want of the means or inclination to build large craft, under the impression that small boats can never be anything else but wet and treacherous.

That a solution to the question "how to build a small boat which shall possess the attributes of a large yacht in all respects, limited only as to power by her small tonnage," has not long ago met with a favorable response, can only be attributed to the prevailing creed that it was useless to expect anything more from 15, 18, 20 or 25 ft. than already achieved in the "open boat."

The GANNET combines the stiffness of the sloop with much of the safety of the cutter. She has 8 feet beam on a load-line of 20, besides depth enough to insure large accommodations for a couple of hands. Her cockpit is roomy enough for four, five or even six. It is shoal, but deep enough for "comfort." She may be knocked down ever so often, but will not fill, as the water will not pass over her cabin door sill. She has a large area of deck forward to hoist and attend to the ground tackle, more than the average open cockpit boat can display. She has a low bilge, and can lie on the mud without harm or inconvenience to those on board. She has a board which gives her practically all that can be claimed on that score. She has her ballast where it will do most good and where it is out of the way. She has an easy body, which makes her easy on her helm. She may be caught out with ladies or children on board, and can house them as required to ride out a snorter under a lee away from home. A meal can be prepared and disposed of under shelter, and storage for articles of clothing and provisions and the numerous accessories of a prolonged cruise finds an appropriate place in permanent quarters.

She is always ready for tripping and a voyage of a week. She is a far drier boat than those of flatter floor, and easier in her behavior in roughish water. She is really a full-fledged, completely furnished floating home.

As to rig, you may give her any plan you most fancy and yet not destroy what has just gone before. Rig her as a sloop or cutter if you think you can master big sails to your satisfaction. If you are doubtful on that point, give her an equivalent and a little over in the cut of a yawl, and but little, if any, speed need be lost in light weather with big topsail and ballooners, as you choose.

With three strakes down the yawl rig takes no slack from sloop or cutter, and will wind on the schooner, lugger, lateen and other substitutes. With the jib on a boom there is not a string more to vex or perplex than in the primitive catboat; for handiness and an ever-ready state to meet squalls, drive unharmed through puffs without varying your course and take risks in so doing, for adaptation to all kinds of weather, to all sorts of sailing, the yawl is particularly suited.

The GANNET is built with oak keel and frame, pine plank and ceiling, and hackmatack knees. Her house and cockpit are pleasing in outline, all neatly finished in yellow pine, varnished, with trimmings, rail, doors and sliding companion of mahogany. The decks are laid in narrow white pine, varnished, which is a great improvement upon the plan of slobbering them with blues, yellows or greens, giving an aged appearance to a boat scarce a week out of the shop, and exasperating to a person of taste with consideration for the fitness of things. Below, the cabin is also fitted in bright yellow pine, and the floor of the cockpit is a counterpart of the deck in this respect. A fresh, smart, agreeable impression and a yacht-like nobbiness are the result. The cockpit, it should be mentioned, is long aft, with an elliptic round, bringing the rudder head inside. This is possible without destroying necessary deck room aft on account of the long overhang, without which the boat would lose materially in the accommodations she possesses.

| | | | |
|---|---|---|---|
| Length over all | 23 | ft. | |
| Load water-line | 20 | " | |
| Beam | 8 | " | |
| Draft without centreboard (aft) | 2 | " | 6 in. |
| Draft with board down | 4 | " | |
| Outside ballast (iron keel) | 1,000 | lbs. | |
| Inside ballast, iron | 2,000 | " | |
| Cabin house (length) | 7 | ft. | |
| Cockpit (length) | 6 | " | 6 in. |
| Headroom in cabin | 4 | " | 6 " |
| Height of cockpit floor above load water-line | | 6 | " |
| Centreboard (length) | 6 | " | |
| Depth of hold | 3 | " | 6 " |
| Freeboard amidships to sheerplank | 1 | " | 6 " |
| Height of rail | | 4 | " |
| Area mainsail | 275 | sq. ft. | |
| Area jib | 70 | " " | |
| Area mizzen | 56 | " " | |

As will be seen from Plate XXXVII., the rig of the GANNET was exceedingly small, the total area of lower sail being only 401 sq. ft., or just the square of the load-line. In light summer weather she suffered in consequence. An area of 500 to 525 sq. ft. would be none too much. The hoist of mainsail could be increased to 18 ft., the bowsprit to 9 ft., and a lug mizzen set nearly half as large again as the jib-headed sail in the Plate. It is proposed to turn the

GANNET into a keel boat for 1885 as an experiment.* An iron shoe 1 ft. deep amidships, weighing 2,300 lbs., will be added below the present keel, and rockered up to nothing at each end. The new rig is shown in the accompanying cut and specifications.

The new rig has an area of 440 sq. ft. in lower sail. The balloon jib, or more strictly the balloon jib topsail, answers also as a spinnaker in running

THE GANNET—SAIL PLAN

free. The spinnaker boom will not ship in a gooseneck on the boom band, but in the deck, forward of the mast, clear of the gear. To this end a piece of gas pipe with collar screwed on top is let into the deck to receive the pin attached to the heel of spinnaker boom by a joint having vertical play, fore and aft bracing being provided for by the pin revolving in the pipe socket. The boom will pass under the jibstay for shifting from side to side. This plan was put into effect aboard the sloop GLEAM by Mr. N. D. Lawton. GANNET'S lower sails are of ten ounce duck, double bighted, mainsail with two rows of reef knittles and jib with one.

* The alteration to keel has proven an entire success. The boat sails as fast as before, and fetches as high, except in very light airs, when she seems to fall away a trifle. The cabin is of course much more roomy without the centreboard trunk. The boat is stiffer and steadier on her helm. No loss in footing can be observed, although skin surface has been increased.

| | | | | |
|---|---|---|---|---|
| Mainsail on luff | 17 | ft. | | |
| Mainsail on head | 12 | " | 6 | in. |
| Mainsail on foot | 19 | " | 6 | " |
| Mainsail on leech | 27 | " | 6 | " |
| Mainsail area | 306 | sq. ft. | | |
| Jib on luff | 23 | ft. | 6 | " |
| Jib on foot | 14 | " | | |
| Jib on leech | 19 | " | | |
| Jib area | 134 | sq. ft. | | |
| Jib topsail on luff | 24 | ft. | | |
| Jib topsail on foot | 13 | " | | |
| Jib topsail on leech | 13 | " | | |
| Jib topsail area | 66 | sq. ft. | | |
| Balloon jib on luff | 30 | ft. | | |
| Balloon jib on foot | 19 | " | | |
| Balloon jib on leech | 29 | " | | |
| Balloon jib area | 260 | sq. ft. | | |
| Topsail yard | 15 | ft. | | |

## II.  IMPROVED OPEN BOAT

### *PLATE XXXVIII*

SIXTEEN FEET LONG ON LOAD-LINE

FOR cruising in the Shrewsbury River, Mr. A. Cary Smith, of New York, designed the compromise keel and centreboard shown in Plate XXXVIII for Mr. E. S. Auchincloss.  She is intended to combine safety without great draft. A weight of 900 lbs. lead was cut up into the wood keel, the centreboard dropping through.

| | | | | |
|---|---|---|---|---|
| Length over all | 19 | ft. | | |
| Length on water-line | 16 | " | | |
| Greatest beam | 6 | " | 5 | in. |
| Beam at water-line | 5 | " | 9 | " |
| Breadth across counter | 3 | " | | |
| Least freeboard | 1 | " | 3 | " |
| Sheer forward | | | 10 | " |
| Sheer aft | | | 4 | " |
| Draft without board | 2 | ft. | 3 | " |
| Draft with board | 5 | " | | |
| Length of board | 4 | " | | |
| Pin from end *L W L* | 6 | " | 9 | in. |

# PLATE XXXVIII

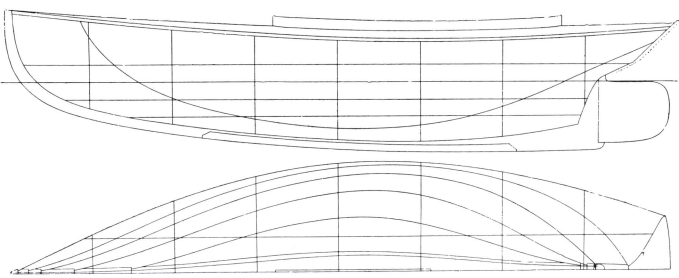

A COMPROMISE SLOOP

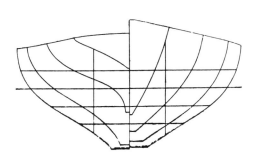

| | | |
|---|---|---|
| Mast from end *L W L* | 5 | ft. |
| Mast, deck to hounds | 16 " | 9 in |
| Topmast above cap | 8 " | 2 " |
| Boom over all | 18 " | 9 " |
| Gaff over all | 12 " | |
| Bowsprit, stem to stay | 7 " | 9 " |
| Area mainsail | 232 sq. | ft. |
| Area jib | 78 " | " |

Air-tight tanks were stowed in the wings to float the boat if filled. The sail area is 125 per cent of the square of the load-line.

Lead ballast fastened to the keel has in recent years become quite common in all types of large and small yachts, and the practice is likely to become general in the future. It played an important part in the international races of 1875 and 1876. Both American representatives, the Puritan and the May-flower, had this feature incorporated in their construction, and in this respect, as well as in regard to rig and some features of model, stand as the principal and most successful examples of compromise between cutter and sloop build and equipment.

*Reeving off Jibtopsl Halliards*

# VIII

# BEAMY CUTTERS

## I. THE DAISY

### PLATE XXXIX

#### TWENTY-FIVE FEET LONG ON LOAD-LINE

THE lines of this English-built yacht will prove of interest in comparison with the keel sloops which have come into general favor in our own waters. The DAISY was built to sail under the load-line rule temporarily enforced in Southampton waters and immediate neighborhood. The influence which that rule has upon modelling is at once detected in the close resemblance existing between the cutter DAISY and the most approved keel sloops of the East. Considerable beam and depth, with a deep keel and enough displacement to act as a counterpoise to the beam and a large rig to correspond, are the principal features of all such boats. The DAISY has, however, the advantage in point of style, as appears from her graceful sheer, straightish topsides and long fantail. With her rocker keel, flush deck, free from encumbering house, and full cutter rig, she is a smarter and rather more ship-shape craft than the sloops of the East.

The fact that small boats on a given length are at a disadvantage with large boats in respect to power and general ability, quickly forced itself upon the conviction of builders abroad, and they were not slow to take advantage of the rule by adding to the size, weight, draft and rig of boats in succession until the maximum bulk on the beam was attained by experiment. To meet the peculiar exigencies of the length rule the DAISY was designed by Mr. Joseph M. Soper, of the famous yard of John G. Fay & Co., of Southampton.

DAISY was built in 1882, and in the Solent matches won for herself an enviable record and kept up her victorious career in American waters in 1884. The spars of the DAISY are necessarily of the most liberal proportion, so that to mitigate their influence in pitching, the mast has been stepped well amidships.

PLATE XXXIX

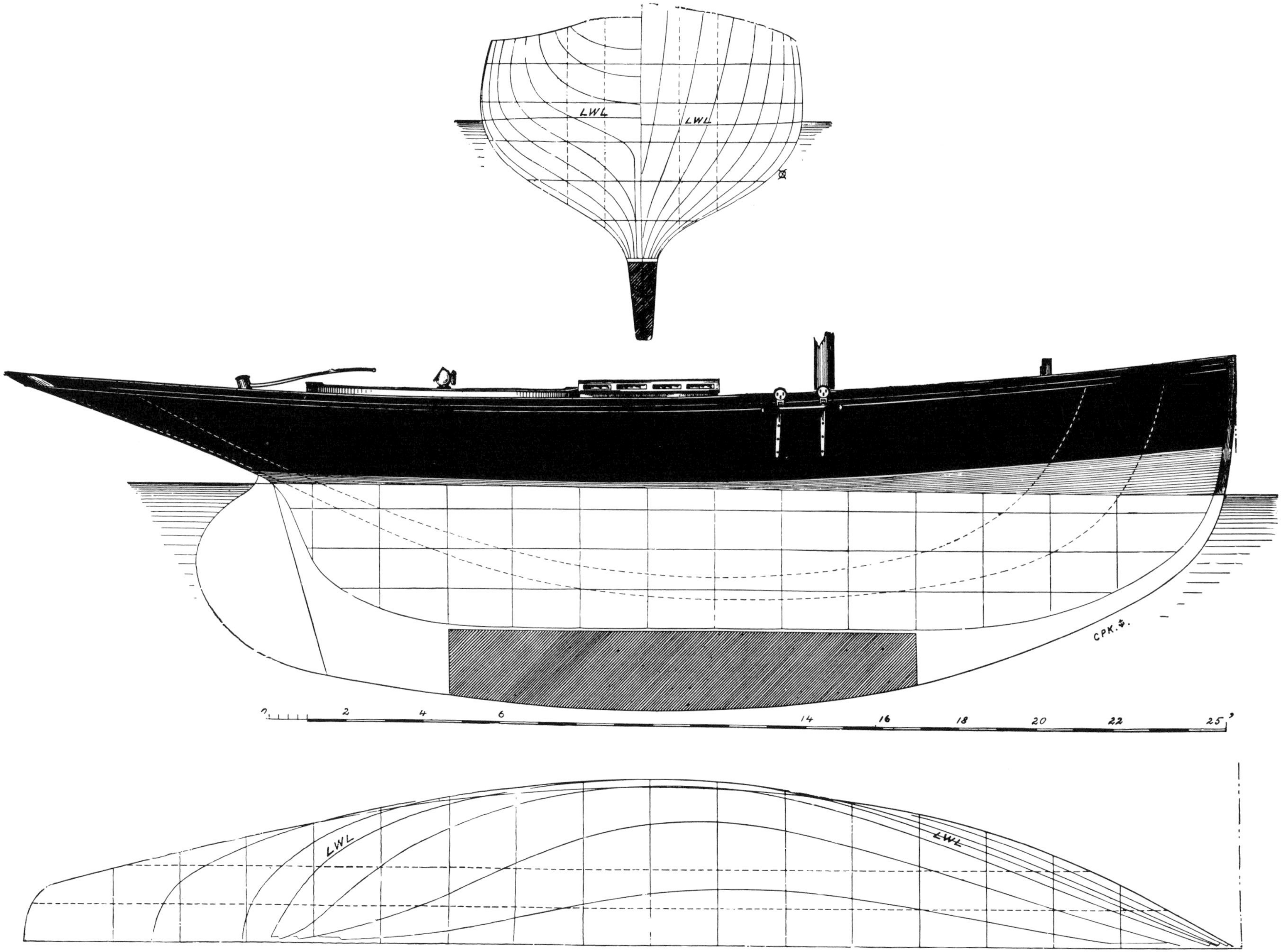

THE ITCHEN CUTTER DAISY

Length over all. . . . . . . . . . . . . . . . . . . . . . . . . . . . . . . . . 32 ft.
Length on load-line. . . . . . . . . . . . . . . . . . . . . . . . . . . . . 25 "
Beam load-line . . . . . . . . . . . . . . . . . . . . . . . . . . . . . . . . 8 " 6 in.
Least freeboard to planksheer . . . . . . . . . . . . . . . . . . . 2 "
Greatest draft . . . . . . . . . . . . . . . . . . . . . . . . . . . . . . . . . 5 " 9 "
Displacement, long tons. . . . . . . . . . . . . . . . . . . . . . . . 7.86 tons
Coefficient fineness to rabbet . . . . . . . . . . . . . . . . . . . 0.36
Ballast on keel, lead. . . . . . . . . . . . . . . . . . . . . . . . . . . 4.38 tons
Ballast inside, lead. . . . . . . . . . . . . . . . . . . . . . . . . . . . 0.25 "
Ratio of ballast to displacement. . . . . . . . . . . . . . . . . 0.59
Area load-line plane. . . . . . . . . . . . . . . . . . . . . . . . . . . 149 sq. ft.
Area midship section. . . . . . . . . . . . . . . . . . . . . . . . . . 20.75 sq. ft.
Area longitudinal section, with rudder. . . . . . . . . . . 120 " "
Area wet surface, with rudder. . . . . . . . . . . . . . . . . . . 320 " "
Area three lower sails . . . . . . . . . . . . . . . . . . . . . . . . . 862 " "
Centre of sails abaft middle *L W L*. . . . . . . . . . . . . 1 ft.
Centre of lateral resistance do. . . . . . . . . . . . . . . . . . 1 " 5 in.
Lower sail per sq. ft. wetted surface. . . . . . . . . . . . . 2.69 sq. ft.
Wet surface per long ton displacement. . . . . . . . . . . 40.7 " "

In Plate XL will be found the rig and a cross section showing method of construction. The disposition of the area, however, is such that the mainsail, especially the boom, is kept within the control of two hands. The weight of the mast is well aft, and topmast can quickly be got rid of by housing or striking altogether for a passage.

### SPARS

Mast from end *L W L* . . . . . . . . . . . . . . . . . . . . . . . . . 10 ft. 6 in.
Rake of mast . . . . . . . . . . . . . . . . . . . . . . . . . . . . . . . . . 0
Mast from deck to hounds. . . . . . . . . . . . . . . . . . . . . 23 " 6 "
Masthead. . . . . . . . . . . . . . . . . . . . . . . . . . . . . . . . . . . . 5 " 6 "
Topmast, cap to shoulder. . . . . . . . . . . . . . . . . . . . . . 14 "
Bowsprit outboard . . . . . . . . . . . . . . . . . . . . . . . . . . . . 15 "
Bowsprit housing . . . . . . . . . . . . . . . . . . . . . . . . . . . . . 5 "
Forestay boomkin outboard . . . . . . . . . . . . . . . . . . . . 2 " 6 in.
Mainboom, over all . . . . . . . . . . . . . . . . . . . . . . . . . . . 26 "
Maingaff, over all. . . . . . . . . . . . . . . . . . . . . . . . . . . . . 20 " 9 "
Trysail gaff . . . . . . . . . . . . . . . . . . . . . . . . . . . . . . . . . . 9 "
Spinnaker boom . . . . . . . . . . . . . . . . . . . . . . . . . . . . . . 30 " 4 "
First topsail yard. . . . . . . . . . . . . . . . . . . . . . . . . . . . . . 23 " 6 "
Second topsail yard. . . . . . . . . . . . . . . . . . . . . . . . . . . 17 " 6 "
Jackyard. . . . . . . . . . . . . . . . . . . . . . . . . . . . . . . . . . . . . 15 " 6 "

### SAILS

The outfit consists of the following: One mainsail, two sizes working fore-sails and one balloon foresail, three shifting jibs, one jackyard (club) topsail,

# PLATE XL

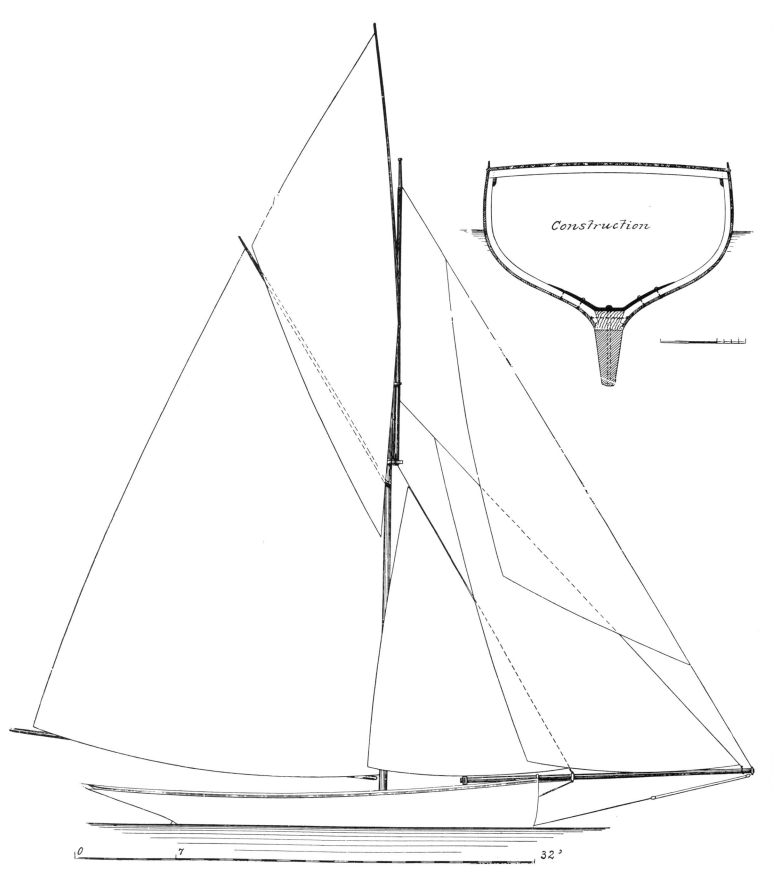

*Construction*

0   7   32'

DAISY—SAIL PLAN

one jib topsail, two sizes yardtopsails, one jib-headed topsail, one spinnaker, one trysail; a total of fourteen sails, with bags and covers for all. The dimensions of the rig illustrated herewith (mainsail, No. 1 jib, large working foresail, and No. 1 yardtopsail) are as follows, all sails being made by Ratsey & Lapthorn, of West Cowes, England:

| | | |
|---|---|---|
| Mainsail on luff | 21 ft. | |
| Mainsail on foot | 24 " | 3 in. |
| Mainsail on leech | 37 " | 3 " |
| Mainsail on head | 19 " | 8 " |
| Roach to loose foot | | 16 " |
| Foresail on foot | 14 " | |
| Foresail on luff | 23 " | |
| Foresail on leech | 20 " | 4 in. |
| Roach to foot | | 8 " |
| Jib on foot | 15 " | |
| Jib on luff | 31 " | 9 " |
| Jib on leech | 24 " | |
| Roach to foot | | 8 " |
| Area mainsail | 542 sq. ft. | |
| Area foresail | 145 " " | |
| Area jib | 175 " " | |
| Area three lower sails | 862 " " | |
| Ratio to square of load-line | 1.38 | |
| Area per sq. ft. wet surface | 2.69 sq. ft. | |
| Area per long ton of displacement | 108.7 " " | |
| Centre lower sails from end $LWL$ | 13 ft. | 6 in. |
| Centre lateral resistance from $LWL$ | 13 " | 11 " |

The yacht has teak topsides and planksheer and oak frame. All deadwood is through-bolted with copper and the hull through-fastened with copper. The iron floors are bolted through frame and bottom plank, and the frame heels are boxed in and through-fastened to the keel. Stem and post of British oak, sided 4¼ in.; main keel, English elm, 8 in. moulded; deadwood of oak; frame spaced 21 in. apart between centres, sided 2 in., moulded 2½ at heel and 2¼ at head, doubled throughout; floors of wrought iron on every frame, the throat taking bolts of lead keel; beams of oak, sided and moulded 3 x 2½ in. Clamp of red pine, 3½ x 1¼ in. Rudder stock of oak, blade of pine. Deck has covering board of teak, 4⅓ x 1⅛ in.; planking of pine, 1½ x 2⅜ in., caulked and payed with marine glue. Outside plank of teak, four strakes; garboards of elm, 1⅛ in. thick. Bulwarks of teak, and deck fittings of same. Fastenings of yellow metal and copper. Bolts of lead keel, 1¼ in. diameter, driven from inside and screwed up from below, and countersunk and plugged. Bright pine cabin. No paint, except the black of the sides and gold bead.

# Small Yachts

The cabin is very spacious considering the room taken up by the cockpit. The floor measures 3 ft. 4 in. between sofas, the latter being 6½ ft. long by 26 in. wide, with sideboards and pantry at forward end of 2 ft. front. The cabin is entered from doors without a sliding companion, the space being occupied instead by a hatch 3½ ft. by 2 ft. Headroom is 5 ft. and 6 ft. under hatch. Forecastle is bulkheaded off from cabin and entered by a sliding door. Has 2 ft. 4 in. floor, a berth on one side, and w. c., sail rack, etc., on the other. A circular hatch 16 in. diameter gives access from deck. The cockpit is 7 ft. long and 2 ft. 6 in. deep. The yacht steers with a tiller of iron wrapped with hide. She is equipped in most complete manner, the chief articles being a Berthon folding dingy; a yawl boat of long flat floor, having great buoyancy and fine construction, with considerable carrying capacity; water tank and brass-hooped deck breaker, box compass, floating compass with brass binnacle, barometer, clock, side lights, anchor and deck lights, flareups, red and green signal lamps, fog-horn, triangle to take place of bell, sea anchor, life belts, patent towing log, buffers for main sheet and anchor, fenders, mops, handlead, code signals in bag, brass rudder head cap, gratings for cockpit; also cushions, stove and belongings, pump, anchors with chain, kedge and two hawsers, swing table in cabin, and the usual supply of the pantry and small stores.

## II. THE VAYU

### PLATE XLI

#### THIRTY-ONE FEET LONG ON LOAD-LINE

A VERY fine, fast, able and roomy cutter is represented in the VAYU, built in 1882, for Mr. C. A. Welch, by George Lawley & Son, of South Boston. Although snugly rigged for off-shore cruising, this cutter has shown a good turn of speed in a breeze. As a family yacht, having all the desirable qualities of a safe, stiff, smart big vessel on the length, the VAYU would be difficult to surpass.

While resembling the Itchen boats of Southampton, England, in general, she has features of her own rather an improvement upon her prototype across the pond. The sheer plan shows her to be bold in conception and in the round up forward and raking post a commendable departure from old school custom. Her topsides show none of the flare or hip of the sloop which so retards headway in rough water, while the sharp lines forward with the tolerably fine run assist ease and dryness and close windedness in a sea.

110

PLATE XLI

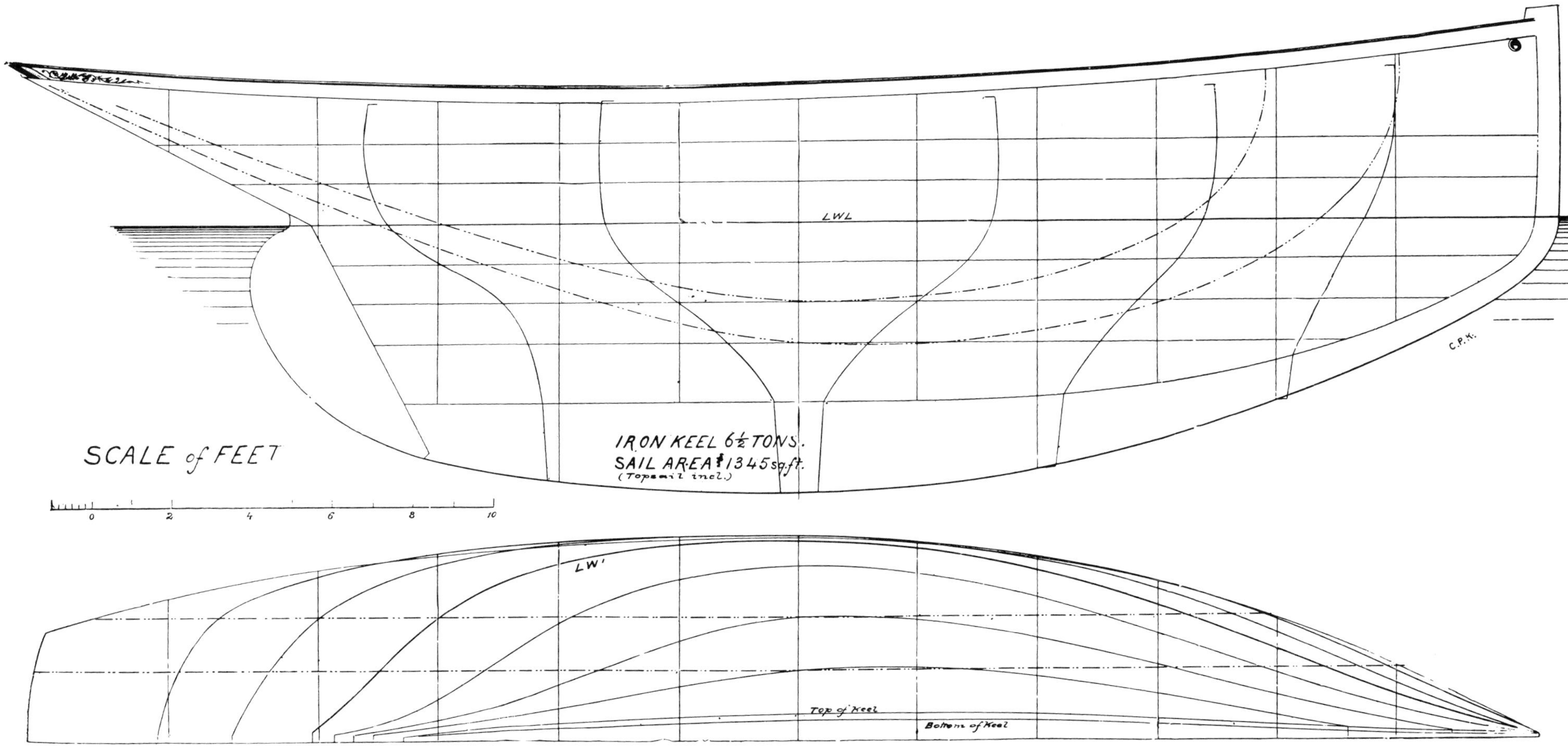

SCALE of FEET

0   2   4   6   8   10

LWL

IRON KEEL 6½ TONS.
SAIL AREA 1,345 sq ft.
(Topsail incl.)

C.B.K.

LW'

Top of Keel

Bottom of Keel

THE CUTTER VAYU

# Small Yachts

The overhang adds much to jaunty appearance and deck room abaft the mainsheet. It is one of those luxuries seldom to be found in our fleet, owing to the imperative necessity of docking under the length rules of the day. It is within bounds to say that no benefit to speed is derived from the last four feet of this overhang, yet the mean length and one-third overhang rules still in vogue would tax these last four feet as equal to a lump in the body a couple of feet in length. Had the Vayu been intended for racing under such rules she could not have indulged in the beauty or utility the long overhang offers, but would have felt obliged to saw it off short and ugly. Luckily no measurement blighted the good looks of Vayu in this respect, and the builders were able to display themselves without hindrance in a nobby fantail. The Vayu is uncapsizable, able in a sea and minus a centreboard casing just where it is not wanted, and under most circumstances will draw less water than if built with a fin.

| | | |
|---|---|---|
| Length over all | 38 ft. | 8 in. |
| Length on water-line | 31 " | |
| Greatest moulded beam | 10 " | 2 " |
| Beam moulded at water-line | 9 " | 9 " |
| Breadth across counter | 5 " | 4 " |
| Depth at side, No. 7 | 7 " | 3 " |
| Least freeboard | 2 " | 11 " |
| Sheer forward | 1 " | 6 " |
| Sheer aft | | 6 " |
| Greatest draft | 7 " | |
| Depth of hold | 6 " | 9 " |
| Displacement | 14.8 tons | |
| Iron keel | 6.5 " | |
| Ballast inside | 2 " | |
| Mast, from stem | 11 ft. | 8 in. |
| Mast, deck to head | 30 " | |
| Diameter at partners | | 7 " |
| Topmast over all | 24 " | |
| Bowsprit outboard | 16 " | |
| Boom over all | 31 " | |
| Gaff over all | 23 " | 6 in. |
| Hoist of mainsail | 20 " | |
| Sail area with topsail | 1,345 sq. ft. | |

She is strongly built. The keel is of well seasoned white oak, 16 in. wide on top and 14 in. on the bottom, the iron shoe below having also a slight taper downward and fore and aft. Frames spaced 12 in. between centres, every third station being shown in the plans. They are double, with exception of seven in the ends, 2 in. sided and 4 in. moulded at keel, tapering to 2½ in. at head, of white oak. Every alternate frame is steam bent. Plank, 1½ in. Georgia yellow pine, 4 in. wide, the topsides being worked in one length fore and aft. Oak beam shelf, 4 x 4 in., the clamps being in a single length and through-riveted to the frames. Decks of white pine 1½ x 1¾ in. wide.

The accommodations are extremely liberal. The deck is flush, no house or cockpit interfering with free passage. There is a skylight over the saloon amidships and a mahogany companion over the main hatch, also a small hatch to forecastle and large bull's-eye to after cabin. The forecastle is 12 ft. long, with standing height; main saloon, 8 ft. 6 in. long, with 6 ft. head room, bulkheaded off at both ends with sliding doors of neat panel frame. The stateroom aft is very cosy, having a double berth on starboard side and handsome bureau and lockers with mirrors on port hand, also improved provisions for washing and a w. c.

It is noteworthy that VAYU has only two-thirds her load-line length for hoist of mainsail and a very long gaff. The canvas is kept low and a close-winded rig is the result. It has proved a great success.

## III.  THE WINDWARD

### *PLATE XLII*

#### EIGHTEEN FEET LONG ON LOAD-LINE

THE object in turning out the WINDWARD was to secure the best all-round average without giving undue prominence to any one quality at material sacrifice in others  A good average in performance, accommodation, cost and utility was the ruling idea in the production of the WINDWARD. It is quite possible to produce something which shall surpass this little cruiser in a particular respect, but the gain would be accompanied with a loss of some kind not consistent with a good average on all points. Less beam, more depth and weight with large rig, or less depth and more beam, would, upon commendable lines, have brought about greater speed. This would have been purchased at increased cost and lack of " elbow room" upon the first supposition, and with disregard for safety, headroom, and seagoing qualities upon the second. Caution is here in place against adopting too great bulk and beam on the length, for, while adding to stowage and area of deck, a slow, unwieldy and leewardly boat is certain to result, and such a boat is about the most unsatisfactory for all purposes but riding at anchor. It is in this respect that failure is most courted when trying to get too much out of the length, and many small cruisers suffer from the evil. The WINDWARD has a maximum of volume on 18 ft. load-line,

PLATE XLII

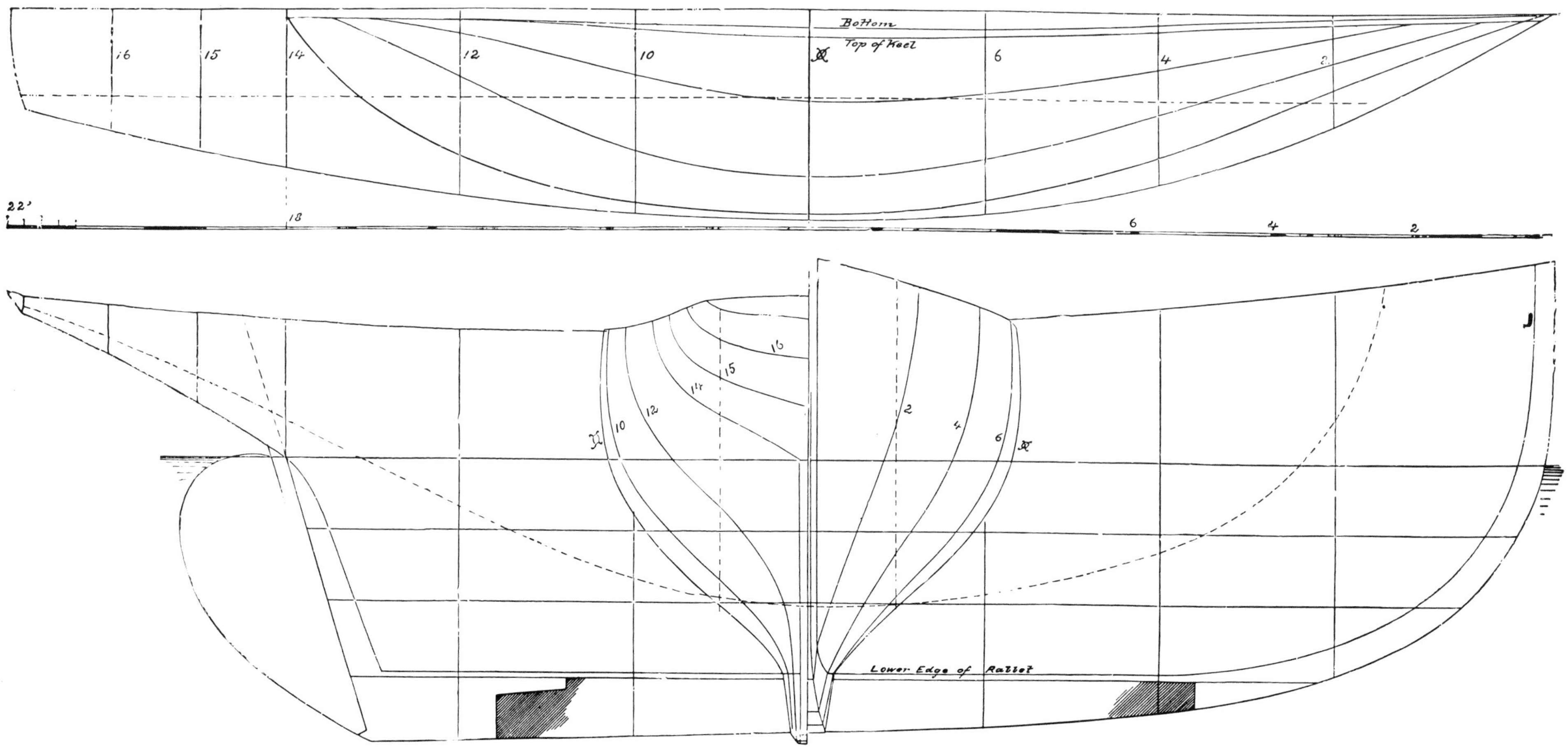

Bottom
Top of Heel

2

3

4

6

8

10

12

14

15

16

18

22'

Lower Edge of Rabbet

THE CRUISING YAWL WINDWARD

beyond which it is not advisable to experiment, unless with considerable reduction in beam, if willing to put up with the features of slim middle body.

The WINDWARD was built by W. P. Stephens, of Staten Island, N. Y., in 1884, for Mr. H. L. Willoughby, with reference to service in Newport and Eastern waters. Fishing, cruising, and general yachting life afloat can be indulged in upon nominal expenditure for keep. Where speed is also an object, a pole sloop rig like that of the COLUMBINE, or a pole cutter with fixed bowsprit and jib hanked to a stay, is to be preferred. She has been tried thoroughly in light and heavy weather, and handles well under full sail, under jib and mizzen, and under mainsail only, requiring with the latter, in very strong winds, a little of the jib to keep her off, but at other times having an easy weather helm under any shift of sails.

| | |
|---|---|
| Length over all | 22 ft. |
| Length on load-line | 18 " |
| Beam extreme | 6 " |
| Depth of hold | 4 " 9 in. |
| Draft extreme | 4 " |
| Draft mean | 3 " 4 " |
| Least freeboard | 1 " 9 " |
| Displacement | 116.6 cu. ft. |
| Displacement in tons, 2,000 lbs. | 3.75 tons |
| Coefficient of fineness | 0.324 |
| Iron on keel | 1,700 lbs. |
| Iron inside | 2,000 " |
| Ratio of ballast to displacement | 0.5 |
| Area load-line plane | 69 sq. ft. |
| Area midship section | 11.2 " " |
| Area longitudinal section, no rudder | 65.6 " " |
| Area wet surface, no rudder | 173 " " |
| Area of rudder, both sides | 11.6 " " |
| $MS$ abaft centre of $LWL$ | 1.5 ft. |
| Centre of lateral resistance do., with rudder | 1.43 " |
| Centre of effort, do | 1.40 " |
| Centre of buoyancy, do | .72 " |
| Centre of buoyancy below $LWL$ | 1.16 " |
| Wet surface, per ton displacement | 49.2 sq. ft. |
| Area lower sails | 376 " " |
| Sail per sq. ft. wet surface | 2.04 " " |
| With topsail | 2.44 " " |

#### DIMENSIONS OF SAILS AND SPARS

| | |
|---|---|
| Mainmast from foreside of stem | 4 ft. 6 in. |
| Mainmast, deck to hounds | 17 " 6 " |
| Mainmast, deck to truck | 25 " |
| Mainmast, diameter at deck | 5 " |

| | | | |
|---|---|---|---|
| Mizzen mast, from fore side of stem | 19 | ft. | 10 in. |
| Mizzen mast, deck to hounds | 12 | " | |
| Mizzen mast, deck to truck | 13 | " | |
| Mizzen mast, diameter at deck | | 3¼ | " |
| Main boom, length | 15 | " | |
| Main boom, diameter | | 3 | " |
| Mizzen boom, length | 7 | " | 9 " |
| Mizzen boom, diameter | | 2 | " |
| Main gaff | 12 | " | |
| Main gaff, diameter | | 2¾ | " |
| Mizzen yard | 6 | " | 9 " |
| Mizzen yard, diameter | | 2 | " |
| Luff of mainsail | 15 | " | |
| Luff of mizzen | 6 | " | 9 " |
| Leech of mainsail | 22 | " | 9 " |
| Leech of mizzen | 11 | " | 6 " |
| Mainsail, tack to peak | 25 | " | |
| Mizzen, tack to peak | 12 | " | 3 " |
| Mainsail, clew to throat | 19 | " | 9 " |
| Mizzen, clew to throat | 10 | " | |
| Jib on stay | 18 | " | |
| Jib on foot | 11 | " | 9 " |
| Jib, hoist | 14 | " | 6 " |
| Topsail, luff | 17 | " | 6 " |
| Topsail, leech | 11 | " | 4 " |
| Topsail, foot | 13 | " | |
| Topsail yard | 14 | " | |
| Topsail yard, diameter | | 2 | " |
| Bowsprit outboard | 7 | " | 6 " |
| Bowsprit at stem, diameter | | 3¾ | " |
| Bowsprit at end, diameter | | 2¼ | " |
| Area of mainsail | 230 | sq. ft. | |
| Area of jib | 85 | " | " |
| Area of mizzen | 61 | " | " |
| Area of topsail | 75 | " | " |
| Total sail area | 451 | " | " |

Table of scantling: Stem and post sided 3 in.; keel amidships, sided 8 in.; moulded, 6 in.; frames, double, 2½ x 2¼ in., at heels, 2½ x 1¼ at heads; first 5 frames single, sided 1½ in., 2¼ at heels, 1¼ at heads, all spaced 15 in.; floors, iron, gal., 3⁄8 x 2½ in.; keel bolts, iron, gal., ¾, spaced 15 in.; clamp, 1¼ x 5 in.; shelf, 1¼ x 4 in.; ceiling, 3⁄8 in.; bilge clamp, ¼ x 5 in.; planking, 7⁄8 in.; deck, 1 in.; fastenings of keel and deadwoods, ½ in. gal. iron bolts.

It will be seen from Plate XLIV that the WINDWARD is underrigged, and could easily carry in her lower sails twenty-five per cent more canvas, which, with a large balloon topsail for light winds, would make the yacht step out in different fashion.

It is a difficult problem in all yachts how to arrange the available space to the best advantage, and the difficulty increases rapidly as the size of the yacht decreases. In comparing the relative accommodations of yachts, it is often forgotten that there is a unit of measurement for all, large or small, by which they must be gauged ; and this unit is the height of a man, or say 6 ft., as the least head room in which the average man can move in comfort. This much at least must be had in a yacht of any size, and more, while desirable, is not indispensable. Similarly, this length, or a little more, is necessary for berths and lockers for sleeping, and a like size for breadth, an excess in any one direction being of little value, unless accompanied with reasonable dimensions in the other two.

For this reason the keel boat of moderate or even extreme proportions permits great advantages over the ordinary shoal type, whether large or small, as taking boats of the same internal capacity in cubic feet, the former offers one clear space from stem to stern, with a fair proportion of height and breadth, offering every possibility to the designer, while the space in the latter is largely taken up by the wings, where it is of little use, leaving a low and confined rat-hole for galley and forecastle, and a similar large and comparatively useless space aft, under and about the cockpit ; and while headroom may be had in the cabin, thanks to a house-like structure on deck, the space under it is sacrificed to that ever-present, always in the way, centreboard. Panel it over, veneer it, put leaves to it and call it a table, put mirrors on the side and call it a bulkhead, it is always there, making two small rooms of a single large one, parting the best of friends, separating each from his vis-a-vis at dinner, taking the space that would, without it, allow gangways, staterooms and closets, and, most of all, a constant source of weakness in an otherwise strongly built boat. Of course, with the diminutive proportions of the craft, whose interior arrangements are shown in Plate XLIII, it is impossible to obtain the comfort of a large yacht, but an effort has been made to secure fair accommodations for two in cruising in the limited space at the disposal of the designer, and in comparing with other types, only those of approximate capacity must be considered.

The space forward of the combined hatch and skylight has a height of 4 ft. 6 in., allowing a man to sit down comfortably while cooking over the oil stove shown on shelf on port side. In the bows are two shelves for paints, boat-swain's stores, etc., just forward of the mast is the chain locker, abaft the mast is a large zinc-lined box for ice. The body of the boat has a height varying from 4 ft. 9 in. to 5 ft. 2 in. under the low trunk, the sides of which at no point are over 9 in. high, while its curved top takes away the clumsy look of the ordinary cabin trunk. The slide is quite long, so that a man can stand on the

# PLATE XLIII

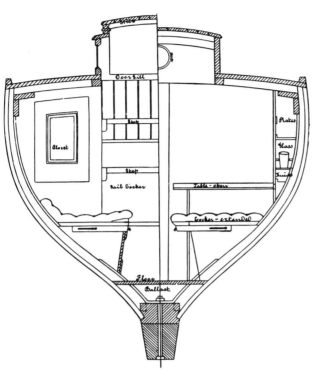

aa. Shelves for stores
b. Bitts
c. Chainlocker
d. Stove
e. Icebox
f. Pantry
g. Table
hh. Lockers
ii. Steps
k. Companion slide
l. Decklight in end of house
mm. Cast ballast
nn. Closets
o. Pump
p. Inlet to tank, with screw plug
s. Water tank, thirty gallons
t. Faucet
u. Sail locker
vv. Lockers at side of cockpit

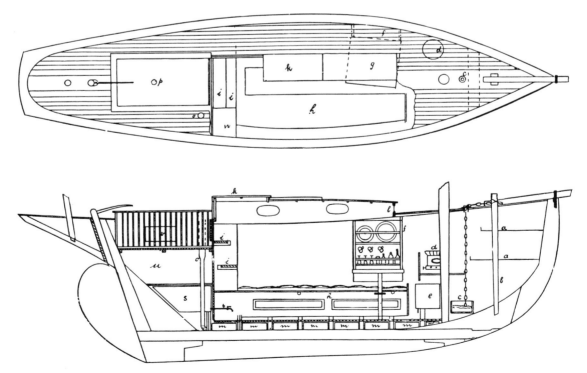

THE WINDWARD—ACCOMMODATION PLANS

PLATE XLIV

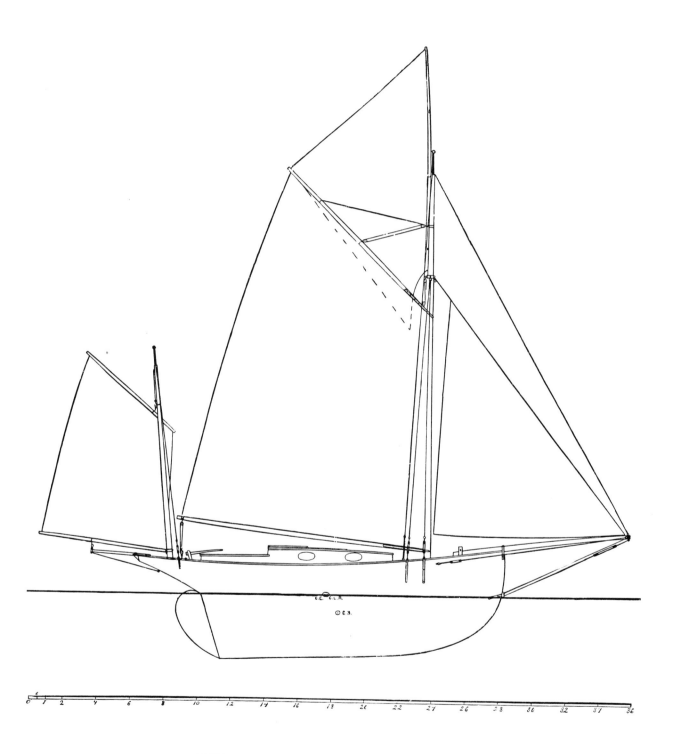

THE WINDWARD—SAIL PLAN

floor in dressing, his head being just out of the cabin. The lockers on each side are nearly 7 ft. long and 24 in. wide for sleeping, the width being increased at night by pieces hinged to each, resting on the slides shown in the drawing, or if three are to be provided for, the entire space between the lockers may be covered over, making one wide bed, decreasing the standing room, but even then giving more headroom than any sloop of similar size.

At the after end of each locker is a large closet for stores, canned goods, clothes, etc., while additional stowage room is provided under the lockers. Instead of a companion ladder, two movable steps are fitted on cleats screwed to the sides of the closets, both being quickly removed and not being in the way when it is desired to reach the sail locker under the cockpit; below which, in turn, in the run, is a water tank holding a large supply, which is filled by a pipe in the cockpit floor, and empties by a faucet in the cabin. On either side of the cockpit are also small lockers, the cockpit rail being wide enough for a seat.

The cabin is well lighted by four oval fixed lights of plate glass, and a five-inch swinging decklight, the latter, also, in connection with a small canvas windsail, giving a current of fresh air when at anchor. The cabin door, the sill of which is on a level with the deck, is hinged to drop down and out, falling against the bulkhead between cabin and cockpit, where it is out of the way, but may be readily closed. At night the slide may be closed, but the door is hooked so as to be open a few inches at the top, making a draft upward and outward, but admitting little or no rain. The door is also fitted so as to drop to a horizontal position, where it makes a seat for the helmsman in bad weather, his legs and a portion of his body being in the cabin, the hatch drawn close to him and a tarpaulin keeping him warm, and all dry below in the cabin.

Where room is so limited it is hard to find a place for the many small articles required on a cruise, especially in the cook's department. An attempt has been made in this boat to combine a table and pantry, as shown on the starboard side of the midship section. A closet, two feet long, fore and aft, is built into the side of the boat, its greatest depth from front to back being five to six inches. In it are several shelves, the top one with racks for plates on edge, the one below for glasses, jars and bottles, with hooks for cups, while the lowest forms a tray for knives, forks, napkins, etc. The front of this closet is about two feet square, hinged on the lower side, and opens downward, being supported in a horizontal position by a leg from the floor. A rim around it one inch high prevents the plates going adrift in a lurch to leeward. Two can sit on the opposite locker and one beside it. It is quickly stowed, takes no room, and offers a convenient place for all crockery and small articles.

The perspective of the WINDWARD, Plate III, will help to elucidate the lead of gear and the boat's appearance under-way.

PLATE III

# IV.  THE  ANETO

*PLATE  XLV*

TWENTY-ONE  FEET  LONG  ON  LOAD-LINE

A SECOND example of small cruising yacht is the ANETO, larger, but similar in essential features to the WINDWARD. She, too, is underrigged for light weather, but in a breeze and jump has been found a smart craft. With a racing suit she could probably give a good account of herself in trifling work as well, her underwater body being handsome and well balanced. Of course something has been sacrificed for headroom, the freeboard being more than required for ability and buoyancy, and unfavorably affecting the Centre of Gravity. She was built in 1883 by W. P. Stephens, Staten Island, N. Y., for Mr. W. H. Eaton, of New York, from plans drawn up by the owner.

ANETO has good airy quarters for a hand forward to take his turn at the helm when foreign bound or to devise ways and means for the inner man through the skillful manipulation of the " doctor's " department in the forepeak. The main cabin has been restricted to 6½ ft. in length to permit washroom, etc., between bulkheads, and the long quarters forward just mentioned. The cockpit is limited to a small well for one person, or for the reception of the nether shanks, waterproof cushions outside the coaming serving for seating purposes. Access to the cabin is had by a sash in the hatch, and a similar arrangement at the forward end leads to washroom and forecastle, all being connected by doorways below. The water tank is located in the run, the space alongside the cockpit being devoted to general stowage. The ice-chest is in the bow, and has a pipe from the tank coiled around the inside for a constant sup-

PLATE XLV

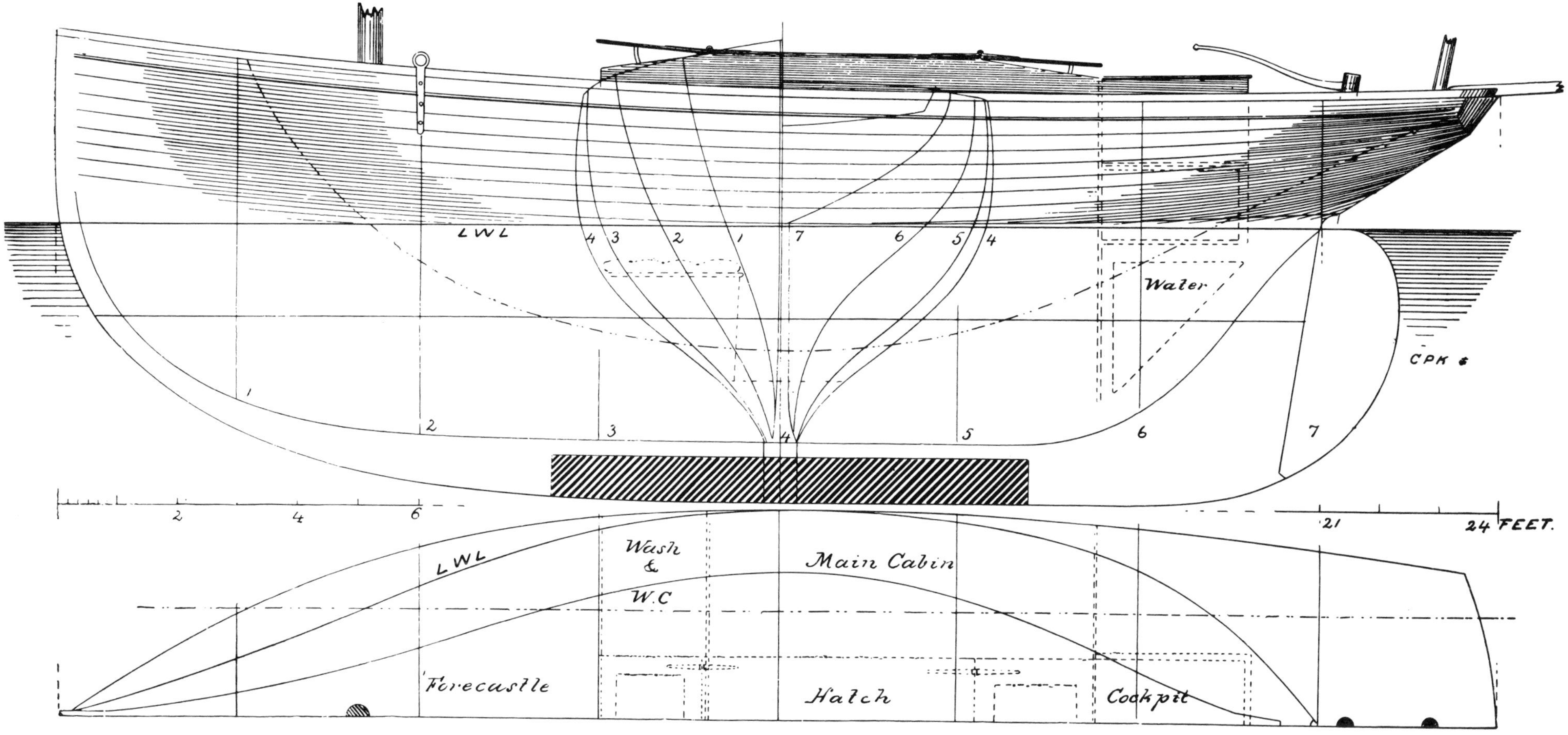

THE CRUISING YAWL ANETO

Water

CPK #

LWL

Main Cabin

Cockpit

Hatch

Wash &

W.C

Forecastle

LWL

24 FEET.

ply of cool water. The wash and toilet-room has one of **A. B. Sands'** clever little pumping arrangements, and a tap to the tank aft enables water to be drawn in all parts of the boat. Cooking gear consists of Adams & Westlake's oil stoves with cast-iron bottoms and fixed covers, especially adapted to yachting wants. The hull inside has been paid with tar, for preservation of the wood and for keeping the bottom sweet. The smell of the tar very soon disappeared, and is not likely again to be perceptible as the boat gets older.

DETAILS OF ANETO

| | | |
|---|---|---|
| Length over all .......................... | 24 ft. | |
| Length on load-line...................... | 21 " | |
| Beam extreme........................... | 7 " | |
| Depth amidships, keel to deck ............ | 5 " | 3 in. |
| Greatest draft.......................... | 4 " | 6 " |
| Least freeboard......................... | 2 " | |
| Displacement........................... | 4¾ tons. | |
| Lead on keel........................... | 1,850 lbs. | |
| Lead inside............................ | 2,550 " | |
| Mainmast, from stem.................... | 5 ft. | 3 in. |
| Mainsail, hoist......................... | 18 " | |
| Mainsail, foot.......................... | 16 " | 6 " |
| Mainsail, head......................... | 14 " | |
| Bowsprit outboard...................... | 7 " | |
| Jib on foot ............................ | 13 " | |
| Jib on stay ............................ | 20 " | 6 in. |
| Mizzen mast abaft end load-line .......... | 1 " | 10 " |
| Mizzen boomkin outboard................ | 2 " | 6 " |
| Mizzen on luff ......................... | 7 " | |
| Mizzen, foot........................... | 8 " | |
| Mizzen, head.......................... | 6 " | |
| Mizzen, leech ......................... | 12 " | |
| Topsail yard .......................... | 14 " | |
| Area mainsail.......................... | 300 sq. ft. | |
| Area jib............................... | 105 " " | |
| Area mizzen .......................... | 65 " " | |
| Lower sail............................. | 470 " " | |

The yacht has no paint but the black on side and a petticoat below water. The deck and interior are in bright wood, the ceiling being handsomely wrought in narrow strips of beaded Georgia pine. Hatch and gangboards of mahogany, very neat in finish.

The details of construction of ANETO are as follows: Keel of clear oak 6 x 6 in., tapering at ends to 4½ in., sided; lead on keel, 6 x 8 in. and 8 ft. long; weight, 1,850 lbs. An oak shoe underneath as a chafing guard. Lead bolted up with ¾ in. composition bolts, 12 in. apart; stem and post and knees of oak, sided 4 in.; frame double sawn, sided 2½ and moulded 2¼ at heel and 1¼ at head; spaced 2 ft. between centres with steamed frame 1½ in. sided between; floor knees of hackmatack, 2½ in. sided; plank of 1 in. cypress below load-line and Georgia pine above, worked in single length fore and aft; bilge strakes of yellow pine; ceiling and bulkheads of same; cockpit lined with sheet lead, with outboard drains and staved up with yellow pine, beaded, with oak cap; planksheer 3½ x 1½ in. oak, the butts of deck plank jogging into it at ends; clamps 3 x 1¼ in. oak; rail, 2 x 1 in. oak; fastenings all copper riveted; deck stuff, 1 x 2 in., selected pine, blind nailed; anchors, 25 lbs. Trotman, and 50 lbs. long shank fisherman's anchor; chain, 3-16 in. link, about 25 fms., with manilla rope for long scope; mast, 5 in. diam. at partners; bowsprit, 3½ x 2¾, egg shape at stem; mizzen mast at deck 3 in. diam.

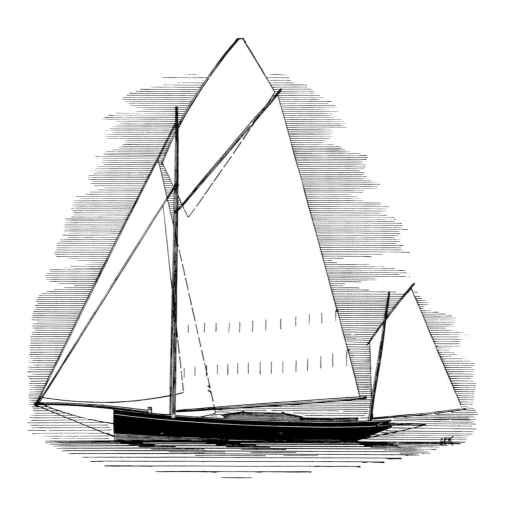

THE ANETO—SAIL PLAN

# V. THE DEUCE

## *PLATE XLVI*

### FOURTEEN FEET LONG ON LOAD-LINE

IN evidence of what can be done in extremely small boats by compromise in all three chief dimensions, the DEUCE, 14 ft. on water-line, has been produced in Plates XLVI and XLVII. The illustrations will explain themselves, like letters denoting the same thing in all the diagrams. Further reference to this little specimen of the cruising family is made in the chapter on Singlehand Yachting.

| | | | | | |
|---|---|---|---|---|---|
| Length over all.......................... | 17 | ft. | | | |
| Length on water-line..................... | 14 | " | | | |
| Beam on water-line...................... | 4 | " | 10 | in. | |
| Breadth across counter.................. | 2 | " | 6 | " | |
| Greatest draft........................... | 3 | " | 3 | " | |
| Least freeboard ........................ | 1 | " | 6 | " | |
| Depth of hold.......................... | 4 | " | | | |
| Headroom in cabin...................... | 3 | " | 10 | " | |
| Width between berths ................... | 1 | " | | | |
| Width of berths......................... | 1 | " | 4 | " | |
| Width of gangway on deck............... | 1 | " | 4 | " | |
| Length of cockpit ...................... | 3 | " | | | |
| Depth of cockpit....................... | 2 | " | | | |
| Displacement.......................... | 1.6 | tons | | | |
| Ballast on keel......................... | 750 | lbs. | | | |
| Ballast inside ......................... | 1,000 | " | | | |
| Mast from stem........................ | 3 | ft. | | | |
| Mast, deck to hounds................... | 14 | " | 3 | in. | |
| Mast over all .......................... | 24 | " | 6 | " | |
| Diameter at deck....................... | | | 3¾ | " | |
| Bowsprit outboard ..................... | 7 | " | | | |
| Boom over all.......................... | 12 | " | 4 | " | |
| Diameter in slings...................... | | | 2½ | " | |
| Gaff, over all.......................... | 10 | " | | | |
| Diameter of gaff....................... | | | 2 | " | |
| Mizzen mast, deck to head ............. | 9 | " | 6 | " | |
| Mizzen boom .......................... | 7 | " | 6 | " | |
| Mizzen yard ........................... | 7 | " | | | |
| Topsail yard........................... | 10 | " | | | |
| Spinnaker boom ....................... | 15 | " | | | |
| Hoist of mainsail....................... | 11 | " | 3 | " | |
| Jib on foot ............................ | 9 | " | 6 | " | |

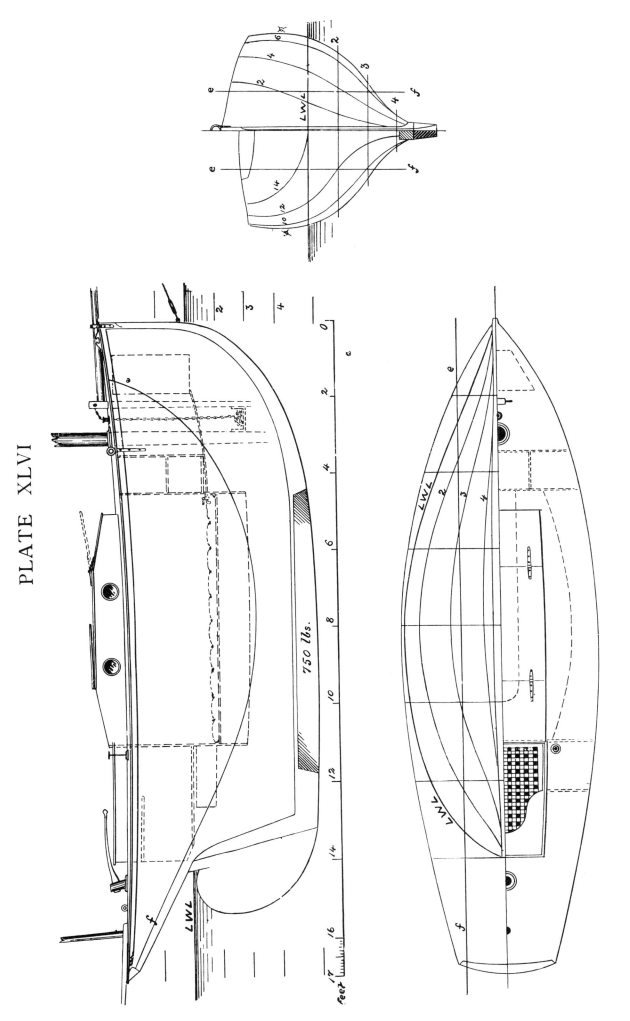

PLATE XLVI

750 lbs.

THE SINGLE HAND YAWL DEUCE

# PLATE XLVII

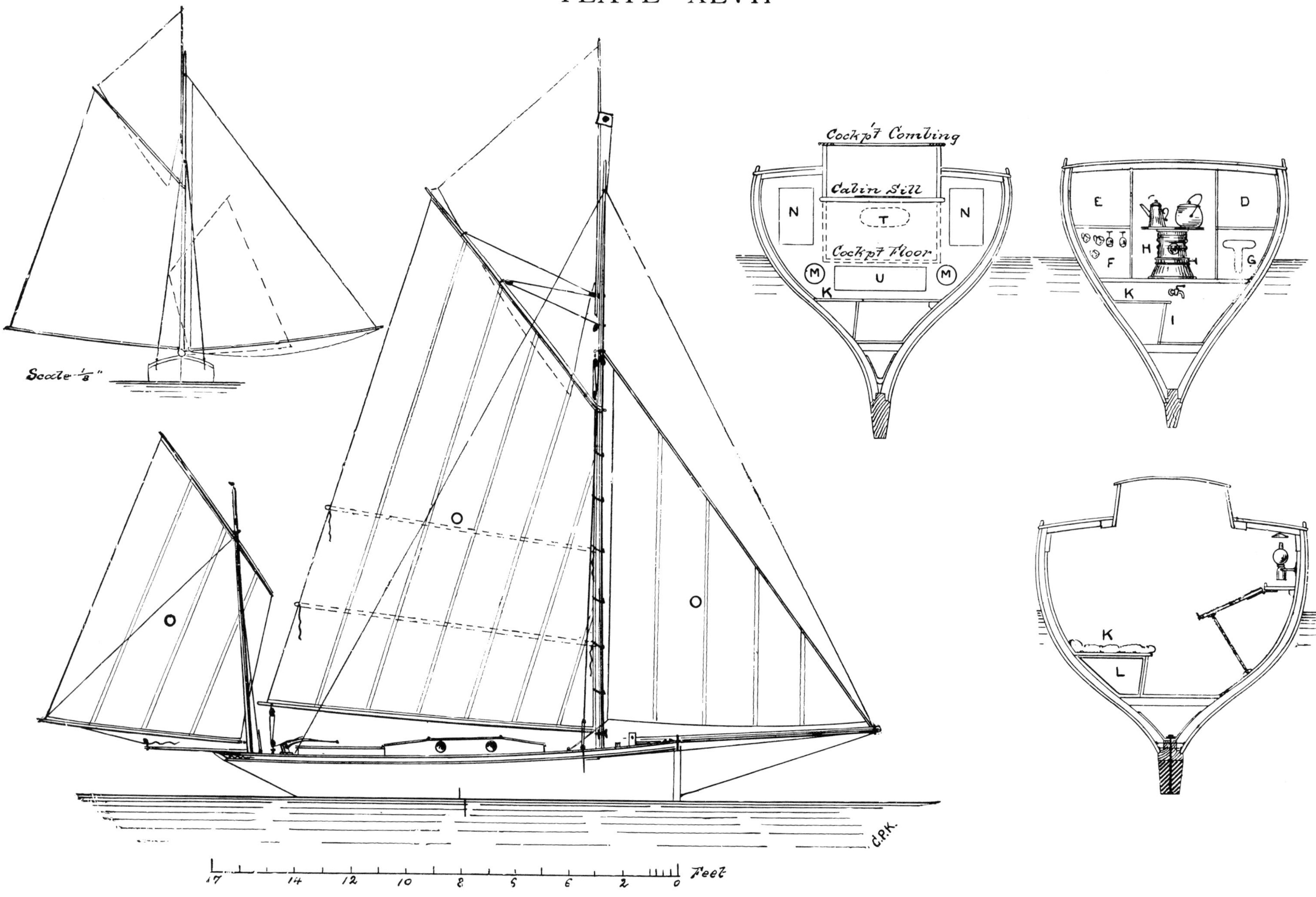

Scale 1/8"
Cockp't Combing
Cabin Sill
Cockp't Floor
N
T
N
M
U
M
K
E
D
H
F
G
K
I
K
L
O
O
O
C.P.K.
17
14
12
10
8
5
6
2
0
Feet


THE DEUCE—SAIL PLAN AND CONSTRUCTION

Hoist of mizzen . . . . . . . . . . . . . . . . . . . . . . . . . . . . 7 ft.
Area mainsail . . . . . . . . . . . . . . . . . . . . . . . . . . . . . . 150 sq. ft.
Area jib . . . . . . . . . . . . . . . . . . . . . . . . . . . . . . . . . . 58 " "
Area mizzen . . . . . . . . . . . . . . . . . . . . . . . . . . . . . . . 48 " "
Area topsail . . . . . . . . . . . . . . . . . . . . . . . . . . . . . . . 40 " "
Area spinnaker . . . . . . . . . . . . . . . . . . . . . . . . . . . . 130 " "
Centre of Effort abaft *C L R* . . . . . . . . . . . . . . . . 3 in.

The cross sections in Plate XLVII are upon the scale of the large plans. The mizzen takes care of itself. That it is feasible in the smallest of boats can be concluded from the universal custom among canoe sailers. In a small yacht, about whose decks you can still readily travel, the sloop's mainsail is within such easy control that the yawl is hardly necessary. Battens rove through bights in the canvas, as shown in the DEUCE's rig, can so quickly be hauled down and held with a turn or two of the earing, that reef knittles are not required. In heavy weather, jib can be stowed, catching a turn about the bunt on the bowsprit by reaching out and the yacht sailed along as a cat under reduced mainsail, a fair balance being preserved, if the sail be given a broad head and plenty of peak.

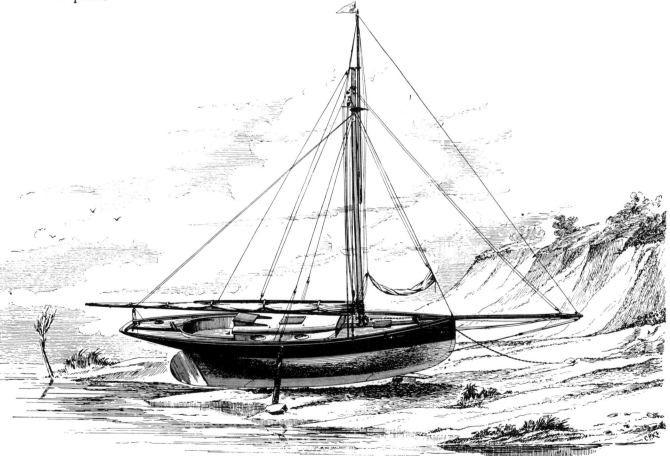

THE REGULAR CUTTER RIG.

# IX

# CUTTERS OF MODERATE BEAM

## I.  THE PETREL

*PLATE  XLVIII*

TWENTY-EIGHT  FEET  LONG  ON  LOAD-LINE

THE PETREL was designed by Mr. John Hyslop, of New York, in 1876, her cross areas corresponding to the ordinates of a "wave curve," Mr. Hyslop having many years previously deduced from experiments upon models the "wave-line area" theory for disposing bulk longitudinally. Not only are the cross areas regulated by such method, but all the water-lines are in themselves wave-lines. Whether the PETREL owes her success to the theory, or merely to the fact that she is clean cut in model and well digested in all her elements, is hardly open to question. A very different boat might have resulted from a less expert person, even living up in full to the theory of wave-line design, for after all, the original choice of displacement and cardinal dimensions and all the features of the yacht individually considered, are matters of judgment for which no governing formulæ are in existence. To these the PETREL owes far more than to subsequent arrangement of bulk. An error of judgment could never have been neutralized by simply making the best of elements badly chosen to begin with.

Her main features can be described as follows: Moderate beam, insuring generally fine form. "Two ends," in place of the long entrance and short, heavy haunches. A rocker keel with raking post, the lowest position to weights, with a high centre of buoyancy, to compensate for moderate displacement, thereby insuring enough sail with the choice of driving the boat upon an easy side. A proper balance between immersed and emersed wedges preserving the same trim as when at a plumb and the ease on her helm which follows. Healthy draft in proportion to displacement. For a boat of her depth the

130

PLATE XLVIII

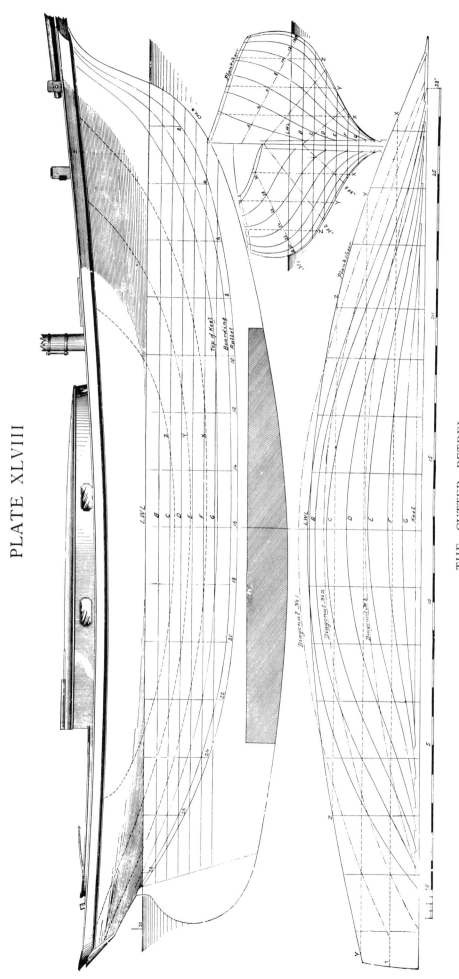

THE CUTTER PETREL

# Small Yachts

Petrel is distinguished by the wonderful ease of her fore and aft sections and her diagonals, as inspection of the plans will substantiate. She has just enough flare to her bow frames to lift dry and clear, just enough tumble home to topsides for a long easy body to drive when heeled under pressure of wind, and her quarters are drawn in just enough for perfect delivery and at the same time ease in her motions. She lifts to everything because free from haunches aft to prevent the depression of her stern. In regard to rig she is a cutter in point of principle, though in some of the mechanical features corresponding to the sloop.

In actual sailing the Petrel is perfection. She is the easiest boat imaginable, and though her lee gangway is awash by the time she is fairly down to her bearings and at her best in a smart breeze, she is remarkably dry to windward. She throws no spray in the hardest drives and rides to her chain like a rocking-chair without tug or snub of the slightest appreciation. She is reasonably able in a chop, and with two cringles down puts in licks to windward, screwing out higher than she points in astonishing style. She is at all times and in all weather fast, jammed high or romping with sheets lifted. There is no difficulty in beaching for a scrub, as a leg is got out abreast the chain plates at high water, and the throat and peak carried broad off to steady as the water falls away. The foresail has a light boom to the foot, the boom working on the sheet as a traveler, so that foresheet need not be touched in beating up.

The rig is found extremely convenient, as it does away with all reefing and bobbing of jib and also gives greater choice of arrangement. The area is quite moderate for the boat's length, and spars correspondingly snug and light with beneficial effect in a head sea. The Petrel heels quickly to her bearings as can be imagined, and until it blows strong is over on her side considerably more than a sloop, but never enough to interfere with perfect control and the management of her gear, or "comfort." And when heeled she goes along about her business in holiday fashion without towing her helm over the weather quarter, and without any gymnastics to keep her on her course.

The rig is depicted on Plate XLIX.

The present mast of Petrel is built of two halves, slightly cored out, glued, doweled and pinned together, with but little taper to masthead. The object was to combine lightness with the stiffness of large diameter. Spars as rigid as they can be stayed with due regard to lightness are now accepted as equally as necessary to smart performance as flat sitting canvas. The Petrel's experiment seems to have been a perfect success, as her mast never buckles, nor does the masthead twist with exposure to the weather, and the stick never "complains." The building of masts may be considered an improvement, but it should be borne in mind that unless accurate and faithful workmanship can be counted

PLATE XLIX

THE PETREL—SAIL PLAN

upon to a certainty, a built mast is a treacherous and dangerous affair. Much weight will not be saved, but weight for weight, greater strength and stiffness can be secured by a competent mechanic familiar' with spar making. PETREL's topmast is fidded to house and the bowsprit reefs in over the wood boomkin. She has two shrouds and backstays each side, and the jib martingale nips under an iron dolphin striker. The boomkin is steadied by an iron rod jumper or bob-stay.

| | |
|---|---|
| Length over all | 32 ft. |
| Length *L W L* | 28 " |
| Beam extreme on *L W L* | 8 " |
| Depth planksheer to garboard on *M S* | 4 " 7 in. |
| Least freeboard | 16½ " |
| Greatest draft | 4 " 10½ " |
| Displacement | 7½ tons |
| Ballast inside | 2,526 lbs. |
| Ballast on keel | 5,474 " |
| Area lower sails | 800 sq. ft. |
| Ratio to square *L W L* | 102 per cent |
| Area mainsail | 522 sq. ft. |
| Area foresail | 132 " " |
| Area jib | 146 " " |
| Mast, deck to hounds | 25 ft. |
| Masthead | 4 " 6 in. |
| Topmast, cap to shoulder | 12 " 3 " |
| Rake of mast | 1 in 21 |
| Main boom over all | 28 ft. 6 in. |
| Gaff over all | 17 " |
| Bowsprit end *L W L* to cap | 5 " |
| Jibboom, cap to stay | 9 " |
| Mainsail on luff | 20 " |
| Mainsail on head | 16 " |
| Mainsail on foot | 27 " |
| Mainsail on leech | 32 " |
| Foresail on luff | 24 " |
| Foresail on foot | 12 " 6 in. |
| Foresail on leech | 21 " |
| Jib on luff | 29 " |
| Jib on foot | 15 " |
| Jib on leech | 20 " 6 in. |

The cabin has 24 in. berths each side, 13 ft. long and 32 in. of floor between. The house overhead is 12 ft. long and only 10 in. high at after end, being kept low for convenience on deck. A square hatch, 16 x 20 in., gives access to the forecastle, in which the stove, pantry and cooking gear are located.

The one exception to be taken is the scant accommodation the PETREL's form and displacement afford. She was built by W. T. Johnson, Port Richmond, Staten Island, N. Y.

## II. THE MERLIN

### PLATE L

TWENTY-FIVE FEET LONG ON LOAD-LINE

THIS yacht was designed by Mr. George H. Ripley, and built for him in 1884, by Daniel C. Bernard, South Brooklyn.

The main objects were safety and accommodation with good speed. The boat has the wave form throughout, the calculations being based on the theories of Mr. Colin Archer. The radius of the construction circle (1 ft. 6 in.) was so selected, however, as to make the centre of gravity of the curve of areas nearly coincident with the centres of buoyancy, etc.

The frame is of white oak, keel sided and moulded 8 in., stem and post sided 4 in., frames all of steamed oak, 2½ x 3 at heels, tapering to 2 x 1½ at heads and spaced 12 in. centre to centre. The bilge clamps and wales are of yellow pine, the plank, 1 in. thick, of white cedar, and the ceiling of white pine. The planksheer is of white oak bent on cold, and the deck of narrow white pine, laid with the side line. The fastenings are all of copper, riveted over burrs.

On deck forward is a hatch opening into the forecastle, over the cabin are companion and skylight in one, and aft a cockpit 5 ft. long. Immediately under the cockpit is a drawer for ice, below which is a water tank in the run. On descending the companion ladder there is a closet to starboard, just aft of which, and partly below the cockpit, is a sail locker; while on the port side there is an extra berth running back beside the cockpit. A narrow door at the head of this berth, in connection with the similar door of the closet opposite, serves to shut off this portion of the boat from the main cabin.

The cabin proper has two lockers, the seats of which are arranged to fold out, making large berths for sleeping. On the starboard side forward are a washstand and mirror, the former provided with a hinged top, making a small table of it if required, and opposite, on the port side, is a space bulkheaded off for a w. c.

A door abreast the mast gives access to the forecastle, where a place is provided for a stove and a berth for one man. The chain locker is just forward of the mast, lessening the weight in the bows.

PLATE L

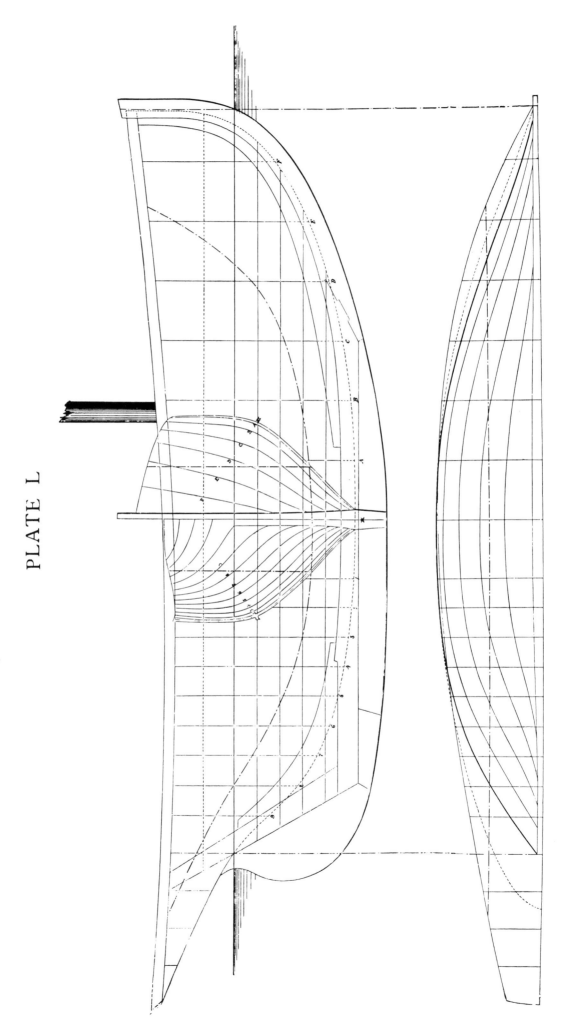

THE CUTTER MERLIN

PLATE LI

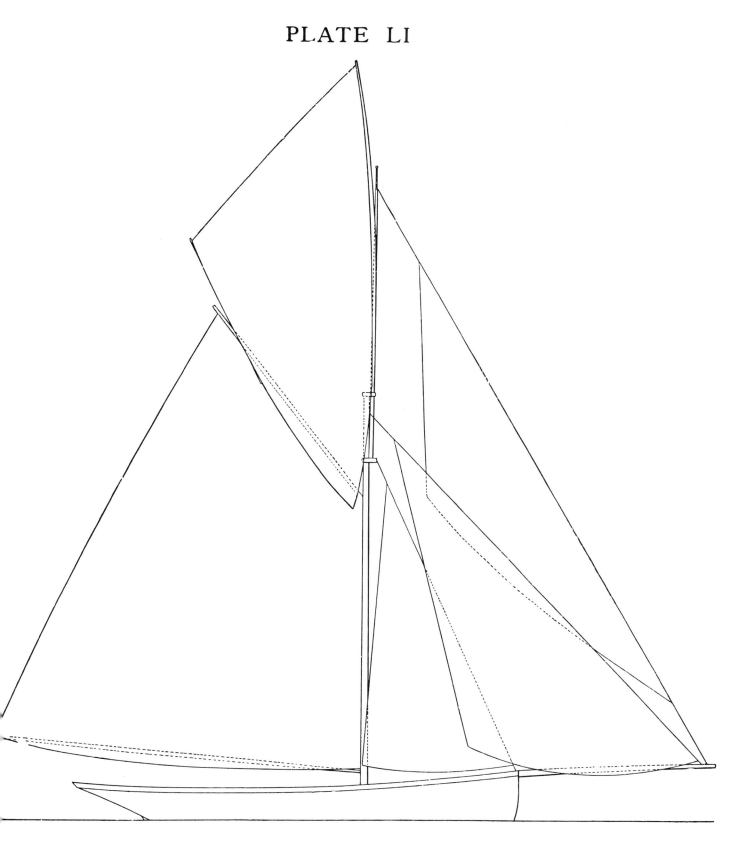

THE MERLIN—SAIL PLAN

Her rig is shown in Plate LI, the sails being from the loft of Wilson & Griffith, New York.

| | | | |
|---|---|---|---|
| Length on *L W L* | 25 ft. | | |
| Length over all | 30 " | 4 in. | |
| Beam extreme | 7 " | | |
| Draft of water | 5 " | | |
| Height of freeboard | 1 " | 11 in. | |
| Midship section aft centre of length *L W L* | 1 " | 9 " | |
| Area load-water plane | 59.79 sq. ft. | | |
| Centre of gravity ditto forward of *M S* | .133 ft. | | |
| Area *M S* | 17.47 sq. ft. | | |
| Centre of buoyancy forward of *M S* | .144 ft. | | |
| Centre of buoyancy below *L W L* | 1.468 " | | |
| Centre of lateral resistance aft centre of *L W L* | 2 ft. | | |
| Centre of effort of lower sails aft centre of *L W L* | 1 ft. 6 in. | | |
| Displacement in long tons | 7.14 | | |
| Ballast inside | 2½ tons | | |
| Ballast outside | 2 " | | |
| Mast, from foreside stem | 10 ft. | | |
| Mast, deck to hounds | 23 " | | |
| Topmast, fid to sheave | 19 ft. 6 in. | | |
| Boom | 26 " | | |
| Gaff | 17 " | | |
| Bowsprit, outboard | 13 " | | |
| Area lower sail | 760 sq. ft. | | |
| Masthead | 5 ft. | | |
| Angle of gaff with horizontal | 51 deg. | | |
| Centre of effort forward of *C L R* | 6 in. | | |
| Mainsail on foot | 25 ft. | 3 in. | |
| Mainsail on luff | 19 " | | |
| Mainsail on head | 16 " | 6 " | |
| Mainsail on leech | 33 " | 4 " | |
| Mainsail, tack to peak | 33 " | 6 " | |
| Mainsail, clew to throat | 30 " | | |
| Jib on foot | 15 " | 10 " | |
| Jib on luff | 30 " | 8 " | |
| Jib on leech | 22 " | 3 " | |
| Staysail on foot | 10 " | 4 " | |
| Staysail on luff | 21 " | 6 " | |
| Staysail on leech | 19 " | 8 " | |
| Topsail yard | 23 " | | |
| Spinnaker boom | 25 " | | |

The MERLIN was found to be somewhat oversparred and will have some of the inside ballast transferred to the keel or the rig cut down a little.

## III.  THE RAJAH

### *PLATE LII*

THIRTY-TWO FEET LONG ON LOAD-LINE

A SOMEWHAT larger yacht of good proportions is the RAJAH, built for **Mr.** J. G. Beecher, of New Haven, by J. J. Driscoll, Greenpoint, Long Island, from designs by Mr. A. Cary Smith, in 1884.   In her the accommodations are on quite a liberal scale.   The forecastle will berth one hand.   Amidships is a cosy main saloon with sofas each side, a w. c. and pantry being bulkheaded off between the two divisions.   The companion ladder leads down at the after end of the saloon, and in the run is a snug stateroom with two berths, the sail locker being abaft of all.   There is 6 ft. under the beams fore and aft, the deck being flush with an **A** skylight over the cabin, a quadrant slide over the companion, and no cockpit.   Access to forecastle and sailroom on deck is from small hatches.   The RAJAH is a handsome vessel afloat, a powerful sea boat, and very comfortable in all respects.   She has shown a good rate of speed.   For general cruising about the coast she is well adapted.

| | | |
|---|---|---|
| Length over all | 40 ft. | |
| Length load-line | 32 " | |
| Beam extreme | 8 " | 6 in. |
| Draft extreme | 6 " | 5 " |
| Least freeboard to planksheer | 2 " | 6 " |
| Displacement, long tons | 13.8 tons | |
| Lead on keel, long tons | 7.3 " | |
| Lead inside, long tons | 0.25 " | |
| Ratio ballast to displacement | 0.55 | |
| Area wet surface, no rudder | 360 sq. ft. | |
| Area three lower sails | 1,092 " " | |
| Sail per sq. ft. of wet surface | 3.03 sq. ft. | |
| Mast, deck to cap | 31 ft. 9 in. | |
| Topmast | 25 " 6 " | |
| Boom | 31 " 9 " | |
| Gaff | 22 " 3 " | |
| Bowsprit outboard | 18 " 4 " | |

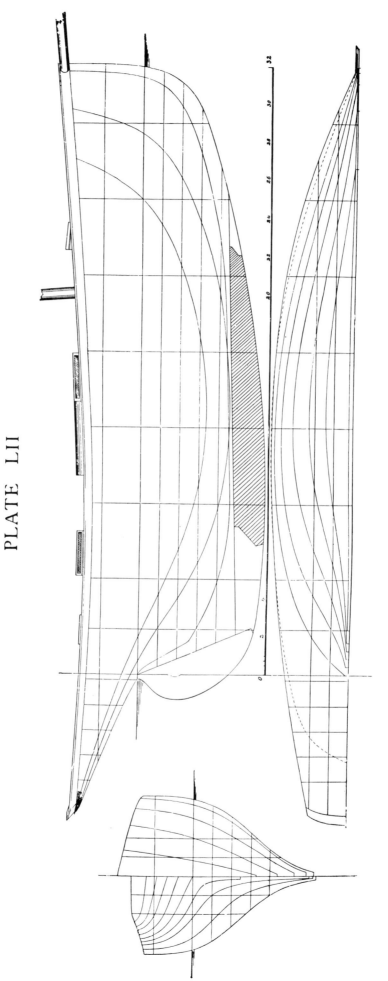

PLATE LII

THE CUTTER RAJAH

# Cutters of Moderate Beam

## IV. THE YOLANDE

### *PLATE LIII*

TWENTY-SIX FEET SIX INCHES LONG ON LOAD-LINE

ONE of the earliest cutters built in America is the YOLANDE, a little gem in construction and finish, launched in 1880 by Henry Piepgrass, of Greenpoint, Long Island, for Mr. M. Roosevelt Schuyler, of New York, who got out her lines, and also superintended the details and fittings. She is a fast, sightly little vessel of more than ordinary excellence in build and equipment. She would have been still better with 3 in. more freeboard, but is quite able as it is, good beam being an offset for want of all the side which later experience has brought into vogue.

| | |
|---|---|
| Length on deck | 31 ft. |
| Length on $LWL$ | 26 " 6 in. |
| Beam | 7 " |
| Draft | 5 " 10 " |
| Ballast on keel | 10,200 lbs. |
| Displacement | 8 tons |
| Area midship section | 14.78 sq. ft. |
| Area load water-line | 118 " " |
| Midship section abaft centre of $LWL$ | 1.3 ft. |
| Centre of buoyancy abaft centre of $LWL$ | 1 " |
| Centre of buoyancy below $LWL$ | 1.4 " |
| Mast, deck to hounds | 23 ft. 6 in. |
| Masthead | 4 " |
| Topmast, fid to sheave hole | 19 " |
| Bowsprit outboard | 14 " 8 " |
| Boom | 25 " |
| Gaff | 17 " |
| Spinnaker boom | 31 " |
| Area of mainsail | 479 sq. ft. |
| Area of foresail | 115 " " |
| Area of jib | 171 " " |
| Total area of sail | 765 " " |

Although the floor in cabin is narrow, the accommodations below are attractive for shipboard life and have been arranged with that in view. With the exception of a cockpit, the deck is flush, the cabin slide and skylight taking the place of a wider and less sightly house top. From Plate LIV the berthing below and the fittings throughout will be apparent, as well as the style of construction, the plans being to scale.

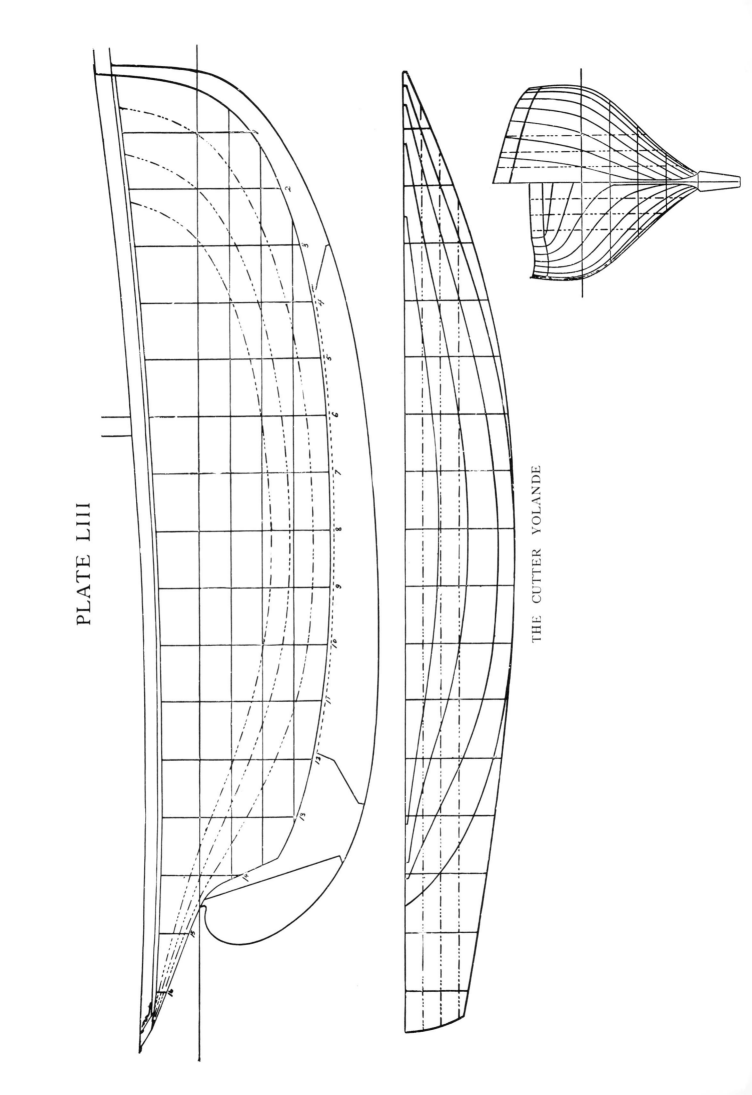

PLATE LIII

THE CUTTER YOLANDE

PLATE LIV

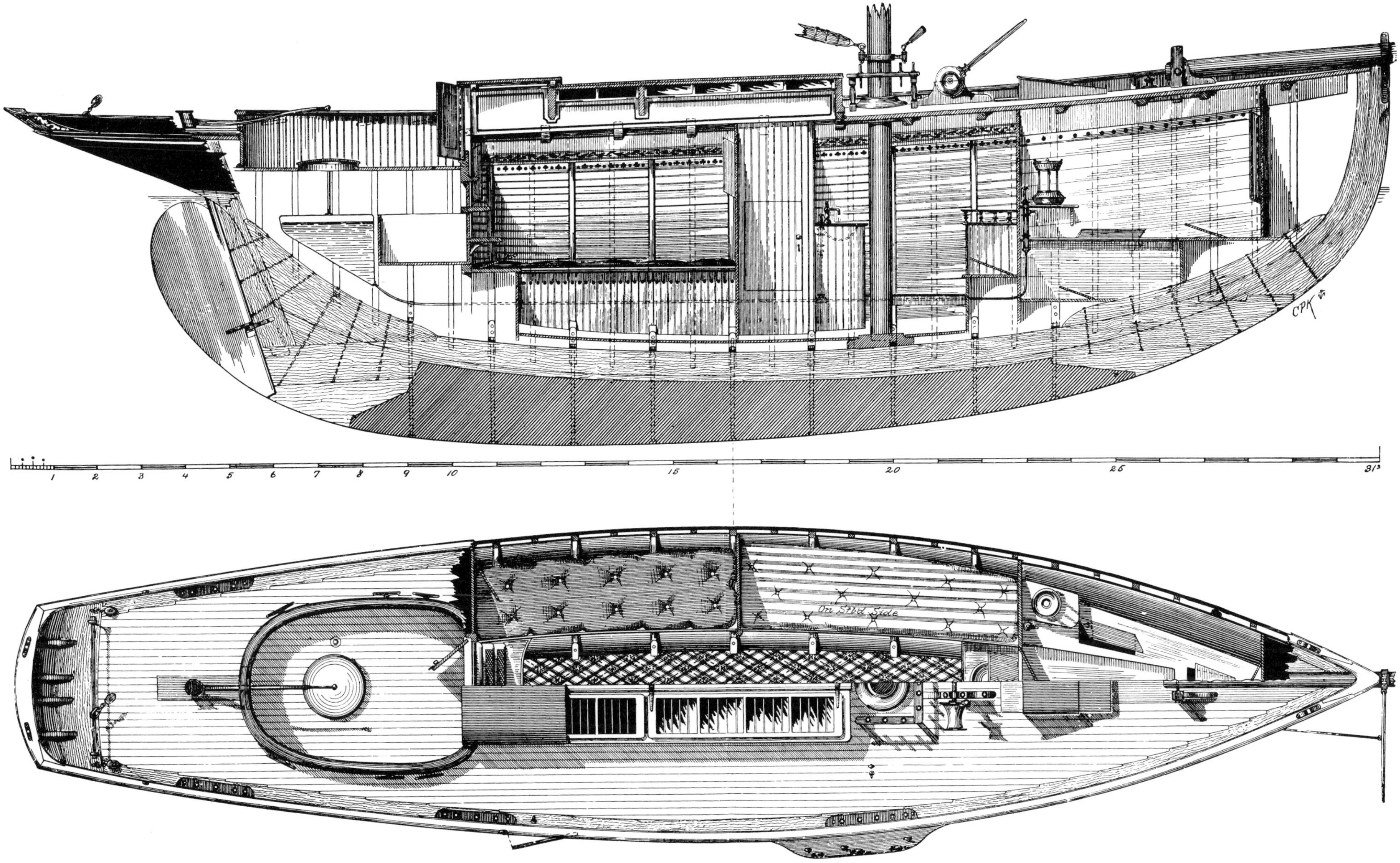

THE CUTTER YOLANDE—CABIN AND DECK PLAN

# Small Yachts

The bitts are keyed in chocks spanning two beams, so that the forecastle is entirely clear, giving a berth for the crew, locker room and a chance to cook on a vapor stove. Water is drawn by a brass hand-pump piped to the tank in the run. A door through the bulkhead leads into the cabin or stateroom amidships, which is 6½ ft. long with 5 ft. 9 in. headroom under the skylight. On port hand is a locker 1 ft. 10 in. face, extending up to deck. The lower portion serves for stowing clothing, while the upper half has a thwartship door opening into the after cabin as a china and wine locker. For the toilet there is also

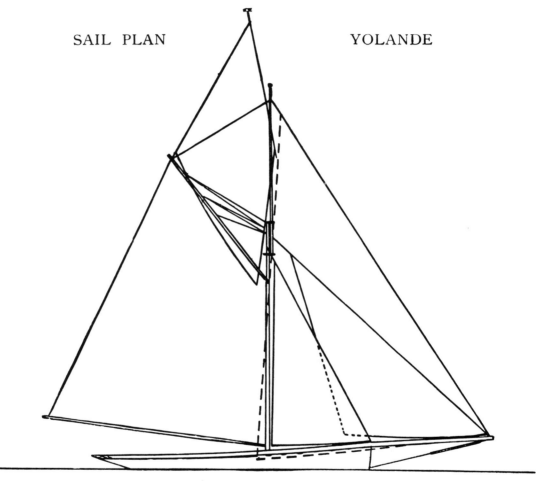

SAIL PLAN                    YOLANDE

a washstand with china basin, supplied by a vertical handpump and faucet. On starboard hand is the owner's berth, with 24 in. mattress, and drawers below. The floor is 18 in. wide. A curtain separates the stateroom from a 6 ft. after cabin with sofas each side. Access to the deck is had by a series of mahogany brackets leading out through the slide into a cockpit 5 ft. long and 3 ft. 6 in. wide, with seating around a mahogany cap of 3 in. Cockpit is 15 in. deep and self-draining. A drawer and water tank in the run leave room above for extra sails and gear passed down through a circular manhole in the cockpit floor.

# Cutters of Moderate Beam

On deck the fittings are appropriate and handsome. Bowsprit ships through a gammon iron over the stem and fids between the bitts supported by knees on forward face. Between the mast and fore hatch is a small "noiseless" winch, of Thayer's pattern, with which to heave in the chain or sweat up halliards. A fife rail about the mast serves for belaying the gear. The skylight is 6 ft. 8 in. long, the two after panels being "blind," over which the cabin slide passes when open. Pin rails, channels, side ports, backstay plates, topmast backstay eyes, fore sheet leader and kneeing of counter above archboard are all shown on the deck plan. Also the "whisker" from stem head giving spread to the bowsprit shrouds. These pass through holes in chocks against the rail abreast the mast and are set up by tackles inboard. Although the YOLANDE has three shrouds a side, two are sufficient.

The ribbing consists of alternate sawed and steamed frames, the former being secured to keel by iron floors, to which the lead keel bolts are set up with large nuts. A stout clamp running fore and aft takes the beam ends. Ventilation is looked after by clover-leaf borings in the upper streak of the ceiling. This is let into the sawed frames half way to add to the room inside, faying against the steamed timbers. The mainsheet is rove with two hauling parts leading through single quarter blocks abreast of the traveler and belayed to cleats on the cockpit coaming. Headsheets make fast to cleats on the fore quarters. The principal specifications are as follows :

Keel, oak, 10 x 8 in. amidships. Stem and post, oak, sided 4 in. moulded as per plans. Frame, oak, single, sawed from natural crook, 2½ in. sided, and 2¼ moulded at heel, tapering ½ in. to head. Spaced 22 in. between centres, with one bent oak frame between; wrought iron floor knees, 2 x ½ in., with two ⅜ in. bolts in each arm, and 1 in. composition bolts for the lead keel. Clamps of oak 7 x 1½ in. ; beams, oak, 2⅞ x 1¾ in., spaced 20 in. ; mast beams, 3 x 1¾, spaced 15 in. Mast partners, 12 x 2½ in., through bolted fore and aft and to four lodge knees. Chock for bitts, 3 in. thick. Bitts, 3 x 3 in. Ceiling, ½ in. Plank, 1 in. cedar. Garboards and topstreak of 1¼ in. oak. Deck, white pine 2 x 1 in. King plank, 12 x 1¼ oak. Covering board, oak, 6 x 1½ in. Mast, 7 in. at partners ; bowsprit, 5¼ in. at stem. Rudderhead, 3½ in. Cap rail, oak, 3 x 1 in. ; hatch coamings, mahogany, 2 in. thick ; door post, 2 x 3 in. ; mast step of lead, 18 in. long, 3½ thick, and 7 in. wide. Channels, 6 in. wide, 1¼ in. thick ; 3 in. deadeyes, with 11 in. spread. Chain plates, 1½ x ¼ iron. Casting for hawsehole is 7½ in. long, let into a chock in the eyes. Gammon iron is 10 in. deep on stem, and 1¼ in. wide. Bowsprit spreader of 1 in. iron, with ½ in. stay. The waist is laid up with ½ in. mahogany against locust stanchions at each sawed frame. Fastenings of ¼ in. yellow metal and plank riveted with copper. The yacht is sheathed with copper to 1 ft. above load-line at stem and 3 in. at post.

## V.  A CRUISING YACHT

### *PLATE LV*

TWENTY-FOUR FEET LONG ON LOAD-LINE

TO supply a demand for a roomy, wholesome cruiser, as large as one hand could control under yawl rig, Messrs. Burgess, of Boston, got out the plans and cabins for a very likely looking yawl of four beams to load-line, of which the following are the chief dimensions:

| | | | |
|---|---|---|---|
| Length over all | 29 ft. | | |
| Length on *W L* | 24 " | | |
| Beam extreme | 6 " | 2 in. | |
| Beam on *W L* | 6 " | | |
| Draft | 5 " | | |
| Least freeboard | 2 " | 3 " | |
| Displacement, 189 cubic feet | 5.4 tons | | |
| Iron on keel | 6,350 lbs. | | |
| Ratio of ballast to displacement | 0.55 | | |
| Area midship section | 14.5 sq. ft. | | |
| Area immersed longitudinal section | 93 " " | | |
| Area load-line | 95.66 " " | | |
| Area wetted surface | 205 " " | | |
| Ratio longitudinal to midship section | 6.4 | | |
| Ratio longitudinal section to load-line plane | 1.03 | | |
| Midship section from end *L W L* | 14 ft. | | |
| Centre of buoyancy from *L W L* | 13.12 ft. | | |
| Centre of lateral resistance from *L W L* | 13.44 " | | |
| Centre of effort from *L W L* | 12.82 " | | |
| Centre of effort forward of *C L R* | 7½ in. | | |
| Mast, deck to hounds | 24 ft. 6 in. | | |
| Masthead and pole | 6 " | | |
| Diameter in partners | 6 in. | | |
| Diameter at hounds | 5 " | | |
| Mainboom | 21 ft. | | |
| Diameter in slings | 3⅛ in. | | |
| Main gaff | 15 ft. | | |
| Diameter greatest | 3 in. | | |
| Mainmast from end *L W L* | 4 ft. 6 in. | | |
| Mizzenmast | 18 " | | |
| Diameter at deck | 4 in. | | |
| Mizzen boom | 11 ft. | | |
| Diameter | 2¼ in. | | |
| Mizzen yard | 11 ft. | | |

PLATE LV

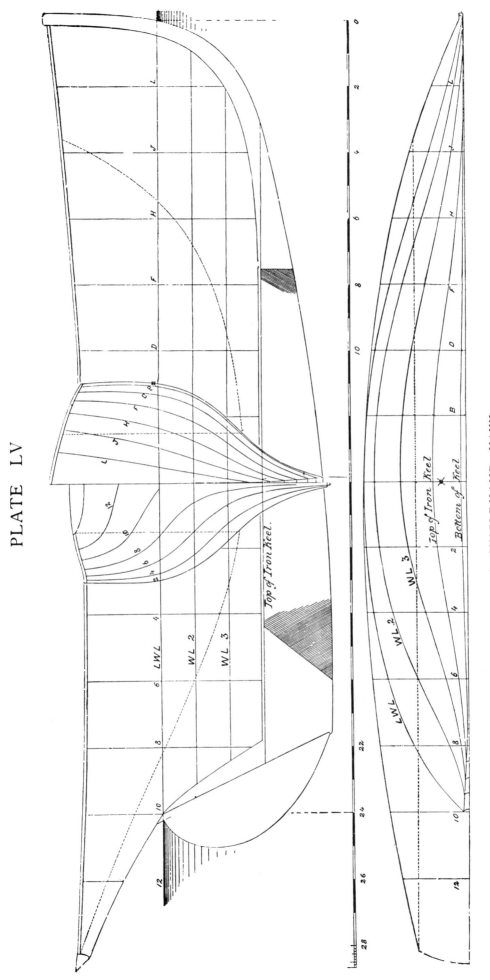

A SINGLE-HAND YAWL

Top of Iron Keel.

Top of Iron Keel
Bottom of Keel

LWL
WL 2
WL 3

LWL
WL 2
WL 3

| | |
|---|---|
| Diameter . . . . . . . . . . . . . . . . . . . . . . . . . . . . . . . . . . . . . . | 2½ in. |
| Bumpkin, oak, outboard . . . . . . . . . . . . . . . . . . . . . . . . | 4½ ft. |
| Bowsprit outboard . . . . . . . . . . . . . . . . . . . . . . . . . . . . | 10½ " |
| Diameter . . . . . . . . . . . . . . . . . . . . . . . . . . . . . . . . . . . | 4¼ in. |
| Area mainsail . . . . . . . . . . . . . . . . . . . . . . . . . . . . . . . 385 sq. ft. |
| Area mizzen . . . . . . . . . . . . . . . . . . . . . . . . . . . . . . . . . 130 " " |
| Area jib . . . . . . . . . . . . . . . . . . . . . . . . . . . . . . . . . . . 154 " " |
| Total lower sail area . . . . . . . . . . . . . . . . . . . . . . . . . 669 " " |
| Sail area per square foot wet surface . . . . . . . . . . . 3.26 sq. ft. |
| Ratio to square of load-line . . . . . . . . . . . . . . . . . . 1.14 per cent |

The rig plan is presented on Plate LVII, and the accommodations on Plate LVI. These explain themselves so readily that little need be said. The cockpit shelters from the weather and is preferred by many people. For ladies it is certainly a great convenience. The sill to the cabin doors is perhaps rather low, but the boat will prove so stiff that it will be all but impossible to sail her cockpit under, and her great buoyancy will insure complete immunity from being run under or "overwhelmed," so that the greater convenience of a low sill may justify its existence in this design. The cabin is as spacious as need be. It is 10 ft. long and 5½ ft. wide across the sofas, with 30 in. floor. Lockers abreast the ladder extend to full height to accommodate clothing and oilskins, while the sideboards and cupboards at the forward end of the sofas afford plenty of room for pantry, linen, writing materials and books. The forecastle is cut off by a curtain shown in the cross section. On port hand is an ice safe and store-room, and shelving, racks, etc., and amidships on top of a large locker over the floor the cooking apparatus is located. A double oil stove of the Adams & Westlake pattern is as good for the purpose as anything else. The chain leads down through a pipe on deck and is stowed forward of the mast. Shelves in the eyes of the boat are suitable for paints, oils, putty, etc. On starboard side is room for a bunk should a hand be shipped. Sails are stowed under the cockpit, and boatswain's small stores, lead-line, etc., in the side lockers and counter. Water in a tank fitted under sail-room floor. Ample ventilation is provided for by the skylight and doors. The cabins in summer will be found cooler than those of a light draft boat spread out on the surface and exposing large area to the sun. Access to the space under the sofa is had by openings closed with narrow curtains. For sleeping the width of the sofas is increased by drawing out a slide and doubling upon it the cushion used as a back rest during the day. The framing of the boat can be understood from the cross section. The keel is very broad, the heels of the frames stepping into it, bolted and further secured by forged iron floors. The outside ballast is bolted up with a diagonal bolt through keel and each iron floor on alternate side, a lag screw going through floor into keel on the other side.

PLATE LVI

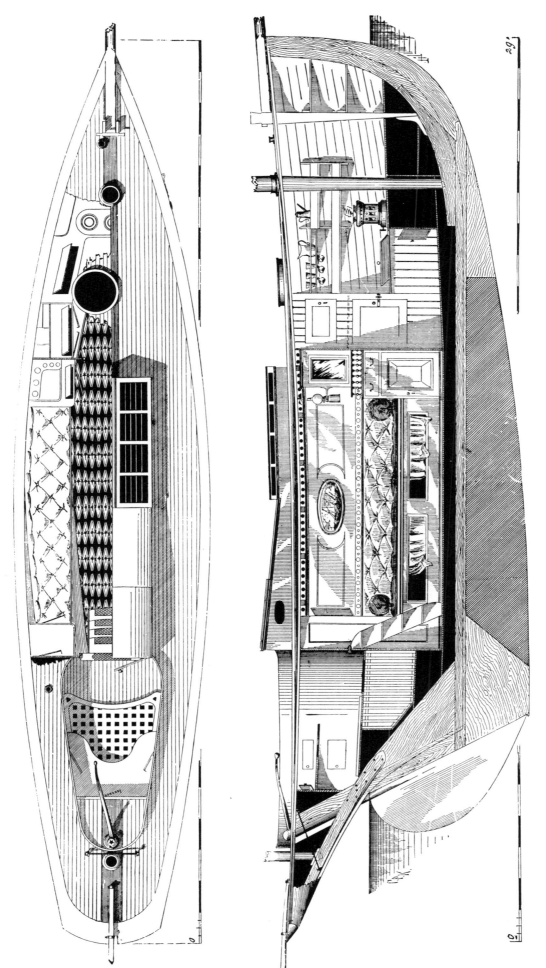

SINGLE-HAND YAWL—CABIN AND DECK PLANS

PLATE LVII

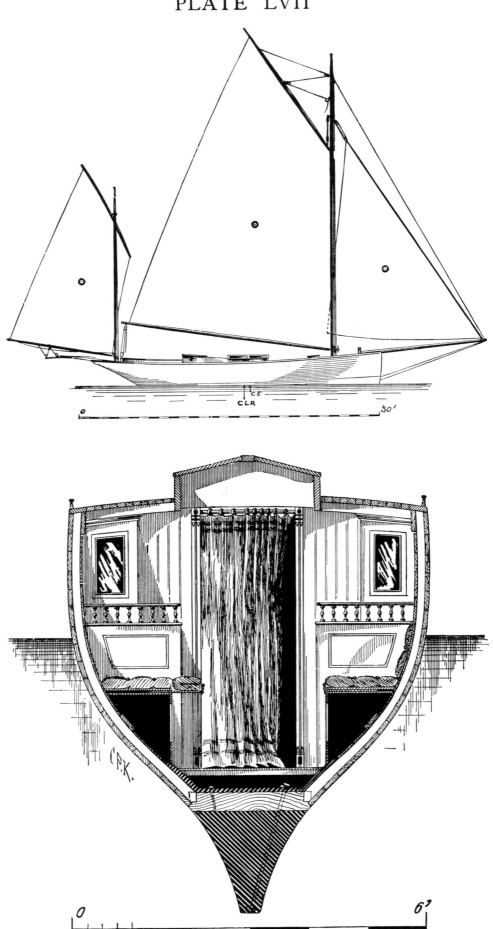

CE
CLR

0                                                    30'

0                                                    6'

SINGLE-HAND YAWL—RIG AND CONSTRUCTION

# VI. THE RONDINA

*PLATE LVIII*

THIRTY FEET LONG ON WATER-LINE

THE RONDINA, designed by Mr. Edward Burgess in 1884, was built by Lawley & Son, of South Boston, for Dr. W. F. Whitney. The general plans of the interior of this boat serve to illustrate the amount of room derived from a judicious combination of length, depth and beam. RONDINA was intended for cruising about the New England coast, for which purpose safety at sea is the very first consideration. For regular life on board a small craft, standing height in the cabin is also of importance, as the constant necessity of crooking the back in a low cabin soon becomes too irksome to be attractive. RONDINA has done considerable knocking about on the coast, having repeatedly visited all the ports between Newport and the Bay of Fundy. Her dimensions are:

| | | | | |
|---|---|---|---|---|
| Length over all | 36 ft. | 4 in. | | |
| Length on water-line | 30 " | | | |
| Beam extreme | 8 " | 2 " | | |
| Draft | 6 " | 6 " | | |
| Least freeboard | 2 " | 3 " | | |
| Displacement, long tons | 12.75 | | | |
| Iron on keel, long tons | 6.00 | | | |
| Ballast inside, iron, long tons | 0.50 | | | |
| Area lower sail | 987 sq. ft. | | | |

Although showing a high side, the cutter makes a smart appearance afloat owing to her long counter and easy sheer.

The forecastle has 5 ft. 8in. headroom under the beams, with good length of floor. Lockers run around both sides, above which two iron-frame swinging berths are suspended. Ice box and refrigerator are on port side, and the pantry and closet to starboard. The main cabin has 5 ft. 9 in. under the beams and a floor 11 ft. long and 3 ft. wide. Sofas on each side, the upholstering being carried up to shoulder height. Linen and wine lockers are against the forward bulkhead, and also a handsome open-grate fireplace with book case above. In the steerage, abreast of the companion ladder, are lockers 6 ft. high for hanging oilers and clothing, also washbowl and toilet appliances. Abaft the ladder is the sail room, ventilated by a grating in the bulkhead. The sails are passed down through a hatch on deck abaft the cockpit. Excellent light and air is secured by an **A** skylight over the cabin.

The berthing arrangements consist of a very handy device. At each end

PLATE LVIII

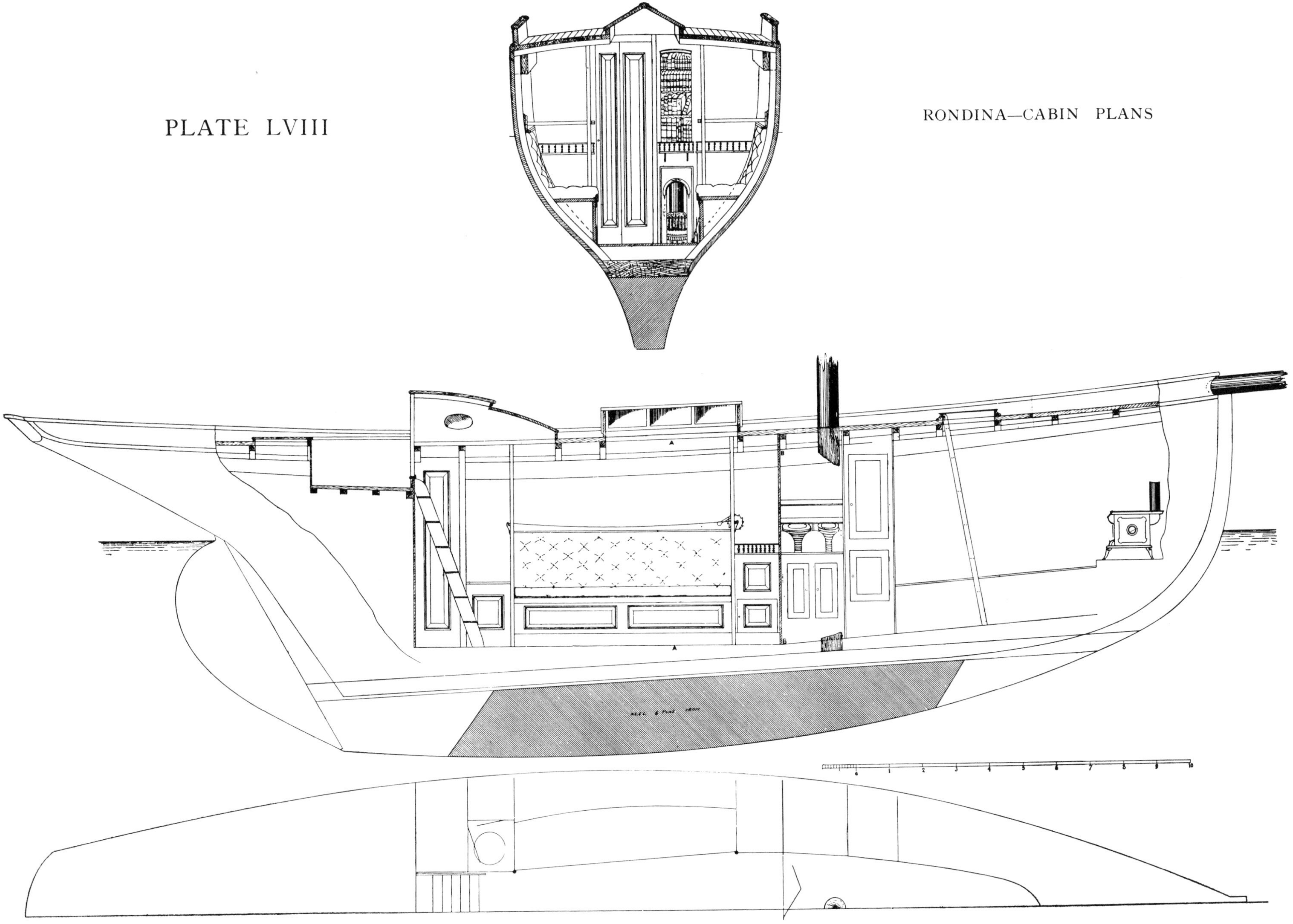

of the sofas are upright pillars or stanchions. Canvas hammocks have iron stretchers laced across the ends. These stretchers fit in journals on the stanchions and at the ship's side. The forward bar has a pawl wheel keyed on the inboard end. When not in use the canvas is rolled up and stowed out of sight. To get the berth ready, the bars are dropped into the journals and a wrench is applied to the forward bar, the canvas being thereby wound up as taut as desired, the pawl and wheel holding it on the stretch.

The internal plans of the large cutter Galatea, designed by Mr. J. Beavor Webb for Lieut. Henn, Royal Navy, and built in 1885 by John Reid & Co., of Port Glasgow, Scotland, will suggest many ideas concerning cabin arrangements which can be adopted in small craft.

The specifications by which the well-known MAYFLOWER, winner of the international race for the America's Cup in 1886, was built, will serve as a guide in making out contracts for small boats. They are as follows:

QUALITY OF MATERIAL AND WORKMANSHIP —In carrying out the specifications it is to be understood that only those materials that are best adapted to speed shall be employed. All the woods must be sound, clear and free from defect. All the iron work, except the floors and frame pieces, shall be galvanized. All spar bands, bolts, braces, the chain and runner plates, bobstay turnbuckles and similar things about the yacht shall be of the best Norway iron.

KEEL —This is to be of white oak, sound and clear. The required siding will be not less than 30 in. The scarf shall not be less than 7 ft. long, bolted with 1 in. yellow metal bolts, and the bolts shall not be more than 1 ft. apart.

LEAD KEEL —This is to be cast in not more than three pieces, with scarfed joints, and bolted with yellow metal 1 in. bolts, nutted on top, not more than 11¼ in. apart. The builder is to cast all ballast needed inside, in such shapes as to fit between the timbers, as laid out upon the plans.

STEM —This is to be of white oak, sound and clear grained, 9 in. sided above and 7 in. below, to work at least 3 in. aft. of rabbet. Both stem and sternpost to be worked fair with plank lines.

FRAMES —They are to be of white oak of natural growth, double and spaced 23 in., and bolted together with ⅝ galvanized iron, box-keyed into keel, and well bolted forward and aft; bolts to go through from one side to the other.

CHAIN PLATE FRAMES —Oak and sided 6 in. in one length. A ⅜ in. iron plate will be 4 in. wide at heel, and 3 in. at head, to be shaped like the frames and fitted between the two halves of each chain plate frame and through-bolted with ⅝ in. nutted bolts. It is expected that six plates will be required. An inverted V-shaped strap of ⅜ in. iron will also be worked on the inside of the frames to distribute the strain on the rigging.

# Small Yachts

FLOORS.—These forward aft of the centreboard trunk will be of the best gun iron and will extend to the deadwoods and will be 5 × 4 in the throat, with arms 3 ft. long, tapering to the top. The centre stringers will be 8 × 4 and the two on each side 8 × 3.

DECK FRAMES—These will be of hackmatack with moulded face and finished bright in cabins 6 (moulded) × 5 (dovetailed), and will go 1 in. into shelf and bolted each end of shelf.

DECK —It will be laid with well-seasoned, clear white pine, free of knots, spiked and 2 3/8 × 2 3/8 laid fore and aft.

BULWARKS —They are to be of dry white pine of one width and stained mahogany inside. They will have a thick lower course 2 × 1 3/4 in. and will be grooved for gilt stripe. There will be three ports on each side.

PLANKING —The garboards will be of 3 in. white oak, the bottoms and bilge of turned clear white oak 10 × 2 3/4 in. The topsides will be of yellow pine 2 3/4 in., and there will be not more than three lengths in any course, except three courses which may be laid in four lengths if thought necessary.

The whole hull is to be carefully joinered and smoothed, and the planking will be thoroughly filled with red lead, and receive two coats of best copper bronze on bottom and centreboard, and three coats of white lead on topsides. Two galvanized iron tanks, one on each side, will be built and put under flooring, capable of holding 400 gallons of water. An improved force pump will be so placed as to drain the lowest part of the bilge and discharge into the centreboard trunk.

The centreboard will be of yellow pine, about 21 ft. in length and 10 ft. in depth, 4 in. thick, with lower course of oak; the whole to be bolted with 1 1/8 steel bolts. Three hundred pounds of lead will be run into the top of the board to sink it easily, and it will be shod with boiler iron, doubled over edges, and worked sharp and fair. The whole board will be hung similar to that of the Puritan. The centreboard trunk will have the lower logs 12 × 6 of oak, and bolted 18 in. apart with 1 in. iron. It will not be sheathed, and the planking will be smoothly finished and beaded.

The mainmast will be made of Oregon pine, and will measure about 80 ft. in length and 20 in. in diameter; the boom of Oregon pine and about 80 ft. long and 14 in. in diameter.

Hatchways and fittings will be finished in mahogany. The cabin below decks will be finished in white and have mahogany trimmings. Aft of the companionway will be a stateroom 7 ft. in length, with two berths and transoms on either side. At the foot of the companionway, which will be immediately entered in going below deck, is the main saloon, 15 ft. in length and of the breadth of the boat. It will be plainly finished and have transoms all around. Forward of the main saloon, on the starboard hand, will be a door

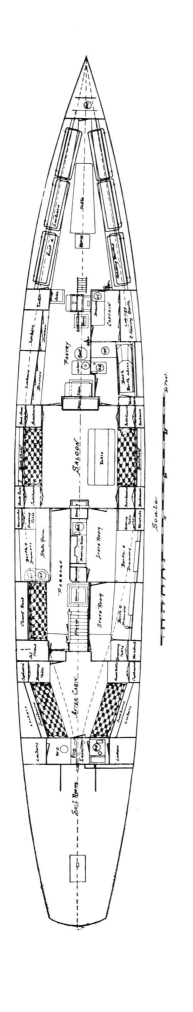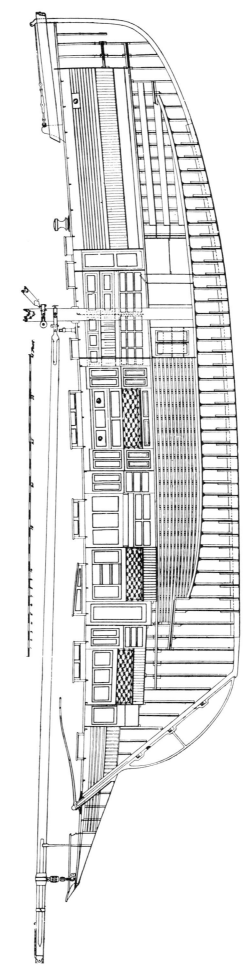

CABIN PLANS OF THE CUTTER GALATEA

leading into the owner's stateroom, 9 × 15½ ft., with a large and roomy berth. On one side will be a fixed basin, the whole to be fitted for convenience rather than show. On the other side (port), corresponding to the owner's stateroom, is a smaller room, entered from a passageway which runs from the main saloon forward. This will be the guests' room and will be nearly square. Adjoining the guests' room, upon the same side of the passage, is a large locker room. Across the passage from this apartment, forward and adjoining the owner's stateroom, is a stateroom to be used by the steward, cabin boy and assistants. Next comes the galley, which is at the end of the passage way. It is of the full width of the yacht and about square. Forward of the galley are the crew's quarters.

The lead on the keel was increased to 37 tons after an experimental trial or two, and the sternpost given additional rake with more rocker to the keel. Her spars are: Mast, deck to hounds, 63 ft.; topmast, 46 ft.; bowsprit outboard, 38 ft.; boom, 80 ft.; gaff, 50 ft. The sails are cut to the following dimensions: The mainsail is 51 ft. 9 in. hoist, 76 ft. 6 in. foot, 48 ft. head. The topsail has 30 ft. hoist, 32 ft. leech, 48 ft. 6 in. foot; foresail, 58 ft. luff, 51 ft. 6 in. leech, 34 ft. foot; jib, 85 ft. 6 in. luff, 61 ft. leech, 44 ft. foot; jibtopsail, 94 ft. luff, 58 ft. leech, 58 ft. foot; spinnaker, 115 ft. luff, 108 ft. leech, 88 ft. foot.

## VII. THE INDRA

### PLATE LIX

#### THIRTY-SIX FEET LONG ON WATER-LINE

THE INDRA, originally christened Melusina, is a handsome specimen of the cruising cutter with moderate beam and iron ballast. She was designed by Mr. Geo K. Boutelle, of Waterville, Me., for Mr. Horace Binney, of Providence, R. I., and built in 1885 by Lawley & Son, of South Boston. The chief characteristic is the commendable way in which ample deck and cabin room have been combined with an excellent and easy form of body without going to excess in displacement in proportion to the boat's beam. To retain the iron on keel within reasonable fore and aft limits the rabbet is struck in along the lower edge of a flat wood keel 2 ft. 6 in. wide amidships, the iron casting being moulded to a continuation of the frames, thereby enabling nearly all the ballast to be carried outside without resorting to an external keel appendage to the hull proper. The midship section has been kept well

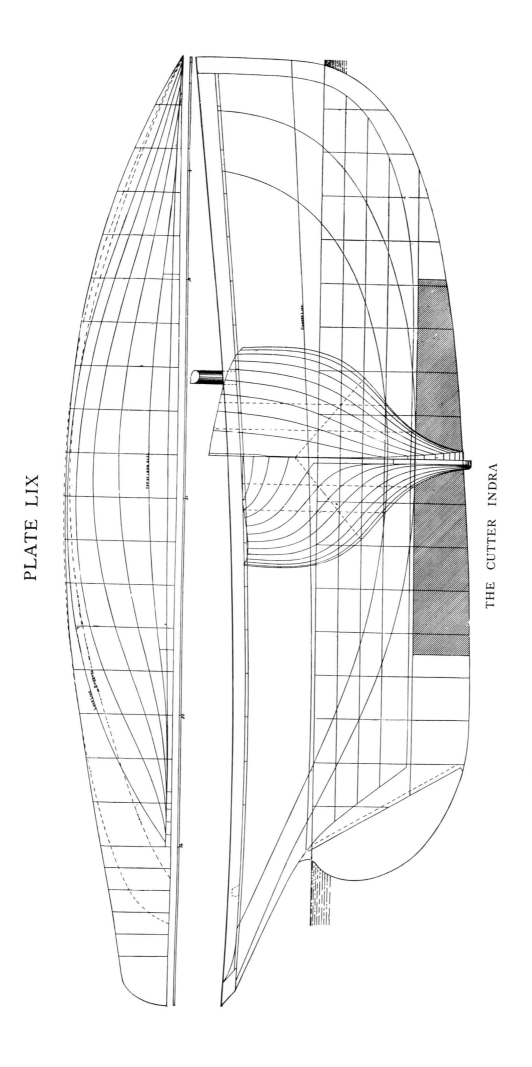

PLATE LIX

THE CUTTER INDRA

forward, and the fore and aft bodies nearly alike in displacement. The sail area, while showing a fairly high ratio to wetted surface, is moderate when compared to the square of the load-line.

| | |
|---|---|
| Length on deck.......................... | 42 ft. 9 in. |
| Length on water-line..................... | 36 " |
| Beam at water-line....................... | 9 " 10 " |
| Beam extreme............................ | 10 " 2½ " |
| Draft, maximum.......................... | 7 " |
| Least freeboard.......................... | 3 " 1½ " |
| Sheer forward........................... | 1 " 8 " |
| Sheer aft............................... | 4 " |
| Breadth across counter................... | 4 " |
| Displacement, long tons.................. | 19.02 |
| Iron on keel, long tons.................. | 9.50 |
| Area midship section..................... | 31 sq. ft. |
| Area immersed longitudinal section........ | 216 " " |
| Area load-line plane...................... | 234 " " |
| Area wetted surface...................... | 501 " " |
| *M S* from end of *L W L*............... | 19 ft. 1¾ in. |
| Centre of buoyancy from end *L W L*...... | 18 " 9 " |
| Centre of gravity load-line plane from *L W L*.. | 19 " 3 " |
| Centre of lateral resistance from *L W L*...... | 20 " 3 " |
| Centre of buoyancy below *L W L*............ | 2 " |
| Mast from stem.......................... | 14 " 9 " |
| Mast, deck to hounds.................... | 29 " |
| Topmast, fid to shoulder................. | 26 " |
| Boom over all........................... | 34 " |
| Gaff over all............................ | 24 " |
| Bowsprit stem to pin..................... | 19 " |
| Topsail yard............................ | 25 " |
| Area mainsail............................ | 895 sq. ft. |
| Area foresail............................ | 178 " " |
| Area jib................................ | 286 " " |
| Area lower sail.......................... | 1,359 " " |
| Area gafftopsail......................... | 346 " " |
| Sail area per sq. ft. of wetted surface........ | 2.71 " " |
| Ratio sail area to square of *L W L*........... | 1.04 |
| Centre of effort from end *L W L*............ | 19 ft. 7 in. |
| Centre of effort forward of *C L R*............ | 8 " |

The principal building specifications are as follows: Keel of white oak 30 in. wide on top, 25 in. on bottom, 8 in. deep amidships. Iron keel bolts are 1¼ in. diameter, spaced 12 in. Frames of oak, double, sided 2¼ in. and moulded 4 in. each at heel and 2½ at head; spaced 12 in. between centres. On each set there is a galvanized wrought-iron floor bolted through keel, frames

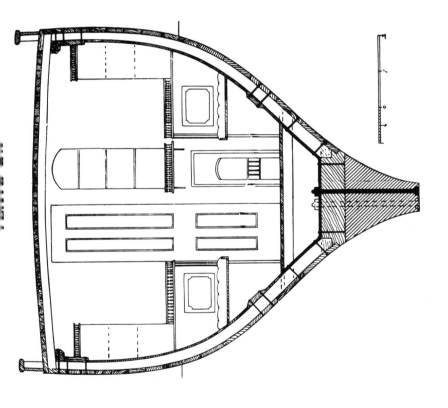

INDRA — CABIN PLANS

and garboards. Stem of oak, sided 5 in. and moulded 9 in.; sternpost of oak, sided 6 in. and moulded 12 in. at heel. Shelf of oak 3 × 4 in., bolted through the sheer plank and resting on clamps 8 × 1½ in., similarly bolted. Bilge strakes 8 × 1½ in., tapering to 5 in. at ends. Planking is of Georgia pine 1½ in. thick with oak garboards and wales. Deck beams 2½ in. square and deck plank 1½ × 2 in. white pine laid straight fore and aft, ship fashion. Bulwarks of mahogany with locust stanchions and elm caprail. Hatches and skylights of mahogany.

A small cockpit accommodates the steersman and two or three passengers. There is a 2 ft. skylight over the after cabin and one of 3 ft. over the saloon, besides the 4 ft. companion slide. The saloon is about 9 ft. square with 6 ft. headroom and 3 ft. 6 in. floor. The after cabin is entered by a door from the steerage, and is 6 ft. 6 in. long with 5 ft. 10 in. headroom under the beams. The water tanks are below the refrigerators in the pantry and abreast of the mast.

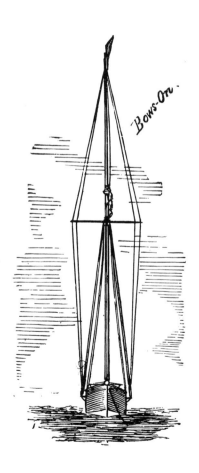

# X

# CUTTERS OF SMALL BEAM

## I.  THE MAMIE

*PLATE LXI*

TWENTY-ONE FEET EIGHT INCHES LONG ON LOAD-LINE

AN experiment in a novel direction has been practically tested in the MAMIE, a boat of triangular sections below water, launched by E. L. Williams, of City Point, South Boston, from his old yard in Lowell, Mass., in 1884. Similar lines with rather more beam were proposed in 1883 by Mr. R. H. Hopkins, of New York, and successfully tried in a model, the lines of which are produced in this connection.

Concerning the objects of the FENDEUR model, Mr. Hopkins wrote in 1883:

" A very important point in such a model is : It is the cheapest plan to build on—straight timbers and broad planking ; which avoids so many seams, decreases the liability to work and leak, making a very strong construction.

" In this design we have a model for smooth and for rough water ; can take the weather on either ; can take heavy rigs or do handsomely under moderate areas ; is non-capsizable ; will possess great momentum, and the more she is driven the more powerfully will she go crushing, splitting through rough water or head seas. In smooth water, for a few hours' recreation, a party of friends can find much enjoyment on her broad flush deck and roomy cockpit, and all the more enjoyable because of her stiffness caused by rapidly increasing beam above *L W L*. In head weather outside, dry quarters will be found in the cockpit, while the boat goes splitting through the seas, not losing her head-way to stop and shake the water from her nose, like the shallow boat, which has to stop and cry every time a sea slaps her face. Below there is ample head and ' elbow ' room, and can be fitted to suit the taste.

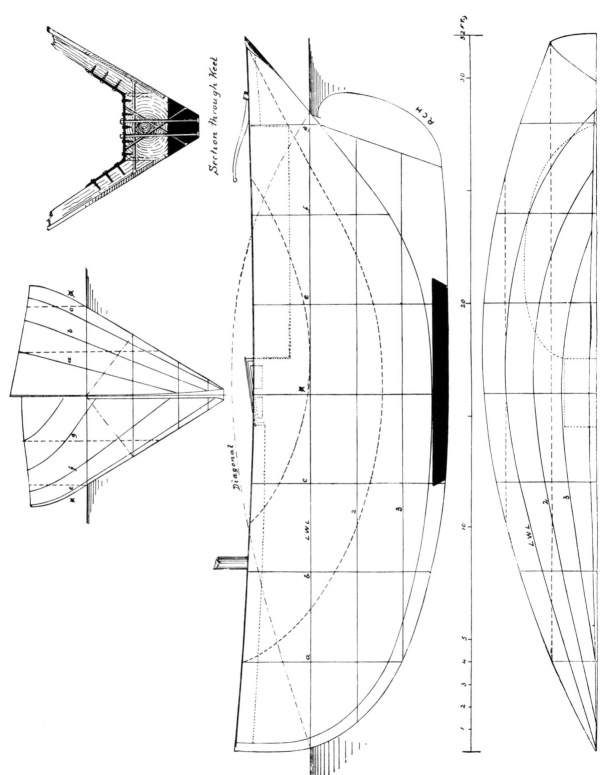

Section through Keel

Diagonal

RCH

LWL

THE FENDEUR MODEL. DISPLACEMENT 10½ TONS

# Cutters of Small Beam

" As to the trials of the model. On October 21st, 1882, when a northeast wind was blowing so hard that everything was reefed down tight and close, large schooners in the lower bay carrying two reefed mainsail and one jib, nothing more, I put the model in the water in Gravesend Bay, close to Coney Island Point, carrying mainsail and jib, both reefed, with topmast on end, and started her toward Bath in heavy, chopping water, which would rise in proportion to her scale six to eight feet high. She went off at a speed varying with the power of the puffs, which at times were heavy enough to heel her to 40°. At such moments it was really wonderful to see her edge bodily to windward, and dig ahead at a speed that required the most lusty pulling on our oars to keep up with her. She ran a little more than a half mile, eating right into the wind, then was put about on the other tack, and delighted the onlookers very much to see the clever manner in which she held up to windward and weathered a long row of buoys and boats lying directly in her course. She carried herself in a very powerful manner, showing great initial stability and a righting power increasing the more she was heeled. Showed no pitching, but drove forward splitting the seas and carrying her sticks steadily and stately, without losing headway like a beamy boat, and not stopping to climb over a sea or smash it down. Her entrance was as clean as could be done with a knife. There was no piling up of water in front to be pushed. Her delivery was as smooth as a duck pond. No dragging of boiling water in her wake. The water closed after her in such a way as to leave no other trace than a tiny rounded ripple right over the rudder. The water at the bow curled right off immediately it was opened, reminding one of a plow turning up the soil and gently pressing it away. She was twice tried in the same manner, and for the same distance, sailing each time more than a mile. The model is a dugout 1 in. thick, and weighs with spars and sails 20½ lbs. She has 8½ lbs. of lead let into the keel outside and conforming to the outlines of the design ; that is, showing no projection like a plank keel. She carried 22½ lbs. ballast inside, making total displacement 51½ lbs. ($L\,W\,L$ is 42 in. x 12 in. greatest beam, and 9 in. greatest draft). October 28th she was sailed again, carrying full lower sails and gafftopsail, the head of the topsail being 70 in. above the deck. She sailed very smoothly, scarcely putting lee scuppers under, and presenting a truly handsome sight. Afterwards was tried for quickness in stays and proved very successful. She appeared to simply heel to the other hand, so slight was the loss of headway, and immediately held her course without first going wide."

It was intended in the FENDEUR to combine, if possible, the advantages of weight, low centre of gravity, fine ends and flush deck of the cutter with as much of the width across deck of the sloop as possible in a structure which should be cheap in framing and easily planked up. Her draft is rather more

163

PLATE LXI

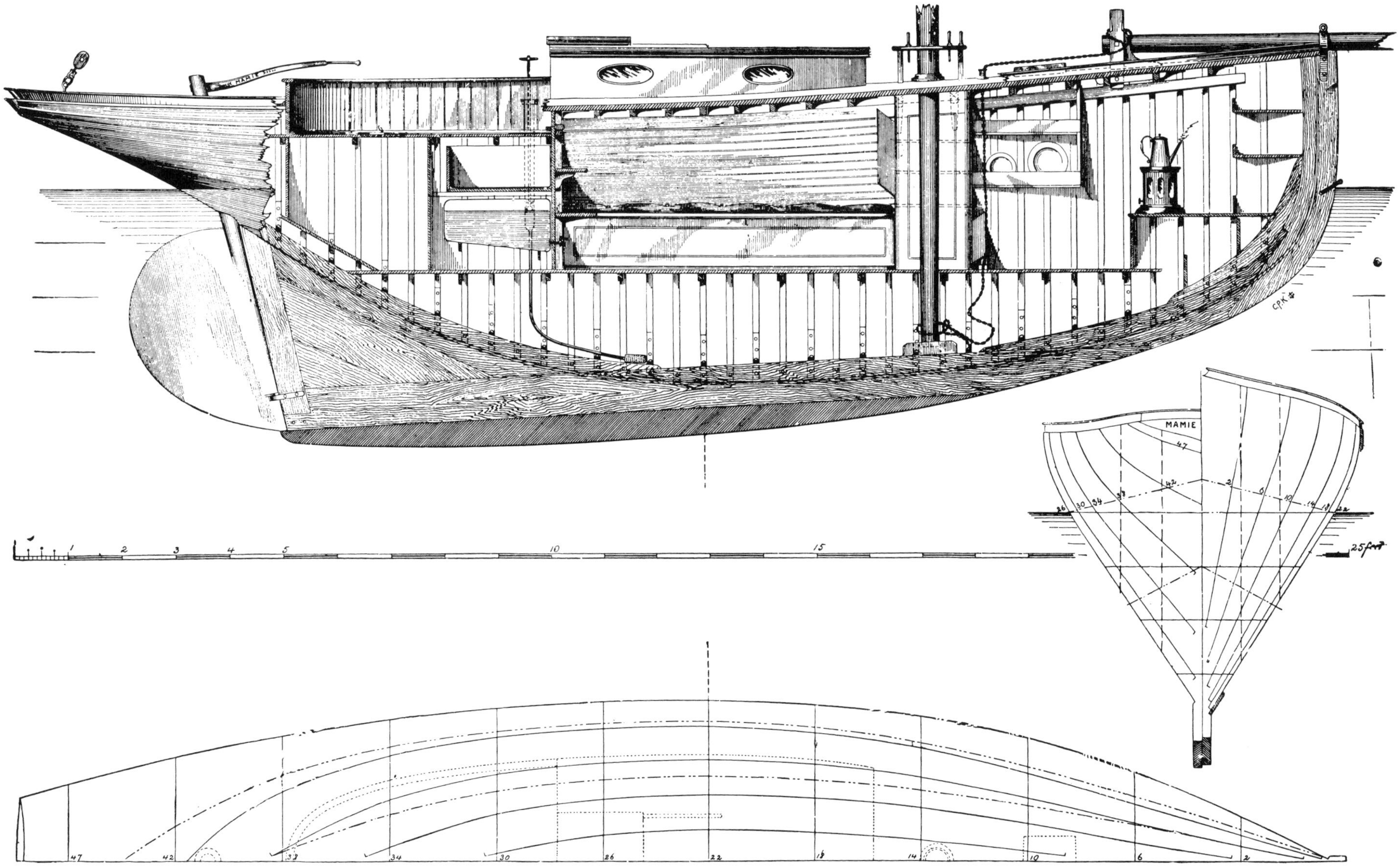

THE CUTTER MAMIE

MAMIE

# PLATE LXII

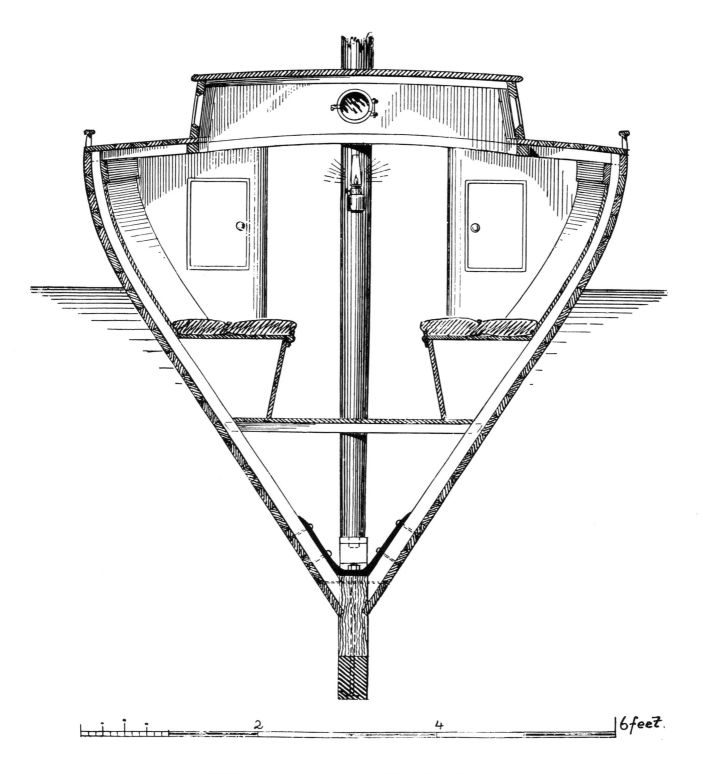

2          4          |6feet.

THE MAMIE—MIDSHIP SECTION

than one-fifth the load-line, or slightly greater than that of the modern cutter. MAGGIE, on 45 ft. load-line, draws 8 ft. MURIEL on 40 ft. draws 7 ft. 6 in. SURF, on 35 ft., draws 7 ft. 4 in. The cabin floor of FENDEUR will be about the same as in a cutter, her berths and wing room rather less and her deck area greater. In respect to rig FENDEUR has in mainsail, jib and small topsail 110 per cent. of the square of her load-line, about one-tenth greater than the racing rig of a cutter. So far as there are any data she seems to heel fully as much as a cutter, but, if uncapsizable, this is a matter of no great moment and may be reduced should practice dictate a smaller rig. The following are the details of the model experimented upon :

| | |
|---|---|
| Length over all | 48 in. |
| Length water-line | 31 " |
| Greatest beam on deck | 15 " |
| Beam on water-line | 12 " |
| Greatest draft | 9 " |
| Least freeboard | 3 " |
| Weight of model | 11½ lbs. |
| Ballast inside | 22½ " |
| Ballast on keel | 8½ " |
| Spars, sails, fittings, etc | 9 " |
| Displacement | 51½ " |
| Mast, deck to upper cap | 47 in. |
| Masthead | 5½ " |
| Topmast over all | 27 " |
| Mainboom | 38 " |
| Gaff | 22 " |
| Topsail yard | 25 " |
| Bowsprit outboard | 15½ " |
| Jib on foot | 25½ " |

In spite of certain structural drawbacks the MAMIE has shown herself a likely craft as far as yet tried. Her keel consists simply of 4 in. flitch and consequently but little outside ballast could be hung thereon. Had it been a 6 in. balk, with the rabbet near the lower edge, the wood projecting inside instead of outside the garboards, nearly three times the weight of iron could have been bolted underneath and rig increased to correspond. Again, the ballast inside is composed of scrap. But if cast to fit would be much lower and afford 8 in. or 1 ft. more head room. In point of type MAMIE is a straight framed cutter with the addition of a shoulder above water. Her bottom, though odd at first sight, differs in reality but little in the frames from a deep cutter. The slight hollow in the floor and the usual round of the bilge have simply been straightened out, a very trifling divergence in form from many an existing and

PLATE LXIII

5     10     15     20     25     30     35     40

THE MAMIE—SAIL PLAN

successful cutter. In the forward and after frames this difference is so small as to amount to scarcely more than an idea.

Report speaks well of her, and in just the way the boat's form would lead one to expect. With weight and fine lines below, she is a steady boat of great ease, holding her way through a sea and also in light, variable winds, owing to great momentum and small resistance. With the low weight and flaring but easy roundish topsides, she is notably stiff after once heeling down to her "sticking point," which seems to be about planksheer-to in good sailing breeze. Beyond this angle she resists. Likewise does she rise to a head sea with much life, as plenty of bulk above water has been provided and the flare all round prevents her dropping deep into a hollow. She is specially dry, throwing no spray, but dipping a little harmless water over the lee bow when pressed in a commotion. She is light on the helm and certain in stays in rough water, also free from yawing when running wide. As to speed, her official trials have not so far been very exacting. Her builder tried her in scrub races and thinks her fast. It can be said with certainty that MAMIE is not a slow boat, and at least up to the average.

Several similar boats are being built at the time of this writing, one of them with more beam, concerning which reports will probably appear in current periodicals.

| | |
|---|---|
| Length over all | 25 ft. |
| Length on water-line | 21 " 8 in. |
| Beam across deck | 6 " |
| Beam at water-line | 5 " |
| Extreme draft | 4 " 8 in. |
| Least freeboard | 1 " 6 " |
| Displacement, about | 4 tons |
| Ballast on keel | 600 lbs. |
| Total ballast | 2.5 tons |
| Mast from stem | 7 ft. 8 in. |
| Mast, deck to hounds | 19 " |
| Diameter at deck | 5 " |
| Topmast over all | 14 " |
| Bowsprit outboard | 10 " |
| Boom over all | 22 " 6 " |
| Gaff over all | 14 " 6 " |
| Spinnaker boom | 21 " 6 " |
| Hoist of mainsail | 14 " |
| Foot of foresail | 7 " |
| Foot of jib | 10 " |
| Area mainsail | 295 sq. ft. |
| Area foresail | 54 " " |
| Area jib | 75 " " |

# Cutters of Small Beam

The rig plan in Plate LXIII, upon being tried for balance, showed the Centre of Effort to be 15 in. forward of the Centre of Lateral Resistance, and slack helm was feared in consequence. The plan was revised.

Jib reduced to 18 ft. luff and 10 ft. on foot; foresail to 7 ft. on foot, and mainsail increased to 14 ft. on head and 22 ft. on foot. With this rig, MAMIE is well balanced, but still light on her helm. Construction will be understood from the midship section in Plate LXII.

She is built with a light, closely spaced frame. Keel, 10 x 4 in. Stem and post, 3 in., sided. Frame sawed, moulded 2 in. at heel, 1¾ at head, and sided 1⅜ in. Spaced 6 in. between centres. Iron floors on every other frame. Plank, ¾ in. yellow pine. Clamps, 3 x ⅞ in. Deck beams, 1¾ in. moulded and 1¼ sided oak, spaced 8 in. Deck, 1¾ x 1 in. thick white pine, laid straight fore and aft. Galvanized iron fastenings.

## II. A SIX BEAM CUTTER

### PLATE LXIV

#### THIRTY-SIX FEET LONG ON LOAD-LINE

THE amount of room to be got out of boats of very small beam is surprising. The depth of narrow boats makes every inch of length available from one end to the other. Something must be given up in the way of "elbow room" in so small a yacht as the cutter illustrated in Plate LXIV, but elbow room is not what is wanted so much as great stowage, even though it be compact. The greatest length for berthing, the privacy of several cabins, and the convenience of standing upright are often valued more highly than wing space or roominess of a kind not contributing in a practical way to any service. As floor in a small boat serves only for passage in and out, more than required for that purpose is waste, and implies a less economic form in regard to accommodations than the same volume so shaped that there shall be no waste of size in any direction, but all of it utilized to the best advantage for the needs of shipboard life. What can be done on 6 ft. beam is shown in Plate LXIV and the cross section here appended.

A very good wrinkle, one now generally followed in narrow yachts, is to keep the sofas in the cabin down to the width required for sitting or lounging, say 15 to 18 in. For berthing at night, turn down from the side an iron frame cot of any width you like, 24 in. being enough for a "square sleep." These swing-cots are made of rectangular shape, say 6 x 2 ft., by screwing lengths of

PLATE LXIV

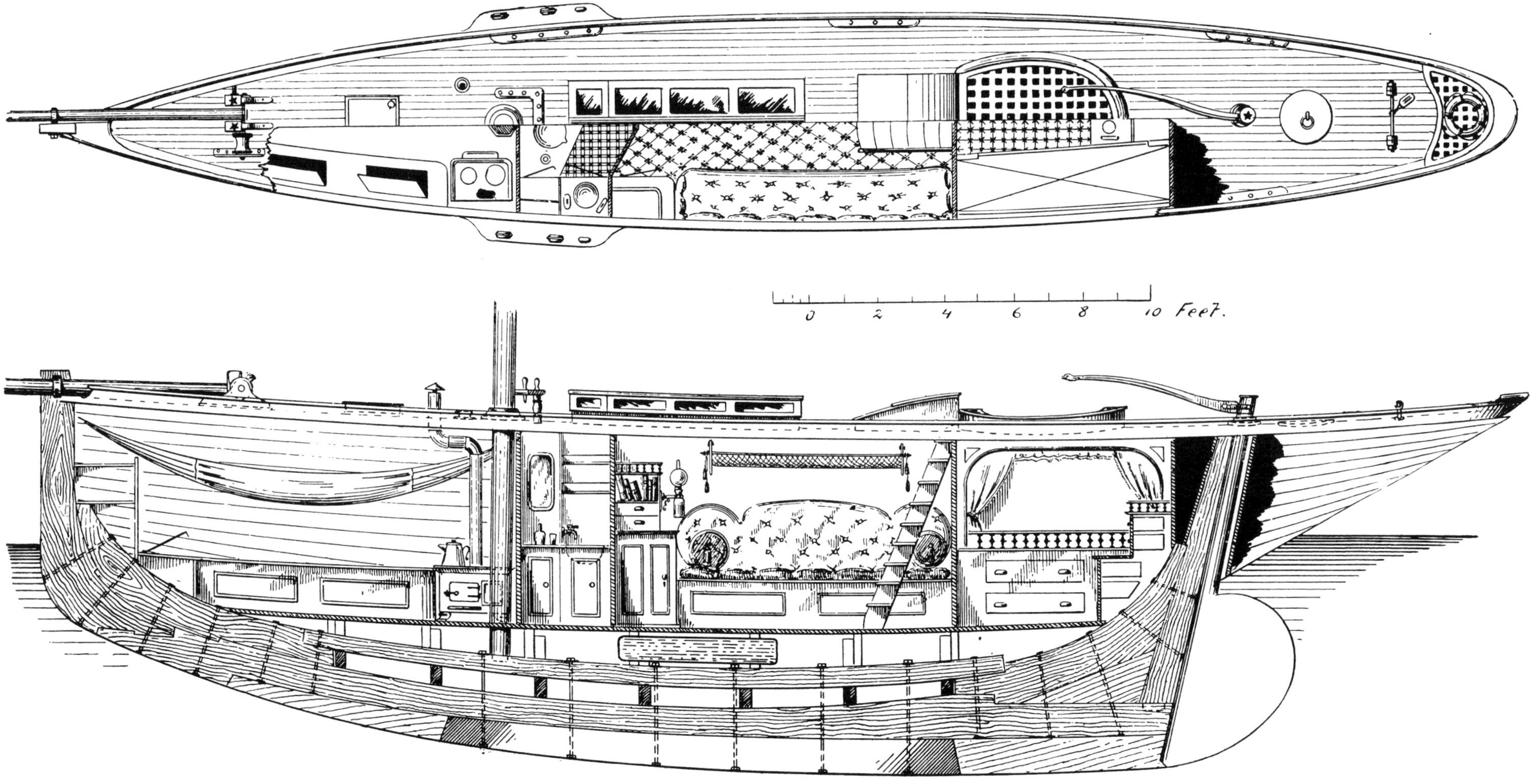

10 Feet.

SIX-BEAM CUTTER

gaspipe into elbows and hung to the ship's side by brackets. Wire netting serves as the bottom to receive the mattress, and when lowered the berth is suspended

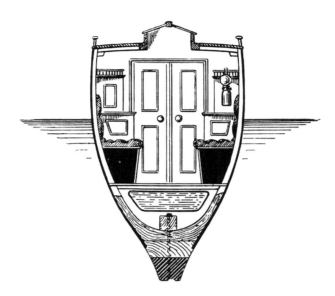

to the beams above by pennants at head and foot. They can be made ornamental, or unshipped for the day and stowed out of sight. The forecastle is

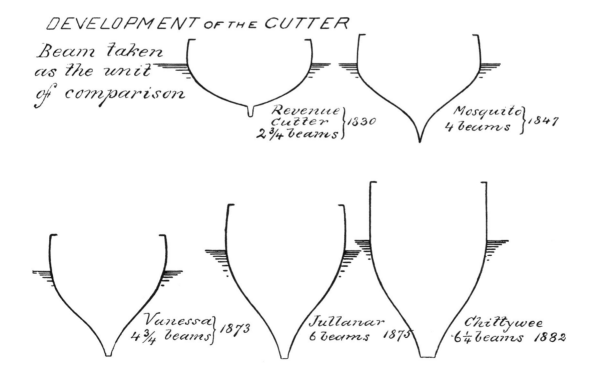

DEVELOPMENT of the CUTTER

Beam taken as the unit of comparison

Revenue Cutter 2¾ beams } 1830

Mosquito 4 beams } 1847

Vanessa 4¾ beams } 1873

Jullanar 6 beams 1875

Chittywee 6¼ beams 1882

similarly provided, and the room occupied by a permanent bunk is economized during day-time. The plans in Plate LXIV and rig in Plate LXV are only of

# PLATE LXV

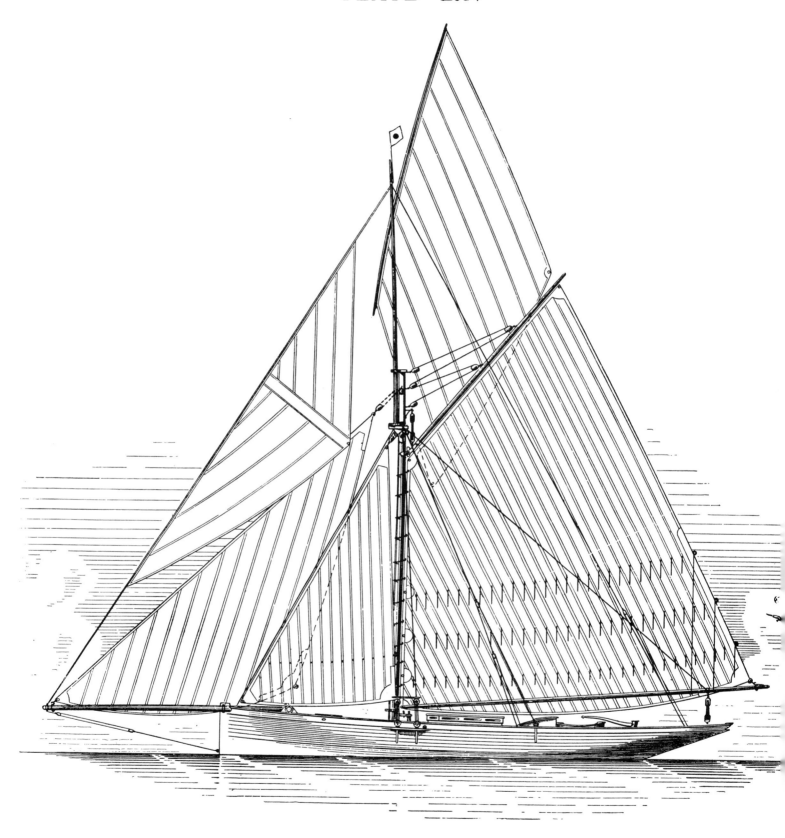

SIX-BEAM CUTTER—SAIL PLAN

a preliminary kind to show the internal arrangements of a proposed vessel 36 ft. long on load-line, 6 ft. beam, 6½ ft. draft, and of about 13 tons displacement, 7 tons to be in ballast on the keel. Boats of this class are subject to much greater angles of heel than broad sloops. To prevent the weather-berth becoming uninhabitable in a fresh breeze, the front of the locker underneath is turned up and hooked, giving the sleeper a regular lee just as much as though he were stretched in the leeward berth on the other side of the cabin. A swing-cot can be regulated to suit by the pennants.

The gradual merging of the old-fashioned beamy, round-sided vessel into the narrow forms, in which yacht designing in Europe finds its best expression to-day, is transcribed by the typical cross sections in the accompanying sketches.

## III. THE SURF

### *PLATE LXVI*

#### THIRTY-FIVE FEET THREE INCHES LONG ON LOAD-LINE

THE SURF is a fine specimen of the family of cruising cutters. She was designed in 1883 by Mr. John Harvey, and built by Geo. W. Byles, of City Island, New York, for Messrs. Rathborne and Zerega.

The main characteristics of the SURF are such as should distinguish well planned vessels. She is remarkable for exceptional "dryness," buoyancy and ease in her behavior. In these respects she is not surpassed by any yacht of her load-line in American waters. Under adverse circumstances, the SURF ships no green water, and positively throws not a drop of spray. She lifts and falls to the seas without violent toss or plunge, but with well cushioned fetch-up in such measured motion that her action may be compared to the gentle swing of a hammock. With 6 short tons of lead on her keel and 3 tons inside, she heels down 35 to 40 degrees in strong lower sail breezes, compelling yachts of the opposite type to reef. This season one more ton has been bolted to the keel and greater stiffness and speed have been attained. But it should be noted, that even at her former extreme angle of heel, which was about planksheer-to, no difficulty was experienced in the perfect control of the yacht, nor was there the slightest trouble in getting about decks, nor even any inconvenience. It is at such times that the chances of falling overboard are reduced to a minimum. With low boom and sail nearly fore and aft amidships, it is impossible to fall to leeward in traveling about the deck, for that is simply to fall into the sail. To fall over the side to windward is very unlikely, for it is to fall " up hill." The

PLATE LXVI

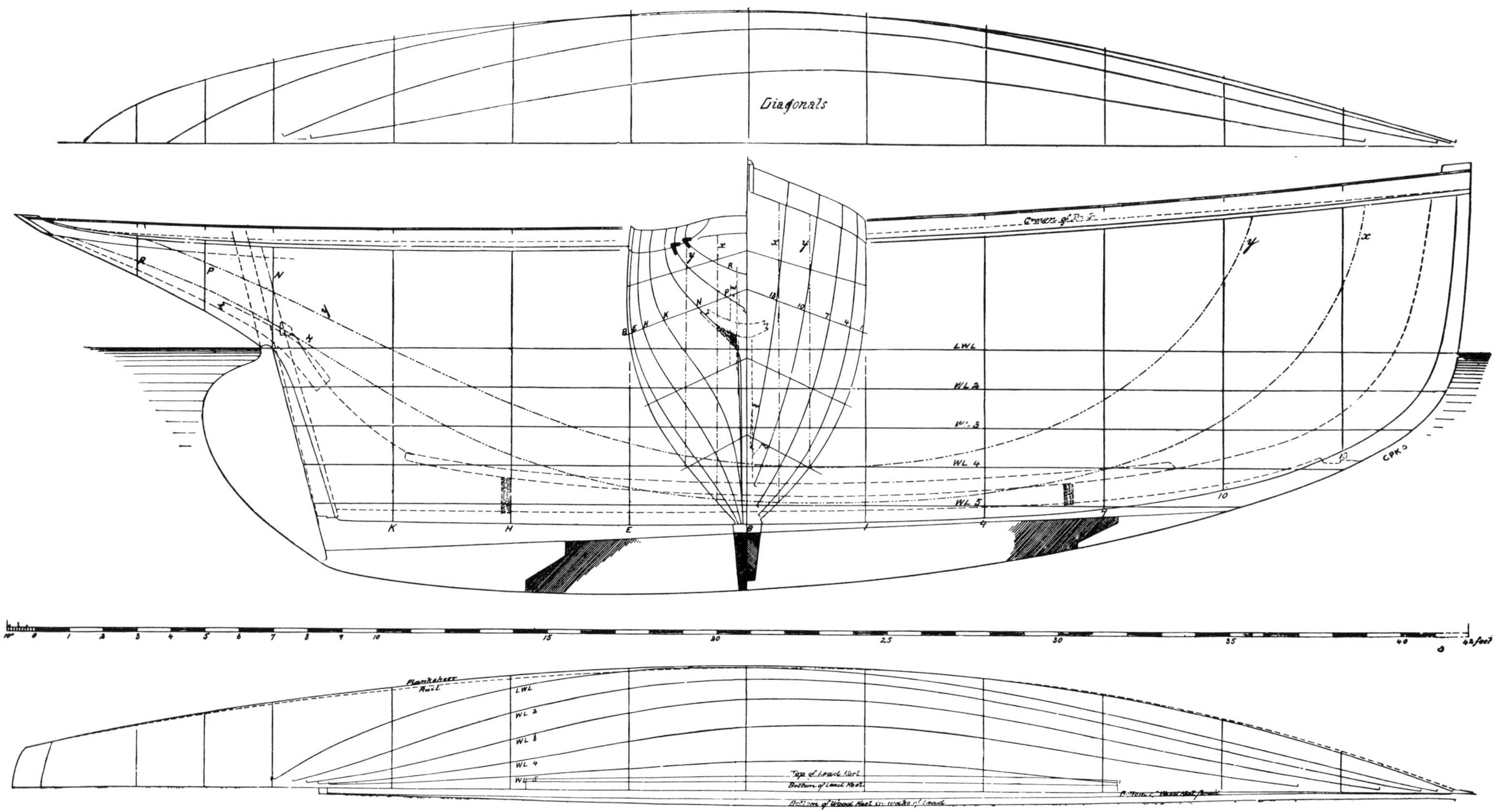

THE CUTTER SURF

easy behavior of the yacht at all times is a safeguard against being tossed over the side, which is a very distant contingency anyway, as the crew get about decks by striding over the low hatches amidships without approaching the rail as in yachts whose decks are encumbered with " houses," and without risk of being tripped by jerky, snappish bringing up. While it may seem almost paradoxical to say that at extreme angles of heel "comfort" is actually at its greatest, such is, nevertheless, the case. To loll about the SURF's decks, with only one or two streaks showing to leeward, is the height of pleasurable indulgence. Reclining, effectively braced with one's weight taken by the feet against the hatch coamings, is to occupy a position similar to lying off on an easy lounge, while the pitch and 'scend of the boat partake of the sensation of grateful rocking in an arm-chair. At all times there is a restful sense of perfect security and squalls lose their terror.

The decks of the SURF are spacious, in spite of her scant beam. When heeled in a breeze, the high weather side forms a shield from rude blasts, which seem to carrom up into the sails, the deck constituting an agreeable lee.

Built for cruising and of more than usual strength, the SURF, though never equipped for racing, has at times given proof of a high rate of speed. She excels in light airs and in a thrash to windward in a jump she revels. With lighter topsides and fittings and a racing rig, there is scarcely any doubt that the SURF would add exceptional speed to her other noteworthy qualities. As a safe, able, comfortable cruiser, fit to voyage at sea, she comes near to per-fection. Although having great stowage and convenience below, she is some-what scant in "elbow room," an evil which seems to be inseparable from excel-lence in much more vital characteristics and to which animadversion has already been made in previous chapters. The exchange of a little elbow room below for positive pre-eminence in other respects seems a sacrifice fully justified by the ends.

At no time does the heel interfere with serving hot meals. Cooking goes on in bad weather, and the productions of the galley are transferred to that great institution in cutter sailing, the "swing table." Dishes are left to take care of themselves in a gale. The passengers around the table quit the festive board without the least concern, and, at his own choice of time, the steward appears on the scene to clear away at leisure. A "swing table" must be seen to be appreciated. It oscillates on central spindles in the standards or legs. From the table a rod loaded with fifty pounds of lead is suspended. This pendulum is the magic charm which wipes out of existence the one objection to cutter sailing, which was really well taken.

The draft of the SURF has been found no hindrance in Sound cruising, and no special attention is given to the matter on board. It is no greater than in the modern keel sloops, common enough in Eastern waters.

# PLATE LXVII

1 2 3 4 5   10   15   20   25   30   35   40   45   sq feet.

THE CUTTER SURF—SAIL PLAN

# Cutters of Small Beam

It is well here to meet a probable query as to what would become of a yacht like the SURF should she ground and be left by the receding tide. During a cruise in the fall of 1883, the SURF attempted to shoot the narrow entrance through the breakwater of Port Jefferson, on a rushing swirl of ebb pouring out like a mill race. This took her on the weather bow and sagged the cutter bodily down upon the gravelly beach, where she struck during half a gale, and lowered sail with all possible haste. An anchor was got out in the fairway with a long scope to swing to upon getting afloat on the flood. As the water left the vessel she slowly settled over on her bilge without apparent strain in any respect and without tumbling over. While on her bilge, all hands enjoyed lunch down below, travelling on the lee ceiling as a floor. When the flood began to make, there was some trepidation lest the cutter might fill before righting. Nothing of the kind happened. The flood rose to the planksheer, came in on deck two or three inches for a few moments, and from that instant the cutter steadily righted with the same freedom from strain she had exhibited in lying

*Hot Dinner in a Blow*

down. Suddenly she worked loose from her bed, and, with tremendous force, was swept round head to the rushing flood, her quarter just clearing the breakwater by a few feet. This was a case where deep draft was the salvation of the yacht. Had she drawn six inches less water her fate would have been sealed, for the ebb would have driven her higher up on the beach in the first place and the force of the flood hurling her against the breakwater would have smashed her to matchwood after working out of the bed in the gravel.

The accommodations below will be understood from Plate LXIX. There is 6 ft. headroom fore and aft. The forecastle is supplied with galley, lockers and a swing cot. In place of the usual rat hole of small yachts, the SURF has a forecastle, light, airy and pleasant, in which the crew is housed with some regard to their comfort. Pantry and w. c. are between bulkheads. The main cabin is amidships, a delightfully cool retreat from the heat of a summer sun. It is most liberally lighted and ventilated from overhead, in which respects

# PLATE LXVIII

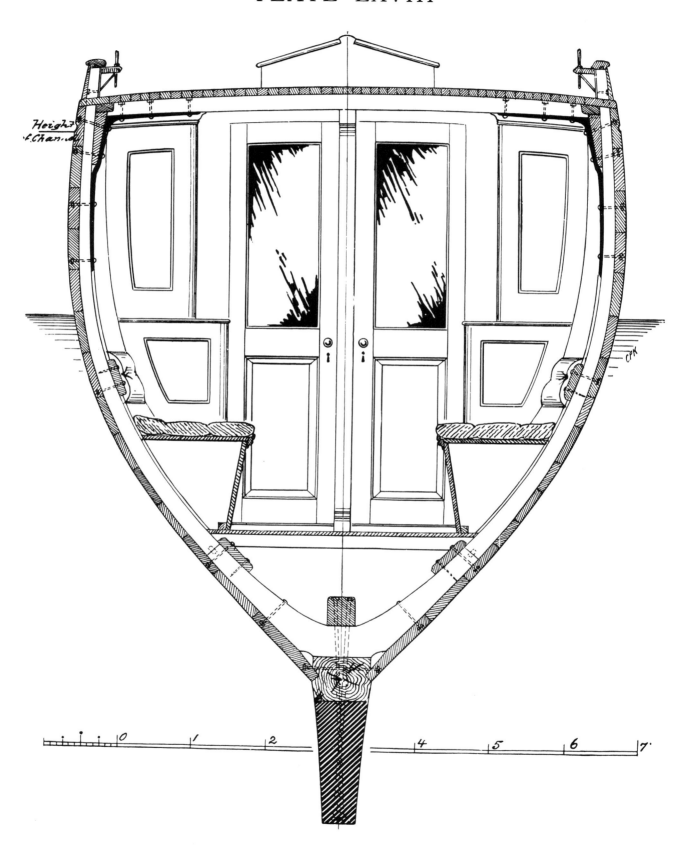

Height
f.Chan...

THE SURF—MIDSHIP SECTION

PLATE LXIX

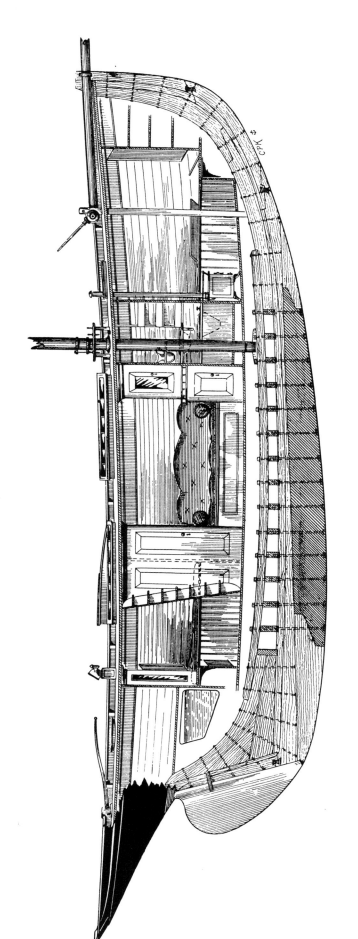

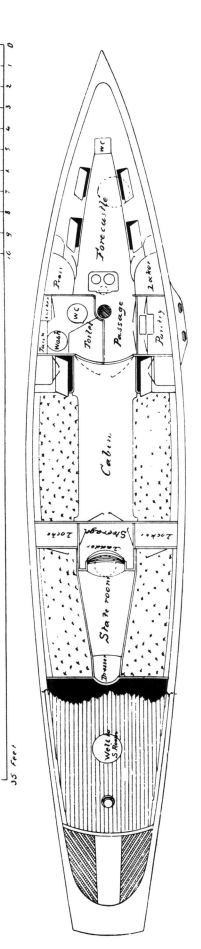

THE CUTTER SURF—CABIN PLANS

there is no room for improvement. The sofas are 6 ft. 6 in. long and 22 in. wide, and ample lockers and sideboards are provided. The companion ladder lands in a small steerage which can be shut off from the cabin by doors. Lockers for oilskins and clothing are built each side of the steerage. The ladder is shipped a little to one side, affording passage into the after cabin, the entrance being closed by a curtain. Two 24 in. berths and shelving make up the furniture aft. In Plate LXIX the ladder is shown as originally fitted. Access to the after cabin was had by pivoting the ladder round to one side.

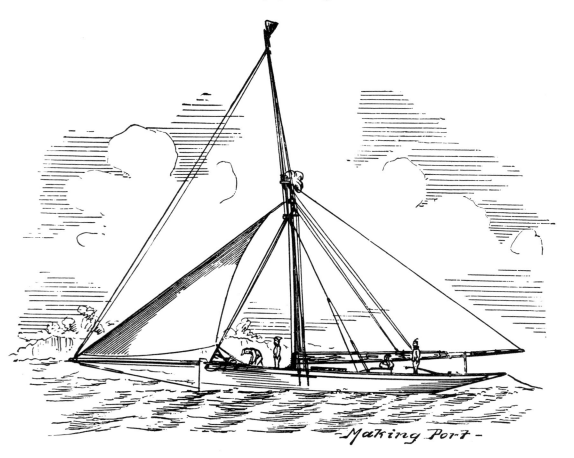

*Making Port*

Although the SURF is particularly well built, probably surpassing in strength and *shipwrighting* anything of her size yet turned out in America, it is a fact that she cost *less* to build and equip than other first-class yachts of her length, of opposite type.

Attention should be directed to her "raking midship section" (Plate LXVI), by which a clean run is brought about. The nature of the diagonals can be studied with advantage, as an index to the boat's dividing lines. They are rather shorter in the fore body than customary in sloops, owing to the greater relative importance of incorporating good clearance in a deep-bodied vessel and the minor importance of fining away the entrance of narrow forms. Experiment seems to indicate connection between weatherliness and a Centre of Buoyancy located further forward, while reaching is improved by keeping the Centre further aft. The SURF's play is to windward. With lifted sheets she is not quite as good. The high freeboard of 3 ft. is well worth having for cruising, though in excess of what is best for racing. From the frame **P** aft, the counter contributes practically nothing to speed, but adds much to deck room and appearance. Under the irrational tax placed upon overhang by some of the more primitive length measurement rules, such handsome finish aft is, unfortunately, still rare in the American fleet.

The rig plan in Plate LXVII shows at a glance the snugness of spars and sails in boats of the SURF's type. Boom scarcely overhangs the counter; bowsprit is but a third of the load-line, and hoist of mainsail less than two-thirds. The SURF is readily worked by one hand at the helm and another to tend gear. While first impressions, got simply from looking at vessels like the SURF, are seldom in their favor, a little experience soon sets the novice right and enables him to appreciate the sterling qualities of a class of yachts steadily winning increased favor in the eyes of the public, and which warrant more than has been said in their behalf in these pages. The Sail Plan shows four jibs to suit varying strength of wind. Three only are requisite along the American coast. The storm trysail is outlined by dashes in the mainsail.

A large spinnaker, 32 ft. on foot, is used in racing. The dimensions of sails are given after full stretching. A working gafftopsail, bent to hoops and furled at the masthead, is preferred for cruising. It will be noticed that SURF's lower sails equal only *eighty per cent* of the square of her load-line. It is common in small sloops to find the area equal to 110 per cent., or more than *one-third* greater. The displacement, draft and freeboard given below refer to the present trim of the SURF, as she has been brought down in the water four inches and a half beyond what Plate LXVI calls for.

Construction of keel and deadwood is found in Plate LXIX, the thwart-ship framing in Plate LXVIII. Keel amidships is 10 in. sided, 8 in. moulded. Stem and post, sided, 6 in., moulded, according to the plans. A keelson, 6 x 6 in., crosses the floors between deadwoods. The frame is double throughout, with long and short arm floors giving shift to each other. The floors are 6 in. in throat, the frames 3 x 2½ at heels and 2 x 2½ at heads, spaced 15 in., dow-elled and pinned. A floorhead streak, 8 x 1½, and a bilge streak, 6 x 1½, stiffen and tie the structure below. A clamp, 9 x 2, tapering, and running the whole length without scarf, has the beam ends dovetailed into it, no shelf being worked, and two thick streaks are also wrought below the clamp. These are not shown in Plate LV.

| | | | | |
|---|---|---|---|---|
| Length over all | .......................... | 42 | ft. | 10 in. |
| Length on load-line | .......................... | 35 | " | 3 " |
| Greatest beam moulded | .......................... | 7 | " | 4 " |
| Beam moulded at *L W L* | .......................... | 7 | " | 1 " |
| Breadth across counter | .......................... | 2 | " | 6 " |
| Greatest draft | .......................... | 7 | " | 4 " |
| Depth at side, frame **H** | .......................... | 7 | " | 10 " |
| Least freeboard | .......................... | 2 | " | 8 " |
| Sheer forward | .......................... | 1 | " | 9 " |
| Sheer aft | .......................... | | 3 | " |
| Displacement | .......................... | 17 | short tons | |
| Ballast on keel | .......................... | 7 | " | " |
| Ballast inside | .......................... | 2½ | " | " |
| Mast from end *L W L* | .......................... | 13 | ft. | 4 in. |
| Mast, deck to hounds | .......................... | 27 | " | |
| Masthead | .......................... | 4 | " | 6 " |
| Topmast, cap to shoulder | .......................... | 18 | " | |
| Bowsprit, outboard | .......................... | 12 | " | 9 " |
| Boom over all | .......................... | 32 | " | |
| Gaff over all | .......................... | 19 | " | |
| Mainsail on luff | .......................... | 22 | " | 9 in. |
| Mainsail on foot | .......................... | 30 | " | |
| Mainsail on head | .......................... | 18 | " | |
| Mainsail on leech | .......................... | 38 | " | |
| Foresail on foot | .......................... | 11 | " | 6 in. |
| Foresail on stay | .......................... | 24 | " | 6 " |
| Foresail on leech | .......................... | 23 | " | |
| Jib No. 1 on foot | .......................... | 17 | " | |
| Jib No. 1 on luff | .......................... | 32 | " | 6 " |
| Jib No. 1 on leech | .......................... | 23 | " | 6 " |
| Area lower sails | .......................... | 985 sq. ft. | | |
| Ratio to square of load-line | .......................... | 0.80 per cent | | |
| Topsail yard | .......................... | 26 | ft. | |
| Balloon jib topsail, foot | .......................... | 26 | " | |
| Balloon jib topsail, luff | .......................... | 49 | " | 3 in. |
| Balloon jib topsail, leech | .......................... | 31 | " | |

The beams are 2¾ x 2½, spaced 22 in. amidships, and 18 in. from mast beams forward. There are five iron hanging knees a side, 1 in. thick in throat and with 18 in. arms, through bolted to clamps, frame and plank, and through the beams to hackmatack lodge knees on opposite side of beams, three bolts in each arm. Hatch framings are 3 x 2½ oak, the mahogany hatch coamings on deck being through bolted to them. A breasthook in the eyes is formed of a heavy oak chock, through bolted from foreside of stem, and also through clamps, frame and plank. The counter is supported by two stout horns, through bolted to the fashion piece, and by two hog timbers strapping several frames forward of the stern post. The fashion piece is also hung by a rod, forked about the post, the two prongs piercing a deck beam across forward face of the stern post, being set up to it with nuts and washers, making a strong and rigid structure of the after end, which can never hog. The lead is hung by ⅞ in. bolts, one through every pair of floors, and rising through the keelson. Iron hog straps are worked over the frames in wake of the runner plates and chain plates. The former take in six frames and the latter arch from floors to wales and down to the floors again, so that "pulling up the sides" is impossible. Garboards are of 1½ in. oak, side plank 1½ in. white cedar and sheer streaks 1½ in. oak. Plank is all through bolted with copper, instead of at butts only, as usual. Deck, 1¼ square white pine, sprung to the sheer. Planksheer, 1½ in. oak, in two 3 in. widths, notched over the stanchions, which are 2¼ sided and 1½ moulded. These support bulwarks 8 in. high, including a broad, stout oak cap rail. Garboards are through bolted to keel and floors with ½ in. copper, making very strong connection. Although the SURF is now in the third year of her commission she has not leaked a drop, and requires sweetening of her bilge by pouring water down the sail room hatch to find its way into the limbers. Rudder head, 4¾ in., cross bolted; bitts, 4 x 2½ in., double, strongly kneed to deck, with 5 in. windlass barrel. Gear bits at mast, 3½ square. The mast is 7½ in. at partners and has *no taper* to the hounds. Bowsprit, 5 in. at stem; boom, 5¼ in.; gaff, 4 in. The mainsail is laced along the foot, but is hauled out by the clew with a traveler about the boom end, and a hemp pendant leading through a sheave, with a tackle underneath the boom to get the foot of the sail on a stretch, or to slack up as desired. Anchors weigh 60 and 105 lbs., the latter being used in cruising with a $\frac{7}{16}$ in. chain, 30 fms. in length. For the light bower there is 40 fms. of 2½ in. warp.

There are two 1½ in. shrouds a side to the mast, with topmast rigging of 1 in. wire. Backstay pendants are 1½ in. wire; runners for same are hemp of 2 in. circumference, with runner tackles of 1¼ in. Bowsprit shrouds, 1¼ in. wire; bobstay chain, ⅜ in. link with 1⅝ in. manilla fall. Forestay of 1¾ in. wire. Double quarterlifts of 1¼ in. Russia white rope to boom. Throat, peak and mainsheet of 1⅝ in. manilla; jib halliards of 1⅞ in. manilla; fore halliards, 1½ in.; jib outhaul, 2 in.; head sheets, 1¼ in. for jib and 1½ in. for foresail. The peak spans on gaff are 2⅛ in. hemp. Topsail halliards, 1¾ in.; topsail gear, 1¼ in., and spinnaker gear the same. Mainsail, foresail and second jib of No. 7 cotton canvas; first or reaching jib of 10 oz. duck. A ten-foot yawl boat, when not towed, is stowed in the gangway without inconvenience.

A matter should be considered in connection with deep vessels like the SURF, though it might have been more properly included in the Chapter on Resistance. It is commonly supposed that vessels must meet with greater resistance with increase of immersion, owing to the hydrostatic pressure of a deep column of water being greater than that of a column having less depth. Thus a vessel immersed 7 ft. is supposed to be driven against the head pressure due to a column of water 7 ft. high, and another vessel of 3 ft. immersion only against the pressure of a column 3 ft. high. Hence the deduction is frequently drawn that the shoaler boat must experience much less resistance to onward motion. Obviously such would be the case but for another fact completely annulling the inference, and this is the *counterbalancing* pressure of the fluid *aft*. A vessel immersed 7 ft., though opposing a 7 ft. head at her bow, is supported *from aft* by exactly *the same pressure*, and she is, for that reason, liable to no " head resistance " due to hydrostatic pressure at all. Neither is the vessel immersed only 3 ft. Both are in balance, as the pressure upon the hull is always in *balance at both ends* and all round the vessel, no matter what her immersion may be. This is the explanation why " direct head resistance " has no foundation in fact and why the true causes of resistance are confined to the three sources of waste discussed in the Chapter on Resistance. Were this not the case, and did vessels really experience resistance from the hydrostatic column against which their bows are driven, it would be impossible to drive a cutter like the SURF at more than *a small fraction* of the speed attained by shoal sloops, possibly not over one-quarter of their speed. Cutters would invariably be outstripped *by hours* in racing, instead of coming in for a full share of the prizes. In fact, the cutter would never have been called into existence, for she would truly have been *impossible*.

*There is no connection between resistance and depth in itself.*

Deep cutters are driven with less sail area at the same speed as sloops of half the depth.

Ultimately a point will be reached where increased depth in the cutter may cause her resistance to equal that of some broad, shoal boat.

But this gradual increase of resistance with increase in depth is *not* to be ascribed to the increased hydrostatic pressure due to the higher column of opposing water, but simply to the additional *work done* in parting the water, in causing it to open around the *additional beam*, forced through as the depth is gradually increased. An increase in resistance due to such a cause is a *very different thing*, and to be ascribed to *beam* and not to the *depth*, which happens to be a purely accidental concurrent attribute. For, the same increase in resistance will be brought about by adding to the beam of a vessel *without* adding to her depth, and therefore *without* increasing the *hydrostatic head*, but merely the *work done* in starting the water for the beam to pass.

## IV. THE SPANKADILLO

*PLATE LXX*

THIRTY FEET LONG ON LOAD-LINE

AS a contradiction to existing prejudices against narrow, deep forms, the English cutter SPANKADILLO stands witness. Built with a view to the greatest cruising efficiency in rough water, she has, in her success, fully sustained the principles followed in her conception. She was built at Dartmouth, South of England, in 1882, by W. J. Hodge, from lines by her owner, Captain H. E. Bayly, and canvased by Horn. In 1883 she was lengthened 3 ft. to put narrow beam to still more thorough trial. In her new form the SPANKADILLO is known as a dry, powerful vessel, which will look at hard weather and turn to windward in a sea which larger boats of opposite type find it difficult to face, much less make anything good against. She confirms the good opinions entertained by those who have had opportunity to arrive at positive convictions concerning yachts of such extreme proportions. The secret of SPANKADILLO'S performance lies in the concentration of her ballast and its low situation, every pound being in lead on the keel and of a length little more than one-third the load line. This overcomes the plunging to which so attenuated a form would otherwise be liable. A fine run and plenty of freeboard enable the cutter to lift well clear to everything, and the high side on small beam keeps decks dry even at extreme angles of heel. Her motions are easy as a rocking chair, and, though snugly rigged for cruising off shore, she has shown uncommon speed. The accommodations are, of course, restricted in breadth, but there is some six feet of headroom below fore and aft, and any amount of useful stowage, which is the main thing in a small vessel, where crowds or dinner parties around a table are out of place. The only use of a cabin in a four-ton cruiser is to have a berth over night or shelter in bad weather. This, with the chance of standing upright, would seem to be a more agreeable average than the wing space and want of head room met with in shoaler boats of more beam, so long as everything cannot be had on such small dimensions without approaching the tub form too nearly for the vessel's good underway.

The SPANKADILLO has a forecastle with berth for one hand, a main cabin with sofas and two swing cots, and a large sail room in the run. For the steersman there is a cockpit, 4 ft. long. A companion, 2 ft. 8 in. long, and a skylight, 2 x 2 ft., are all the obstructions on deck. These are so low that they can be stepped upon, or straddled, and do not interfere with free travel fore and aft or athwartships.

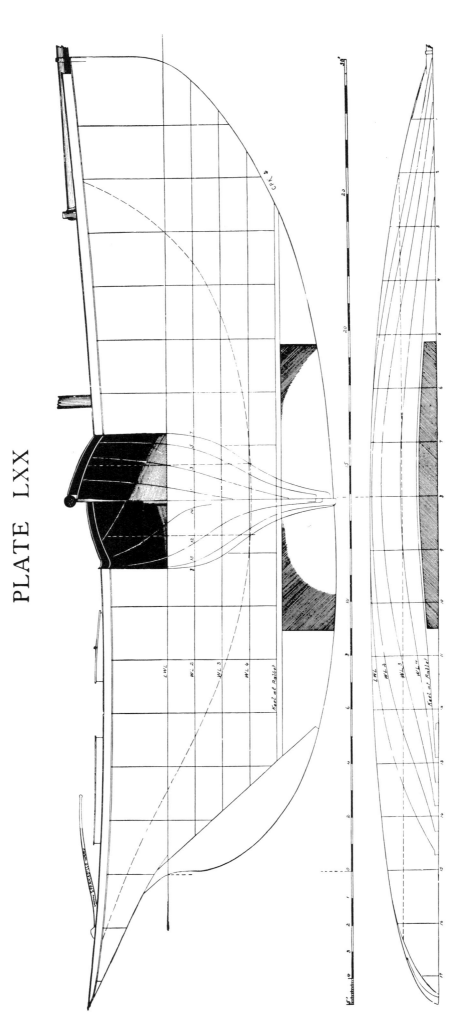

PLATE LXX

THE CUTTER SPANKADILLO

The round up forward and rake to posts are necessary in a flat sided vessel of such draft. SPANKADILLO works like a top, stays like a catboat, and holds her way in fore-reaching, so that she is always under full control of the guiding mind at the stick. Her chain locker is close to the mast. With topmast struck and bowsprit reefed, the cutter can be made exceedingly snug to do away with laboring in a steep sea. In this respect she excels. Her construction is light, but the hull is thoroughly riveted.

| | | | |
|---|---|---|---|
| Length over all | 36 ft. | | |
| Length on water-line. | 30 " | | |
| Beam extreme. | 5 " | | |
| Draft extreme. | 6 " | 2 in. | |
| Depth at side, No. 11. | 6 " | | |
| Least freeboard. | 2 " | | |
| Sheer forward. | 1 " | 4 in. | |
| Sheer aft. | | 6 " | |
| Displacement. | 8.5 tons | | |
| Ballast on keel. | 5.5 " | | |
| Mast from stem. | 12 ft. | 6 in. | |
| Mast, deck to hounds. | 20 " | | |
| Topmast, fid to sheave. | 18 " | | |
| Bowsprit, cranze to shoulder. | 13 " | 9 in. | |
| Boom, mast to sheave. | 26 " | | |
| Gaff, mast to earing hole. | 18 " | | |
| Topsail yard, between earing holes. | 18 " | 6 in. | |

Attention may be called to the short boom of 26 ft. on 36 ft. length over all; to the hoist of 17 ft. 6 in. on 30 ft. water-line, and to the bowsprit of 13 ft. 9 in. on 30 ft. water-line, all of which are exceeded by 20 to 50 per cent. in boats of opposite form.

## V.  THE  MADGE

### *PLATE LXXI*

#### THIRTY-NINE FEET SIX INCHES ON LOAD-LINE

THE first vessel to prominently prove beyond question the perfect feasibility of obtaining the highest rate of speed in all sorts of weather from the narrow and heavily ballasted forms developed through the instrumentality of the peculiar " Thames " measurement rule was the Scotch ten-ton cutter MADGE.

From her advent in American waters, in the fall of 1881, may be dated a new period in the world's yachting.

PLATE LXXI

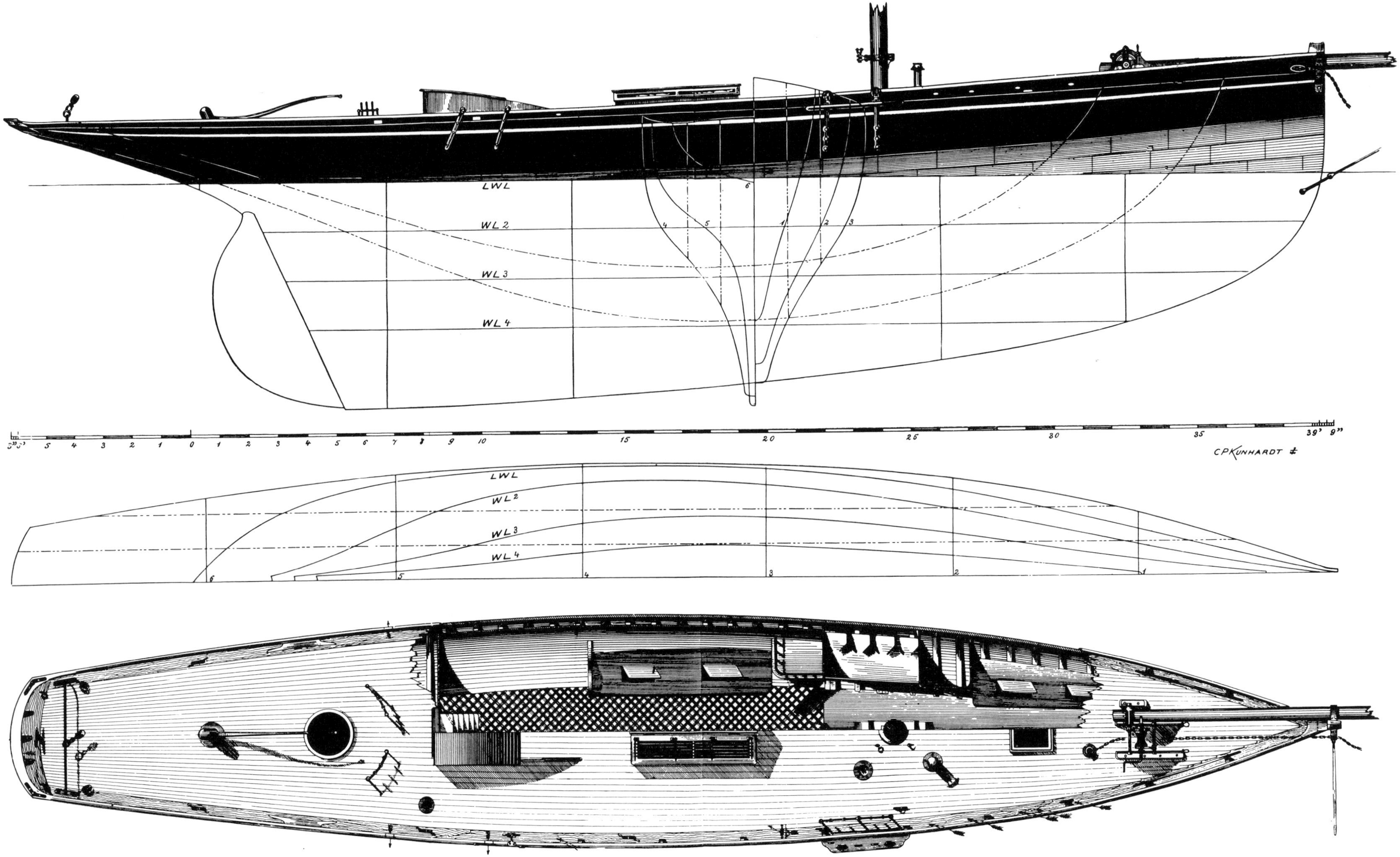

C.P.KUNHARDT ‡

LWL
WL2
WL3
WL4

LWL
WL2
WL3
WL4

THE CUTTER MADGE

# Cutters of Small Beam

Not only was the success of the MADGE a most welcome relief to all hands abroad, but also a totally unexpected revelation on this side of the Atlantic.

It was a relief to British yachtsmen, for it set at rest the doubts as to whether the new-fashioned cutters really were fast, or only made to appear so judged through such notoriously falacious standards of comparison as the Thames, and, later, the Yacht Racing Association Rule. Designed especially to evade these rules, and to enter the lists with an advantage in size over her competitors, for which the rules compelled no accounting, it remained an open question how the MADGE, and all of her type, would compare with other shapes of hull when not permitted to smuggle in size unpaid.

Of the seven matches the MADGE sailed in American waters but one was lost, and that owing to an accident. Without entering into a detailed consideration of these races, quite enough was discovered to establish definitely this fact: The type represented in the MADGE was capable of paralleling the highest performance yet attained by any other style of fashioning.

While persons in their private capacity had already reached just this conclusion, the American public at large declined to admit that weight and depth could hope to make even a respectable showing opposed to the light displacement, great beam and small draft universal in yachts of American origin. Up to the very moment of the first start, the proposition of racing the MADGE against our sloops was held up to ridicule. Accomplished facts, however, could not long be denied. The victories of the " ten tonner," supplemented by those of many other similar vessels, since her arrival, have removed the " question of type " from the realms of speculation and settled the issues under that head. It has become evident that, upon the assumption of equal perfection in design, " type " does not enter as a consideration unless something abnormal be attempted beyond the average American centreboard sloops on the one hand, or beyond the modern British " racing cutter " on the other. As between regular representatives of these classes, the result hinges upon perfection of detail in the individual boats and not upon broad distinctions of type, as supposed, until the MADGE appeared upon the scene. Under circumstances properly to be mentioned as exceptional, such as light airs or gales, especially with sea, an innate advantage does seem to rest with the boat of least beam and greatest weight, but in reaching in smooth water, the sloop has the call by a trifle. This is probably more truly to be ascribed to the inefficiency of head sail with sheets lifted, and not to differences in hull. The cutter, with mast further aft, suffers greater loss on this one point of sailing than the sloop with less area in jibs.

Illogical and unfair as the British rules of measurement have been, a tribute to their accidental blessings is due. But for those rules, it is doubtful whether the modern racing cutter would ever have been evolved, and the world might have missed much of the light thrown upon naval architecture in recent years through their performance.

It is not too much, then, to claim a fresh period of enlightenment from the appearance of the MADGE in American waters. Though want of time to fully digest a new and somewhat startling dispensation and also the limitations of local surroundings have prevented close approximation to the MADGE's proportions in the majority of boats recently built, it is none the less true that old dogmas, long cherished as irrevocable truths, have been thrown overboard for later and sounder conceptions brought forth through the revelations the MADGE vouchsafed us. Antipathy to depth and weight have almost disappeared. In all principal features, the design and rig of most new vessels has undergone radical modification in the gradual adjustment of exploded preferences to the recent lessons of practice which the MADGE was first to exemplify with a force that was challenging. With more time this new movement will keep gathering in force, and is destined to run its course as long as additional experience warrants still closer approximation in type and equipment to the modern racing cutter. Now that prejudice has been cleared from the horizon, intelligence at the wheel may be trusted to pilot in the new channels, till experience in the future orders the popular drift towards the type of the MADGE to round to.

In Plate LXXI, the lines and interior of this cutter are produced from actual measurements. She is striking in the ease and fairness of her form and in the unity of purpose evident throughout. She is distinct from other cutters in her strong individuality. A long entrance at and about the load-line is compensated for by a midship section of considerable rake to provide sufficiently clean run. Closing the displacement is economically effected through reasonably fine lines below and easy upward sweep of the buttocks, due to carrying the main breadths forward in the lower water-lines in succession. In spite of the roundish $L W L$ under the quarter, no overhanging haunches destroy balance of bulk when heeled, as the side from midships aft is kept plumb until the body proper is drawn away into the counter. The load-line has been kept full with a view to aiding stability, and with "in and out" wedges nearly alike, disturbance to trim and wake are avoided. Handsomer bow and buttocks than those of the MADGE are seldom to be met with, and her main diagonal will be entitled to equal praise.

A feature of this cutter, and of all racers from the same source, is the scant freeboard and extremely light deck and fittings, saving of weight in topsides being the object. Unquestionably, the gain is quite material where the highest speed is the goal of the designer. For cruising and all round satisfaction, more side would be a benefit in promoting drier decks. Though the MADGE is a wet boat compared to so wholesome and able a craft as the SURF, she throws no spray and is on an average a drier vessel than sloops of same load-line. Like all of her kind she is distinguished for ease and graceful motion in her behavior and the comforts thereon depending. The interior furnishing is of the simplest and lightest possible, which applies also to hatches on deck.

Forecastle accommodates three hands in swing cots. The main cabin has low sideboards and two sofas. At present the accommodations are being rebuilt, with a stateroom aft for cruising. The rail is 8 in. high forward, supported by every fourth frame head projecting above the planksheer from the bow to midships, abaft of which the rail tapers away to 2½ in. at the quarter, requiring no lateral support. It is surmounted by a light half round oak cap of 1¾ in., included in the heights mentioned.

| | |
|---|---|
| Length over all | 46 ft. |
| Length on load-line | 39 " 9 in. |
| Greatest beam | 7 " 9 " |
| Beam on load-line | 7 " 8 " |
| Breadth across counter | 4 " 1 " |
| Depth, bottom of keel to planksheer, No. 5 | 9 " 7 " |
| Least freeboard, No. 5 | 2 " |
| Sheer forward | 1 " 6 " |
| Sheer aft | ½ " |
| Greatest draft | 7 " 8 " |
| Rake of post | 3 in 7 |
| Displacement, approximate | 16.5 tons |
| Ballast on keel | 10 " |
| Ballast inside | 0.5 " |
| Mast from end *L W L* | 15 ft. 4 in. |
| Mast, deck to hounds | 28 " |
| Masthead | 5 " 3 " |
| Topmast, fid to sheave | 25 " |
| Bowsprit outboard | 20 " |
| Bowsprit, cranze to fid | 7 " |
| Boom over all | 36 " 2 in. |
| Gaff, saddle to earing-hole | 25 " |
| Topsail yard | 24 " |
| Spinnaker boom | 38 " |

The specification of scantling is as follows: Keel of English oak, 16 in. sided and 10 in. moulded amidships. Stem and post 6 in. sided at head. Knee over scarf of stem is 4 ft. 6 in. long, 4½ in. sided, with six ½ in. copper through bolts. After deadwood knee, 4½ in. sided. Frame of oak, 5¾ in. at heel, tapering to 2¾ in. at head and 2 in. sided, single, spaced 32 in., with two steamed frames between, 1¾ in. moulded and 2 in. sided. As shown in the plans, there are double frames abreast and abaft the mast. These take the chainplate bolts. Between the faying surfaces of these two pairs, the spacing is only 24 in. with one steamed timber between. The chainplate fastenings are 5/8 in. bolts, set up by nuts over iron straps on face of frames. These straps are 2 in. wide and full 1/8 in. thick. Forward one jogs up over the clamp, the upper bolts coming through the latter. The after strap is turned under the after mast beam as an iron knee, having an arm 14 in. long. To further stiffen the structure in wake of the chainplates, a short chock is wrought inside the upper edge of the clamp, to span several frames. The chock is 2 1/2 in. thick, oak, extending 32 in. forward of mast and 48 in. abaft, and is bolted through to the clamp itself. Clamps are 10 x 1 1/2 in., without any shelf or thick streaks, tapering to 5 1/2 in. at stem, where a 2 1/2 in. chock between them serves as a breast hook.

The regular frames are tied across the keel by heavy wood floors 7 in. deep in throat and sided 3 in., the steamed timbers being connected to keel by wrought iron floors 1 in. thick, with arms 1/2 in. thick. Bolts for lead ballast are 1 1/4 in. composition, set up with deep-thread nuts and washers, and spaced from 24 in. to 30 in. apart. Smaller thrust bolts, 3/4 in., are driven diagonally through lead and wood keel every 30 in. Over the floor rides an 8 x 8 in. oak keelson. Only the main cabin is ceiled with 1/2 in. matched pine. There are no floorhead or bilge streaks inside.

The mast beams are oak, 5 x 2 1/2 in., one 2 in. from fore side of mast, the other 19 in. abaft after side. Half-beams, 4 1/4 x 2 1/2, are laid in between. The partners are composed of a chock 1 in. wide forward of mast and 3 1/2 in. wide abaft, set between short carlins, in which the half-beams head. These chocks, in connection with the carlins, are framed out octagonally to receive the mast wedges, which taper to 1 in. on bottom. From forward mastbeam to next beam forward is 20 in.; the next spacing forward is 30 in. Next beam forward is across fore side of forecastle hatch, or 5 ft. 6 in. forward of centre of mast. An angle iron beam 2 1/2 x 2 1/2 with wrought iron knees is screwed to underside of a light beam 20 in. forward of the hatch beam, with the knees secured to a frame. A heavy wood beam, 5 x 2 1/2, is run across 11 in. forward of this, strapped to the frame with bar iron 2 x 1/2 in. Wood chocks 2 3/4 x 1 in., span three forward beams on underside to take the bolts in standards of the windlass on deck. All the forward beams are tied to frame with 2 x 1/8 strap iron fastened with large screws.

Abaft the after mast beam to next beam at forward end of cabin skylight, the spacing is 30 in. This beam is 2 1/2 x 2 1/2. A similar beam crosses at after end of skylight, the spacing between the pair being 4 ft. Then follow two, spaced 40 in., the after one crossing at sailroom bulkhead. The quarter-deck beams are spaced 48 in. Between all these beams two light oak strap beams, 2 1/4 in. wide and 3/4 in. thick, are screwed up to the deck plank with two brass

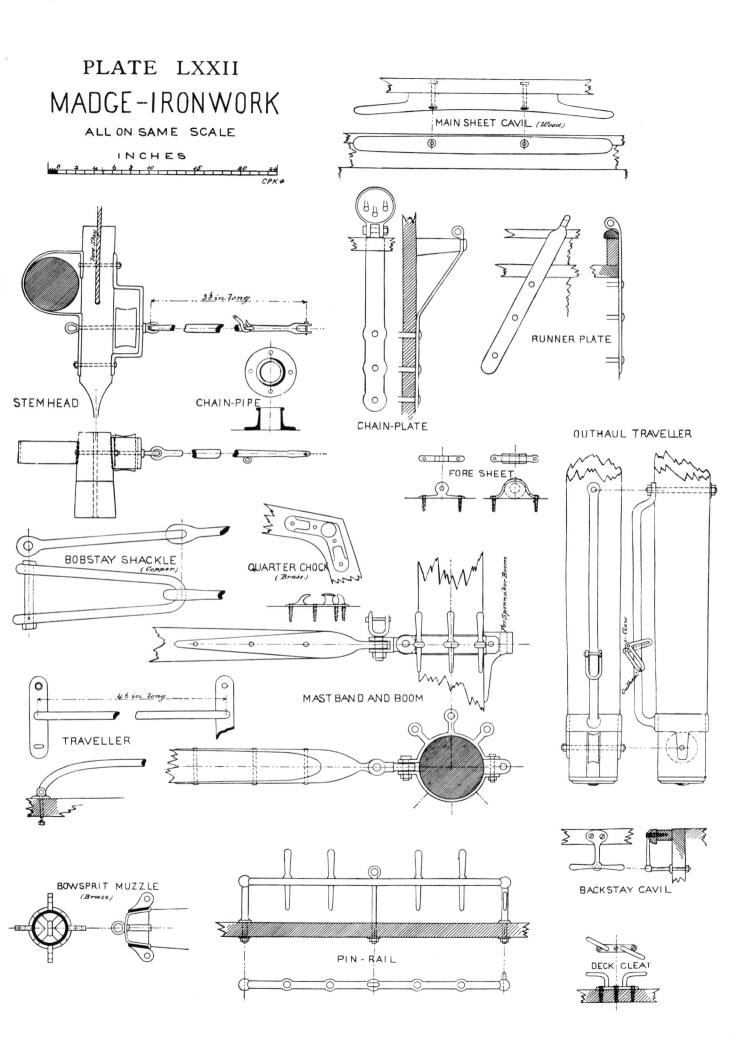

PLATE LXXII

MADGE-IRONWORK

ALL ON SAME SCALE

INCHES

MAIN SHEET CAVIL (Wood)

STEMHEAD

CHAIN-PIPE

CHAIN-PLATE

RUNNER PLATE

OUTHAUL TRAVELLER

FORE SHEET

BOBSTAY SHACKLE
(Copper)

QUARTER CHOCK
(Brass.)

MAST BAND AND BOOM

TRAVELLER

BOWSPRIT MUZZLE
(Brass)

PIN-RAIL

BACKSTAY CAVIL

DECK CLEAT

screws to each plank. They serve simply to tie the plank and are not kneed to the side. The beams at ends of cabin skylight are secured to the clamp by light iron knees ½ in. thick in throat, with 6 in. arms, two screws in each arm. All beams are merely laid on the clamp, not cut in or dovetailed, but fastened down. The mast step is 32 in. long, 7 in. wide, and held down to the keelson by two iron straps ⅜ in. thick and 2 in. wide. The mast heel is hooped 3 in. up with 2 x ⅛ iron, the tennon being 2½ in. thick, wedged fore and aft in the mortise of step. Garboard, 1¾ in. ; side plank, 1½; waterways of teak, 6 x 1½ in.; deck plank, 1¼ x 2½ wide, with taper towards ends, butting into the waterways. Diameter of rudder head, 4½ in., with 3 in. slot for tiller. Channels 5 in. wide, 1½ in. thick, with 20 in. spread between deadeyes. Forecastle hatch coamings rise only 1 in. above the deck. They are 1¾ in. thick, with a rubber bead let in. The hatch cover is a flat galvanized iron plate ⅛ in. thick, with a frame of bar iron round the under side ⅜ in. thick and 1½ in. wide. This fays down watertight on the rubber bead when the hatch is screwed down to a cross bar below. Skylight is 26 in. wide and 4 ft. 2 in. long. Coamings at side 4 in. high, 2 in. thick, with a gutter gouged along upper edge. The centre cap of the hatch is 8½ in. high. Two lights, in 3 in. framing each side, protected by five rods rove through three light iron arms turning up on pins through small iron lugs screwed to the frame, as the plans explain. Companion slide is 12 in. high at after end, 24 in. across coamings, which are 1½ in. thick. The opening from sill to headledge is 28 in. Slide cover is 36 in. long. Long cleats, screwed to frame heads in the bow, are ¾ in. thick and 1½ in. face. Mainsheet cleats are 28 in. long, with 6 in. arms and 1¾ in. thick in throat, 2 in. face, bolted to rail, as in plans, the top coming flush with rail. Location of holes in rail for head-sheets, jib topsail sheets, scuppers, and location of iron work, deck lights, etc., can be got from the plans, as well as the height to which the copper is carried above load-line. Specification of iron work is given in Plate LXXII. Mast head iron work is of proportions similar to the fittings of the SURF, illustrated in the Chapter on Rig.

The MADGE was designed by G. L. Watson, and built in 1879 by him at Govan, Scotland, for Mr. James Coates, Jr. She made a hit as a racer around the British coast for two seasons until "outbuilt" under the Y. R. A. tonnage rule.

# VI.  A  CUTTER  BY  W.  FIFE,  JR.

## *PLATE  LXXIII*

### THIRTY-NINE  FEET  THREE  INCHES  LONG  ON  WATER-LINE

THE handsome design in Plate LXXIII was contributed by Mr. W. Fife, Jr., of the celebrated yard of Fairlie, Scotland, where many of the fastest British racing yachts have had their origin.    Although intended for a vessel of 52 ft. water-line to race in the 55 ft. class on sail area and length measurement, the same plans are applicable to a yacht of smaller dimensions.    This cutter belongs to the medium type, having a load-line length of four and two-thirds times the beam, proportions which will prove satisfactory in every respect.    The displacement and draft are not excessive and no greater than in some of the modern sloops, while the sail area and spars are moderate in comparison with those of wider boats.    Adopting a scale of one-quarter inch to the foot, the plans serve for a boat 39 ft. 3 in. water-line, nearly the same length as the cutter MADGE in Plate LXXI.

| | | |
|---|---|---|
| Length over all | 50 ft. | 6 in. |
| Length on water-line | 39 " | 3 " |
| Beam extreme | 8 " | 6 " |
| Beam on water-line | 8 " | 3 " |
| Draft extreme | 7 " | 2 " |
| Displacement, long tons | 16.50 | |
| Ballast on keel, long tons | 10 | |
| Ballast inside | None | |
| Mast, deck to hounds | 28 ft. | 6 in. |
| Mast from end *L W L* | 14 " | 9 " |
| Topmast, fid to sheave | 23 " | 4 " |
| Bowsprit beyond end *L W L* | 21 " | |
| Boom over all | 36 " | 9 " |
| Gaff over all | 24 " | 9 " |
| Spinnaker boom | 34 " | |
| Topsail yard | 27 " | |
| Area mainsail | 986 sq. ft. | |
| Area foresail | 225 " | " |
| Area jib | 288 " | " |
| Ratio lower sail to square *L W L* | 1.03 | |

The hull should of course be built as light as possible consistent with strength, so that much of the displacement may be utilized for ballast.    A

PLATE LXXIII

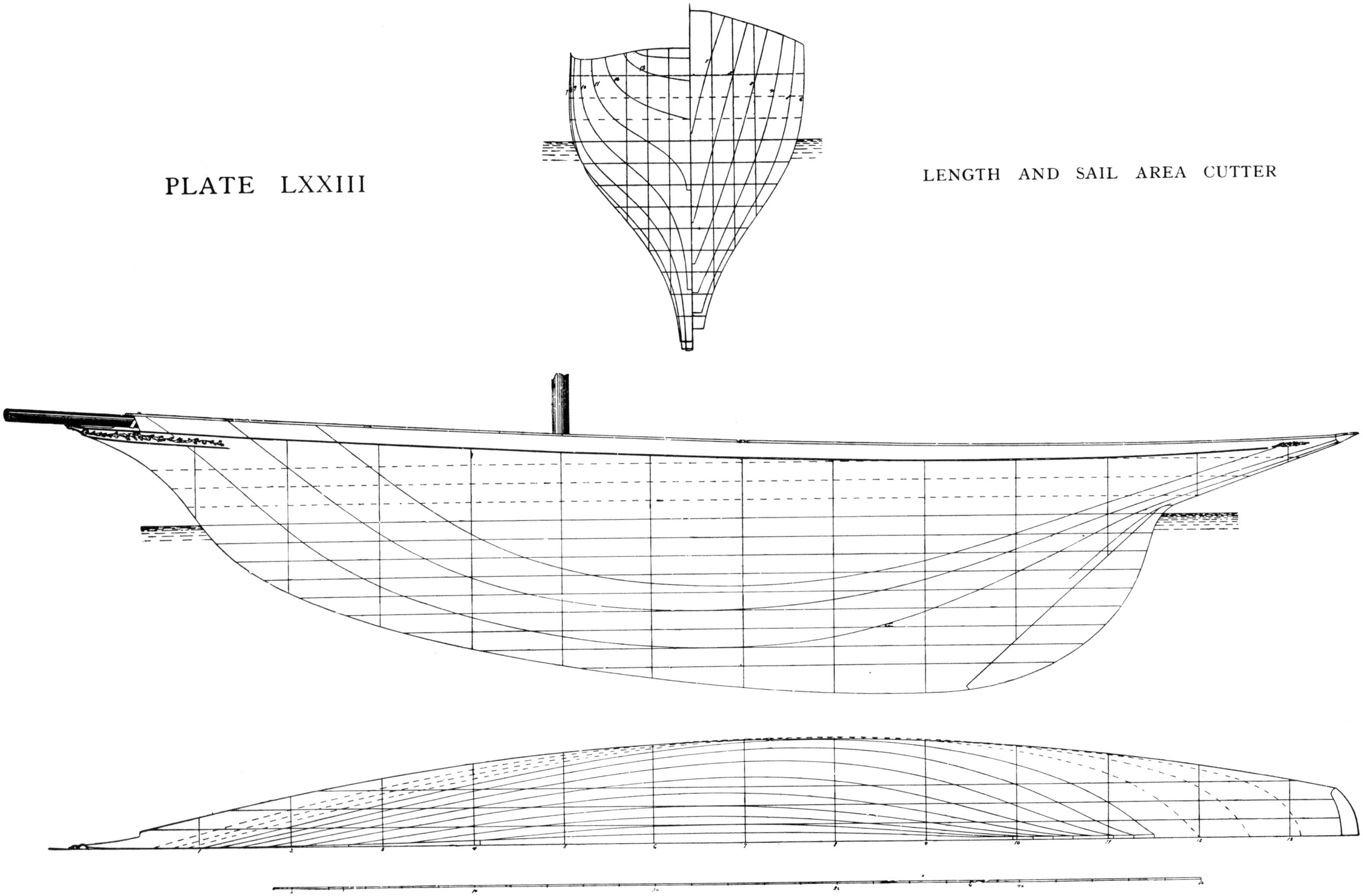

# PLATE LXXIV

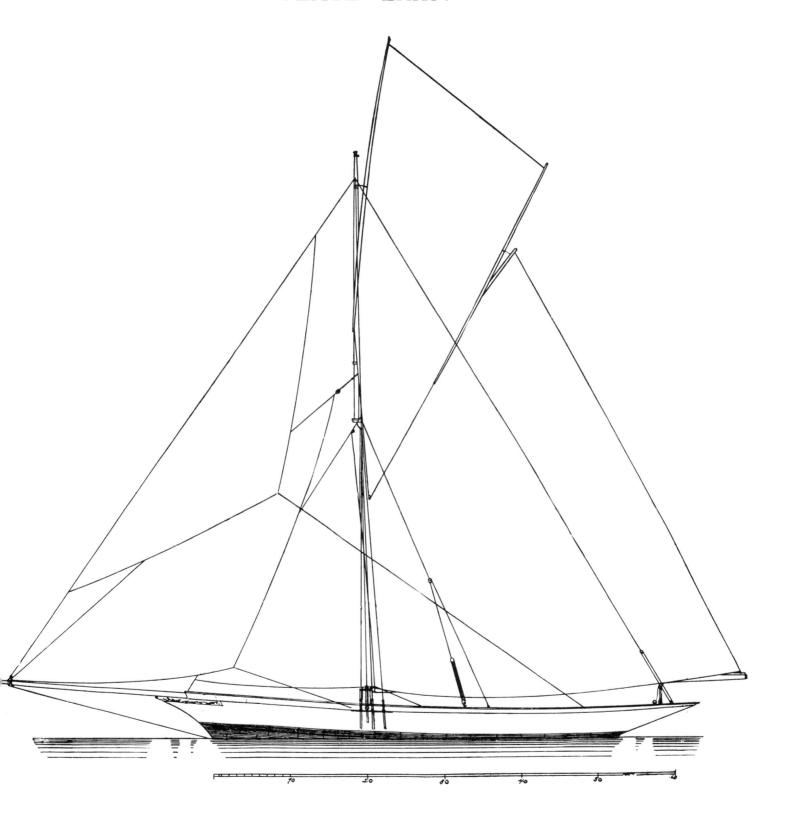

SAIL PLAN—LENGTH AND SAIL AREA CUTTER

strong back bone well connected with the frames by iron floors and through-bolted from out to out of garboards, with intermediate frames steamed and wrought-iron hogging arches should be the system followed. Soft woods should not be countenanced, except white pine for the decks.

## VII. THE JENNY WREN

*PLATE LXXV*

THIRTY-THREE FEET NINE INCHES LONG ON WATER-LINE

THE plans of this cutter show to what extent beam can be dispensed with if compensated for in depth, large displacement and low ballast. The WREN was built in 1885 by Simpson and Denison, of Dartmouth, from designs by Mr. R. E. Froude of the Admiralty experimental station at Torquay, England. As a racer she has been quite successful. She shows no straight amidships, but has a round to frames and water-lines which, with her clipper stem and light counter, make her an exceedingly handsome vessel afloat. A peculiar feature is the manner in which the keel line has been dropped to secure extra depth to the lead keel. The accommodations are narrow, but reach fore and aft with headroom under the beams. The cabin is entered from a cockpit. Length on water-line, 33 ft. 9 in.; greatest beam, 5 ft. 5¾ in.; greatest draft, 7 ft. 7 in.; displacement, 11.4 tons, 7.5 of which go to the lead keel, there being no inside ballast.

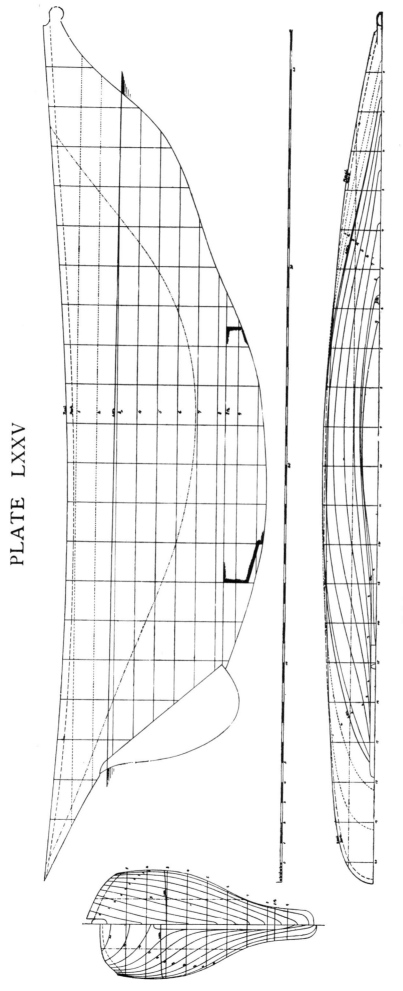

PLATE LXXV

RACING CUTTER JENNY WREN

# XI

# YACHTS OF SPECIAL CLASS

## A CRUISING SCHOONER

*PLATE LXXVI*

THIRTY-FIVE FEET LONG ON LOAD-LINE

THE schooner GAETINA was built in 1883 for Mr. W. O'Sullivan Dimpfel, C. E., of Baltimore, Md., as an all round yacht for summer and winter work upon the Chesapeake and for knocking about the coast. Safety, simplicity, economy and room suggested following the lines of a " Penzance lugger" and the rig of a pilot boat.

After giving the yacht a twelve months' trial her owner reported favorably concerning her behavior and general adaptability to his purpose. The GAETINA exhibits in her water-lines a close likeness to the Penzance fishing craft, but she was given 1 ft. of extra depth to her benefit. She has been found a good sailer in her own waters, easy, dry and comfortable, with liberal arrangements below, as the illustrations indicate. With iron ballast stowed in blocks under the cabin floor and a pole mast rig she was also very economical in first cost. The sail plan shows a large lug on the fore in dotted lines. This sail the owner devised for light winds, and under this and jib she can be sent along with mainsail in the gaskets. The splicing of her rigging is "metallic" all through. For hard weather also a trysail and storm jib, which have both been brought into requisition in the lower half of the Chesapeake, which is more of a sea than a bay. The GAETINA is especially good in light winds and airs in spite of her draft and thirteen tons of displacement. Her owner often sails her singlehanded between Baltimore and his residence in the country, near the mouth of the Choptank, a distance of sixty miles.

The accommodations include a small steerage with the companion aft, leading into an after state cabin 7 ft. long with a berth on each side. The saloon is reached from this through doors, and is 9 ft. long, with extra wide sofas of

PLATE LXXVI

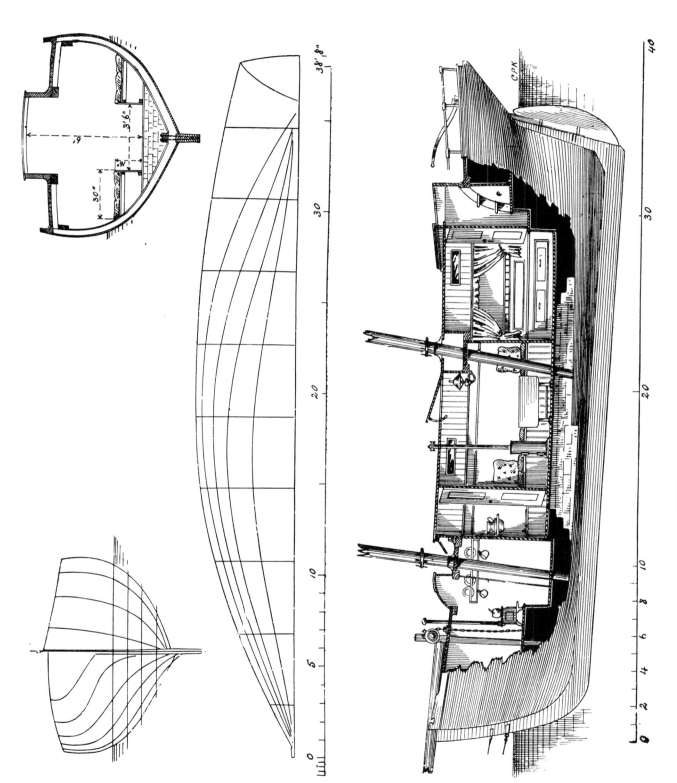

38' 8"

30

20

10

5

0

CPK

40

30

20

10

8

6

4

2

0

9'

3' 6"

3'

30"

THE SCHOONER GAETINA

30 in., having 3 ft. 6 in. of floor between and 6 ft. under beams. Between cabin and forepeak are retiring room and pantry. A hammock can be swung from foremast to the eyes for the paid hand, who has access to the deck by means of an iron ladder and quadrant hatch overhead.

| | |
|---|---|
| Length over all | 38 ft. 8 in. |
| Length on *L W L* | 35 " |
| Beam extreme | 11 " 3 " |
| Draft at heel | 6 " |
| Least freeboard | 2 " 10 in. |
| Displacement | 13 short tons |
| Ballast | 6 " " |
| Area lower sail | 950 sq. ft. |
| Hoist of mainsail | 25 ft. |
| Hoist of foresail | 24 " |
| Mainboom | 23 " |
| Bowsprit outboard | 10 " |

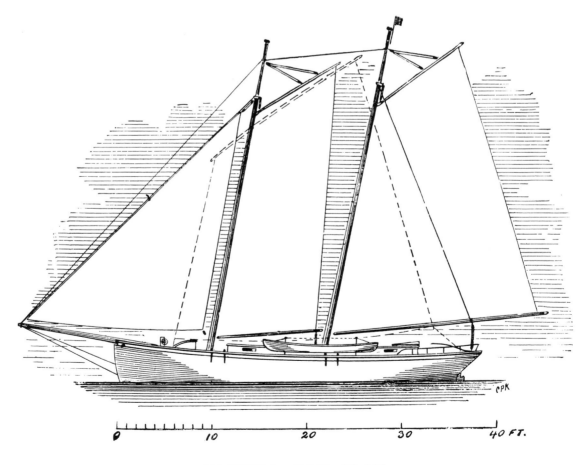

GAETINA—SAIL PLAN

## YAWL AND SCHOONER COMPARED

*PLATE LXXVII*

IN many small schooner yachts, especially in those of Eastern waters, the original rig of the famous AMERICA is still preserved. This consists of three lower sails, a gaff topsail over the main, and often a maintopmast staysail between maintopmasthead and the foremasthead. A foretopmast is usually added. This rig is very handy for a short crew, but does not give sail spread or choice of arrangement enough for racing. It is still the prevailing rig of fishermen and working boats. As a notable vessel, the lines of the AMERICA are herewith appended. By increasing beam and modifying depth, as may seem preferable in a small boat, the same general characteristics can be preserved and a handsome fair body insured.

To compare the yawl rig with that of the schooner, the hull in Plate LXXVII has been resparred according to the plans in Plate LXXIX. Two principal advantages of the change will be apparent. There is no mainmast to interfere with room below and no weak partners through the cabin roof. The larger area of the yawl's mainsail, more nearly approaching that of a cutter or sloop, is certain to add to the speed and closewindedness of the design. The superior handiness of the yawl has already been fully examined in the chapter dealing with Rig and its Principles.

Some important changes have also been made in the hull. The post has been plumbed up so as not to drive the mizzen too far aft for a secure step in the overhang, and the draft has been increased 8 in. by an external lead keel of 4,000 lbs., through which the centreboard drops. The latter has been increased to 11 ft. length and 5 ft. drop. To correspond with this the lower sail area has been enlarged from 836 to 1,050 sq. ft., or 1.03 of the square of the load-line, a very material improvement in all respects, and one which shows how unjustifiable inside ballast is in a yacht, unless the lightest possible draft is a necessity of first importance. All other considerations, such as safety, speed, room, counsel outside ballast under the building keel.

A broad inference can also be drawn from the altered arrangements. The lower the ballast is hung the more sail can be carried, with increased speed in consequence. Or, what is the same thing, the lower the ballast the more beam can be reduced and the same sail area carried as before, greater speed resulting from the diminished resistance of smaller beam. This is the theory underlying the design of cutters and the true explanation why many cutters, despite narrower beam and larger displacement, have shown themselves possessed of equal possibilities in the way of speed with the wider, lighter and shoaler sloops.

The draft of our schooner is 3 ft. 2 in.; that of the yawl 3 ft. 10 in. The cases where this increase could not be accepted are so few, that in the future yachts with inside ballast will become rare exceptions to the general rule. Certainly a yacht with inside weight must be regarded like a bird with clipped wings.

TABLE OF SPARS AND SAILS

| | | |
|---|---|---|
| Centre of mast from end $L W L$ | 8 ft. | |
| Mast, deck to hounds | 26 " | 9 in. |
| Topmast, cap to shoulder | 19 " | |
| Mainboom over all | 24 " | 6 " |
| Maingaff over all | 21 " | |
| Mizzenmast, deck to hounds | 17 " | 9 " |
| Mizzenboom over all | 15 " | 6 " |
| Mizzengaff over all | 11 " | |
| Boomkin outboard | 5 " | |
| Bowsprit beyond end $L W L$ | 16 " | 6 " |
| Centre of mast to forestay | 13 " | 6 " |
| Forestay to jibstay | 10 " | |
| Area mainsail | 560 sq. ft. | |
| Area staysail | 135 " " | |
| Area jib | 130 " " | |
| Area mizzen | 225 " " | |
| Area lower sail | 1,050 " " | |
| $C L R$ abaft end $L W L$ | 19 ft. 7 in. | |
| $C E$ abaft end $L W L$ | 18 " 11 " | |

It will be noticed that the Centre of Effort is forward of the $C L R$, but upon heeling a little the balance will be right for an easy weather helm.

PLATE LXXVII

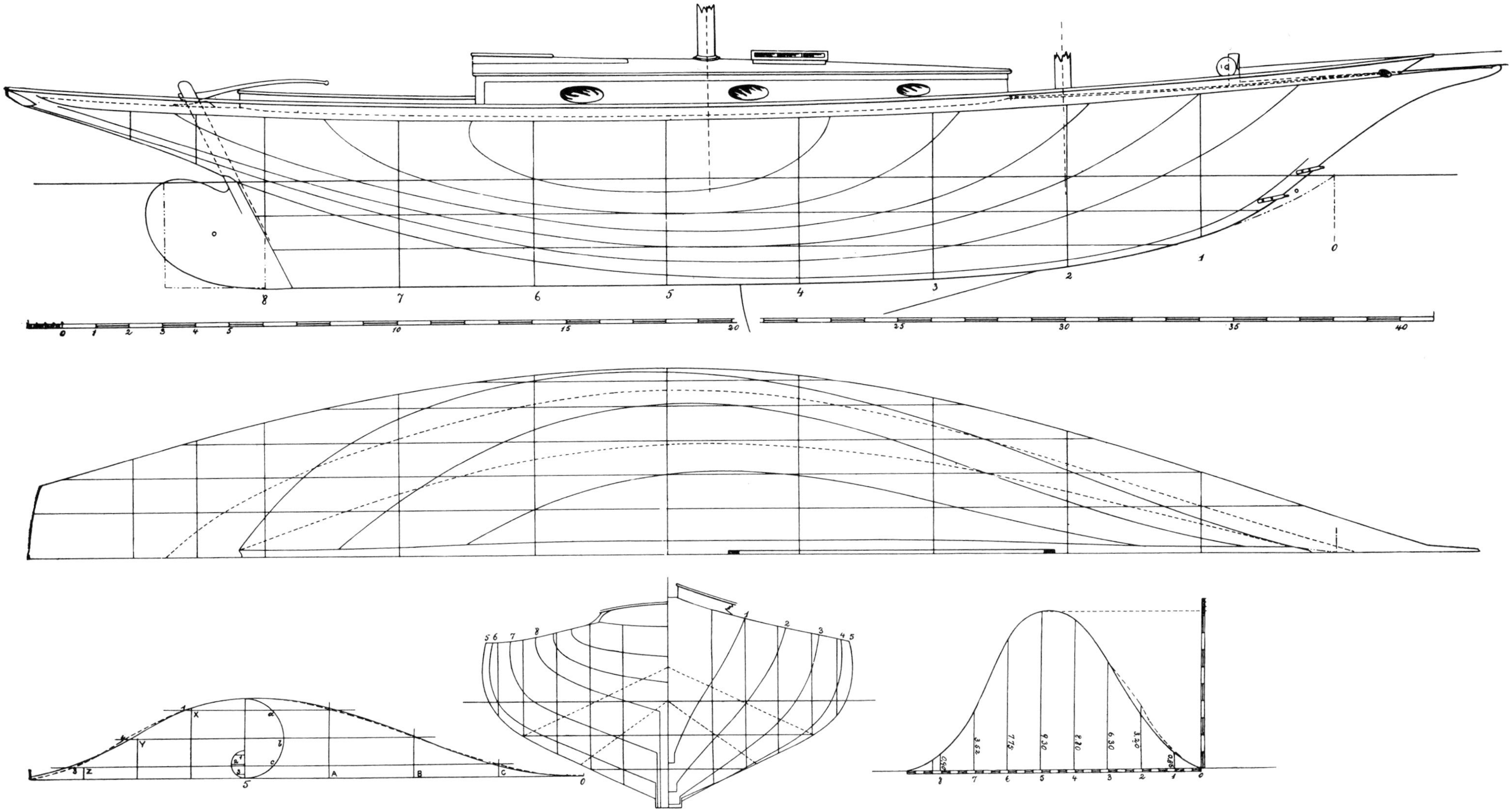

LIGHT DRAFT CENTRE-BOARD SCHOONER

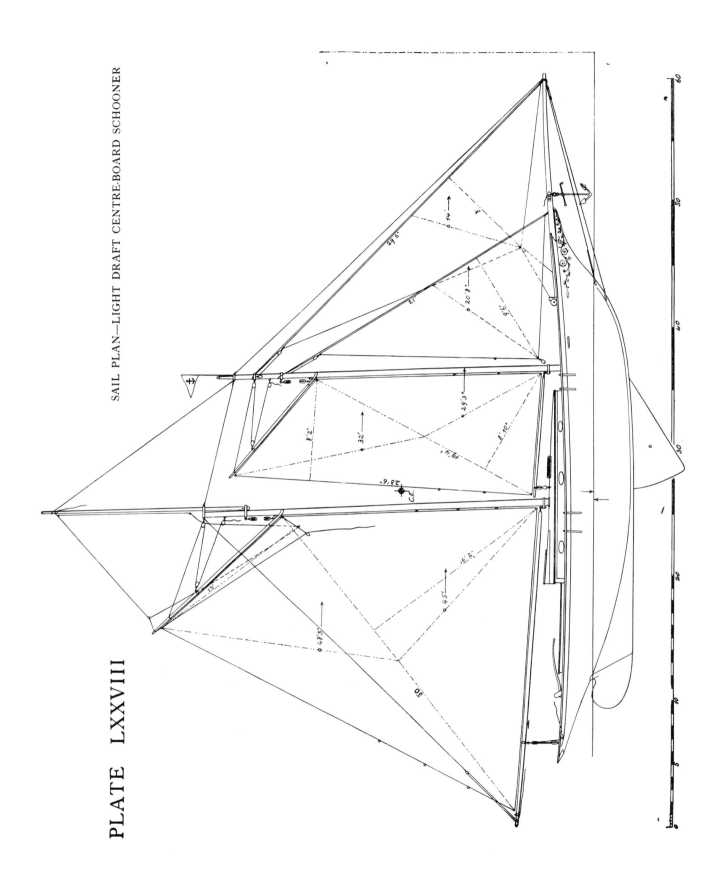

PLATE LXXVIII

SAIL PLAN—LIGHT DRAFT CENTRE-BOARD SCHOONER

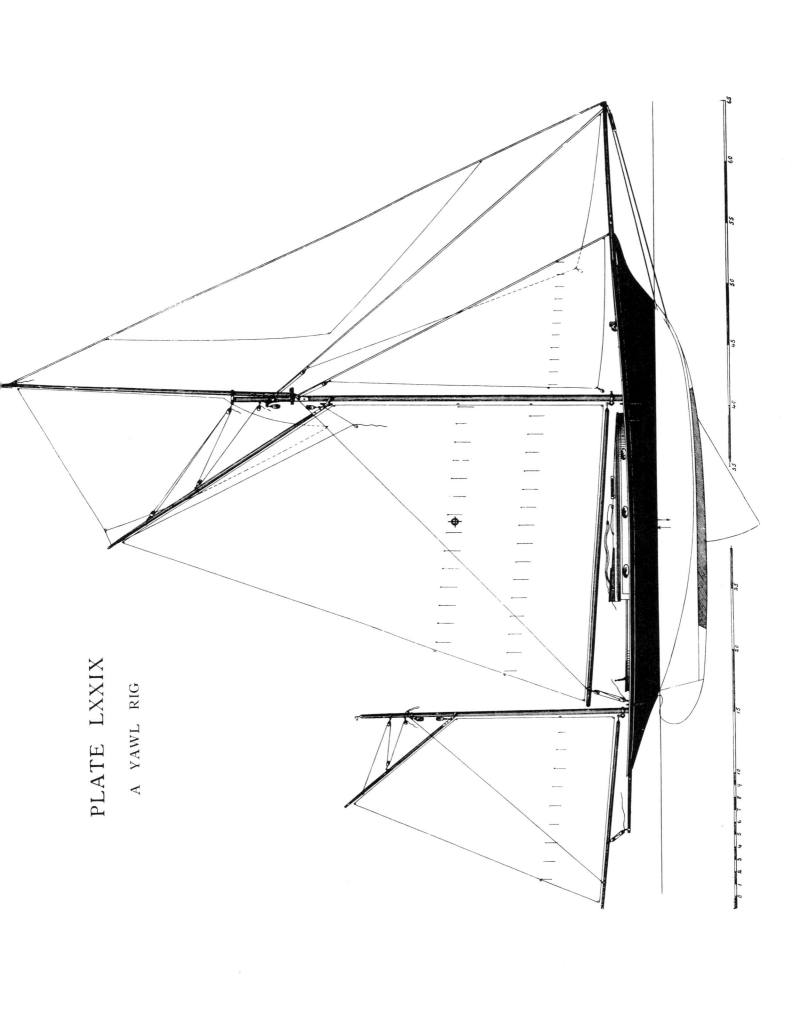

PLATE LXXIX

A YAWL RIG

# Small Yachts

## SHARPIES OF LONG ISLAND SOUND

THE construction of a small sharpie is very simple. Make a midship mould from the drawings. Get out the rabbeted stem and apron, or knee for same, and the sternboard. Hold the stem, midship mould and sternboard in proper position by battens. Then spring the plank from stem around midship mould to the sternboard and fasten with galvanized nails an inch apart. When the sides are complete, turn the boat over and crossplank the bottom. Then put in frames, trunk and fittings.

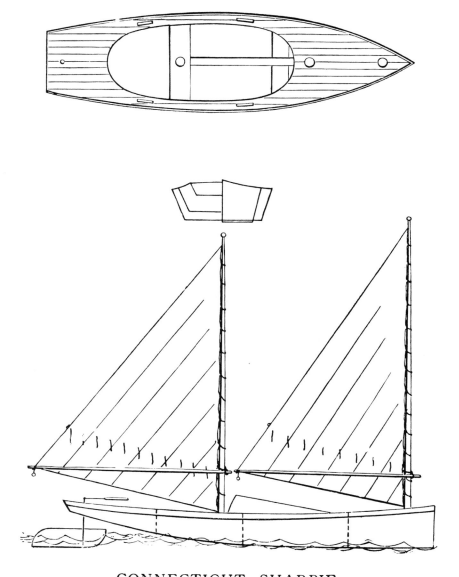

CONNECTICUT SHARPIE

# Yachts of Special Class

The latest practice in sharpies for yachting purposes conforms to the dimensions in the following table:

### DIMENSIONS OF SHARPIES

| | | | | |
|---|---|---|---|---|
| Length over all............... | 15 ft. | 20 ft. | 25 ft. | 35 ft. |
| Length on water-line.......... | 13 " | 17 " | 22 " | 30 " |
| Greatest width across deck..... | 4 " | 5 " | 6 " | 9 " |
| Greatest width across floor..... | 3 " 6 in. | 4 " 3 in. | 4 " 9 in. | 7 " |
| Depth amidships.............. | 1 " 2 " | 1 " 3 " | 1 " 6 " | 2 " 6 in. |
| Draft without board........... | 4 " | 6 " | 9 " | 1 " |
| Foremast..................... | 18 " | 23 " | 29 " | 39 " |
| Luff of foresail............... | 16 " | 21 " | 26 " | 36 " |
| Foot of foresail.............. | 6 " | 10 " | 13 " | 18 " |
| Mainmast.................... | — | 22 " | 27 " | 38 " |
| Luff of mainsail.............. | — | 20 " | 25 " | 35 " |
| Foot of mainsail............. | — | 10 " | 12 " | 17 " |
| Length of centreboard........ | 5 " | 7 " | 9 " | 11 " |

The rigs above are of the leg of mutton pattern. Larger sharpies are rigged with gaff sails or with yards, as shown in Plate LXXX. The scantling for boats, as recommended by Mr. Clapham, is given below:

TWENTY-FOOT SHARPIE --Frames of oak, 1¼ in. square, spaced 18 in. Bottom plank, 1 in. pine; side plank, 1¼ in.; stem of oak; bed logs of centreboard trunk, 6 × 2 in. oak; headpieces, 2 × ¾ in.; siding of trunk, 1½ in. pine; centreboard, 3½ ft. wide and 1¼ in. thick; skag, 1¾ in. thick; thwarts and coamings, 1 in. thick. The rudder is of the balance kind, 4½ ft. long and 8 in. wide.

THIRTY-FOOT SHARPIE —Frames 2 in. square, spaced 18 in. apart. Bottom plank 1½ in. thick, 6 in. wide. Side planking 1½ in. thick, put on in two broad strakes with patches at ends for the sheer as necessary. Bed logs of trunk, 7 × 3 in.; headpieces, 1 × 2 in.; sides of trunk, 2 in. thick; centreboard, 4 ft. wide, 1¾ in. thick; deck beams, 2 × 2 in.; skag, 2½ in. thick; rudder, 6 ft. long and 10 in. wide.

FORTY-FIVE-FOOT SHARPIE —Frames 2½ × 2½ in., spaced 15 in.; bottom plank, 1½ in. thick, 6 in. wide; side planking, 1½ in., put on in 4 to 6 in. strakes. Headpieces of trunk of oak, 2 × 1 in.; sides of trunk, 2 in. thick; centreboard, 4¼ ft. wide, 2 in. thick; keelson of oak, 4 × 9 in., bolted with ⅝ in. iron; deck beams, 2½ × 2 in.; deck plank, 1 in. thick; rudder, 8 ft. long and 18 in. wide.

# A LARGE SHARPIE

*PLATE LXXX*

FIFTY-THREE FEET SIX INCHES ON LOAD-LINE

THE general introduction of sharpies along the coast and in other climes was for a long time neglected, because the originators along the Connecticut shore did not consider themselves shouldered with any special mission to go proselyting. Within the last few years, however, the interests of the oysterman have expanded, and the sharpie, as part and parcel of a regular outfit for the trade, has found her way into Southern waters, and bids fair to receive very wide recognition. In a limited degree, she likewise found a footing among boats used for pleasure sailing, more particularly where sailing was pursued along shore in connection with hunting and fishing. Being light and showing only small sail, the original sharpie was not over good to windward and much given to "pounding" in a chop. After modifications, Mr. Thomas Clapham, of Roslyn, L. I., has been able to meet the requirements of regular yachts in a greater degree, so that the modern yacht-like sharpie is often preferred for shoal water

RIG OF SMALL SHARPIE

# PLATE LXXX

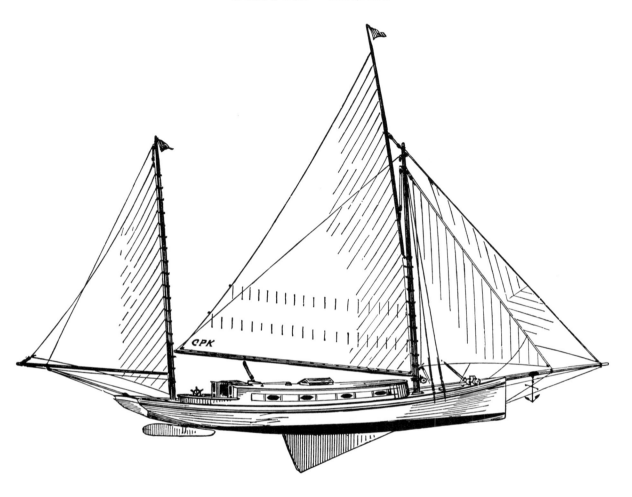

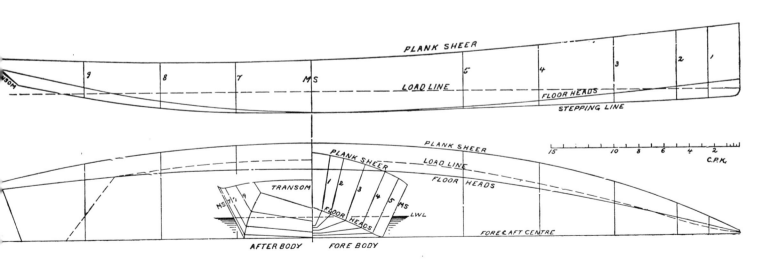

THE NONPAREIL SHARPIE

navigation, especially about the lagoons and inlets of the Southern coast. Experiments have been lately made with compromise keel and centreboard sharpies and report speaks well of the alteration. Lead keels outside will add to the safety of sharpies, as in their earlier form they were prone to sudden upsetting, but whether speed and handiness will be improved is not so certain. More or less deadrise is also introduced in the latest examples and the rig has undergone evolution from the primitive sprit to gaff sails and jibs, all the equipment and fittings being likewise brought up to the regular yacht standard.

For handiness in shoal water, the small hull, flat bottom, and light rig of the sharpie are advantages which sportsmen will appreciate. A great deal is

LARGE SHARPIE UNDER SAIL

claimed for the sharpie as a full substitute for regular yachts at less cost and draft, but these claims lack confirmation and may be left to future experience to settle. It would be opposed to the lessons of practice, should such small bodies and rigs on a length be accepted as the equal in general ability of yachts of more power. Sharpies of large beam have been tried, but they are deficient in good qualities, unless deadrise be introduced, whereupon they become "skipjacks," much the same thing as a hard bilged sloop.

The following are the details of a centreboard sharpie 54 ft. water-line and 14 ft. beam, 1 ft. more than the boat shown in Plate LXXX. They serve as a guide to others of similar proportions, large or small.

| | |
|---|---|
| Length over all | 60 ft. |
| Length on water-line | 54 " |
| Beam extreme | 14 " |
| Greatest beam from stem | 40 " |
| Depth at mast | 5 " |
| Least freeboard | 2 " 5 in. |
| Displacement | 4.3 tons |
| Ballast inside | 3,000 lbs. |
| Draft without board | 20 in. |
| Draft with board | 8 ft. |
| Length of board | 16 " |
| Area mainsail | 900 sq. ft. |
| Area jib | 325 " " |
| Area flying jib | 190 " " |
| Area mizzen | 360 " " |
| Total lower sail | 1,775 " " |
| Ratio of sail to square *L W L* | 55 per cent. |
| Mainmast, deck to hounds | 38 ft. |
| Diameter at deck | 10 in. |
| Diameter at hounds | 7 " |
| Length of masthead | 3 ft. |
| Mainmast, from stem | 14 " |
| Main to mizzen mast | 38 " |
| Mainboom | 37 " |
| Diameter | 6 in |
| Mainyard | 37 ft. |
| Diameter | 6 in. |
| Mizzen mast | 37 ft. |
| Diameter at deck | 9 in. |
| Mizzen sprit | 22 ft. |
| Diameter | 4 in. |
| Bowsprit outboard | 20 ft. |
| Bowsprit housed | 4 " |
| Diameter at stem | 8 x 10 in. |
| Mainmast to jibstay | 24 ft. |
| Mainmast to flying jibstay | 32 " |

These dimensions refer to the yawl rig in the Plate. The schooner has been tried, but is not quite so weatherly. The side timbers of a 60 ft. sharpie are 4 x 4 in., spaced 18 in. apart. Bottom frame consists of four fore-and-aft keelsons mortising into edge keelsons shaped to the side of the boat and into which the heels of the side frames also step. Trunk logs for the centreboard are framed in between the two middle keelsons. Planking, 2 in. yellow pine. Two ⅝ wire shrouds to mainmast and none to the mizzen. The accommodations will consist of a main cabin having a berth in each wing and sofas inside, starboard and port staterooms 8 and 6½ ft. long, a w. c. and forecastle. The general stowage is quite liberal besides.

The details of an open Connecticut sharpie built in New Haven are as follows: Over all, 36 ft. 1 in.; beam, 6 ft. 3 in. on bottom and 7 ft. on top. Depth at bow, 3 ft. 2 in.; depth amidships, 27 in.; draft amidships, 6½ in., round stern; centreboard, 10½ ft. long and 5 ft. wide at after end. Cockpit, 32 ft. long, yellow pine grating on floor; bulkheads of black walnut and ash. Foremast, 38 ft. long; mainmast, 35 ft. long, 6 in. diameter at partners, 1½ in. at head. Sheaves in masthead for halliards. Racing foresail with 10 ft. club, working foresail with 5 ft. club, also used as racing mainsail. Steps fitted with brass collars, extra step for working with one sail only. Awning, oilskin tent for cruising; brass rowlocks; forepeak, 4 ft. 7 in. wide, 6 ft. long, 3 ft. high. Lockers in stern.

Details of a 45 ft. improved sharpie: Length over all, 45 ft.; beam, 11 ft. 6 in.; depth at stem, 5 ft.; depth amidships, 4 ft.; stem, apron and stern of oak; keel and keelson solid oak, 6 x 10 in.; timbers, 2 x 2 in., of oak, and 15 in. apart; side and bottom plank of best clear white and yellow pine, 1½ in. thick; plank rail of oak; deck of clear white pine laid narrow and curving with flare; fastenings of best galvanized iron; centreboard of hickory or oak, 15 ft. long; cockpit finished in hardwood, oiled; cabin the same; house, 9 x 15 ft., with headroom of 5 ft. 6 in.; masts and spars of best spruce; balance rudder with wrought-iron stock and tiller; all iron work attached to rigging galvanized; four berths in cabin, with space for two more forward. Cost of all complete, as above, $1,000, according to amount of extra finish. Such a boat will draw, with board up, 12 to 15 in. of water.

The simplest form of sharpie is a sharp-bowed, flat-bottomed boat, built by nailing two planks, which form her sides, to a plumb stem at the one end, and to a single piece of hardwood plank at the other. The sides are sprung around a temporary midship section, which is to remain in place until her thwarts are in and bottom planking secured. The latter are simply nailed athwartship to the lower edge of the boards which form her sides. She should have some inches flare amidship, which flare should be carried aft to the stern, and her bottom should be sloped up aft from amidship, so that she will leave the water easily. She may be decked over to suit her owner's taste, and her sheer cut to suit his eye. She has no keel or skag of any kind. Her rudder is made from a single plank of an elliptic shape, hung on an iron rudder-post which passes up through her stern. The rudder should be so hung that about one-third of its area is forward of, and two-thirds of it aft of, the iron shaft or stock.

Such a boat should be 30 in. in height at stem, 20 in. in height amidships, and carry a graceful sheer her entire length. Beam amidship, 5 ft. on deck, 4 ft. 3 in. at bottom. Width at stern to suit the eye. These figures are for a boat 20 ft. in length. Centreboard at least 7 ft. long by 3 ft. wide. No position fore and aft can be assigned the centreboard, as its place will be governed by amount of camber to the boat's bottom. Rig to be of the triangular or leg-of-mutton type, and consists of foremast and mainmast, dressed tapering, from full size at deck to 2½ in. diameter at head. Foremast should be stepped as near to stem as is possible. Mainmast 12 ft. aft of foremast, the mainmast somewhat the shorter, thus reversing the usual schooner rig. The sails are bent without boom, but with a sprit, which is stretched across from sheet to mast. Width of foresail, 11 ft.; do. mainsail, 9 ft.

The style of sharpie most in use about New Haven is described in the following :

Length, 33 to 35 ft.; breadth, about 5 ft. 9 in. to 6 ft. on the bottom; depth amidships, about 24 in.; at the stem, 36 in.; and 12 in. perpendicularly at the stern. The stem is a piece of oak, sometimes as much as 15 in. wide, and 6 in., or even 8 in., thick at the top. The lower end is dubbed thinner, so as to give a little flare to the sides. These are usually made of wide plank pieced up at the bow and stern to get the required sheer. Through the first third of the length the flare is increased as rapidly as possible to 3½ in. to 1 ft. of free-board, and more gradually toward the stern, where it is about 4 in. to 1 ft. Of course the flare of the sides, combined with the bend, gives a considerable camber fore and aft to the bottom; the neglect of which, by unaccustomed builders, has caused many failures through the excessive rocker given by shaping the lower edge wrong.

The stern is sometimes square, at others round. When square it is set with a great rake, not less than 45 deg.; when round it is nearly plumb, and becomes quite light by being carried further out by the curve. The centreboard is long, and, as the boat is narrow, should come above the rail to get the needed surface.

The forward deck extends to within a foot of the centreboard, the intervening space being filled by a thwart, which is notched to receive the case, and has a mast-hole for stepping a sail in heavy weather. It also affords a convenient step to climb up from the bottom to the deck.

The after end is decked some three or four feet, and the intervening space has a washboard 7 in. to 9 in. wide, with a combing rising two or three inches above, the whole opening being trimmed out to an oval form. About a foot from the after end of the centreboard the mainmast steps through a very strong thwart, well secured and supported at the ends. The rudder is of peculiar form, known as the balanced rudder. The stock is of round iron or steel, passing through a tube flanged at one end to the deck, and at the other to the bottom, so as to be tight; split and spread below to receive a plank from 4 ft. to 6 ft. long, and 12 in. to 15 in. wide, shaped off on the forward end, which extends some 12 in. to 18 in. by the stock, so as to clear the bottom, and rounded on the lower edge to prevent catching. The stock is generally made of sufficient length to allow the rudder to be lowered in a sea-way, giving a better hold. The head of the stock is squared to receive a corresponding socket on the tiller. The usual style of rig is with two leg-of-mutton sails. The foremast is shipped as near the stem as possible, and for racing the sail is cut so as to reach several feet abaft the mainmast, the clew being cut across and a short club attached, extending from the leech to the foot. This is done to increase the sail without adding to the luff. The booms are not laced, but are sprits which cross from the clew to the mast about five feet up and are stretched by a light purchase at the mast. The mainsail, of course, extends several feet over the stern. Their management is very different from that of a catboat, resembling that of a racing boat with large jib. Being narrow they are rather crank and in fresh breezes must be eased by slacking the foresheet, as too sudden easing of the helm slews the stern so swiftly as to take in water before the boat rights in answer to relief from pressure. Of course such boats require quickness of judgment and action in the sailor.

Their cost is less than any other boat of the same capacity. All the space inside is available for yachting purposes, what little ballast is needed being usually a tier of bricks or paving stones. The clew of the foresail being necessarily cut high, gives room for more height of cabin than is usually attained in other boats, and every inch is of such form as to be useful Owing to their flat bottom it is scarcely possible to injure them by pounding on the sand, as the water forms a cushion.

The chief objection is that they are unsafe in unskillful hands. They sail, like all narrow boats, on the side when it blows, and though fast when properly built, they are seldom successful in the hands of amateur builders.

Considerable latitude in proportions and details exists, each boatman having his own views as to what is best. The CARRIE V., built by Lester Rowe, of Fair Haven East, Connecticut, a fast sharpie of local renown, corresponds to the following:

Length, 35 ft.; breadth of beam is amidships, and is 8 ft. on deck; flare of sides, 4 in. to the foot; width of stern, 4½ ft., just before it commences to round, and 10 in. deep; depth at bow, 36 in.; 14 in. sheer; 11 ft. centreboard; decked over 10 ft. forward and 4 ft. aft; washboards, 12 in. wide amidships; length of rudder, 6 ft., and 18 in. deep; greatest draught of water, 6 in. amidships; bow lifts 4 in. out of water. In her racing trim she carries a 45 ft. foremast, 6 in. diam.; 40 ft. mainmast, 5½ in. diam.; both tapered to 1½ in.

at mastheads. Length of bowsprit, 17 ft.; 22 ft. between spars; hoist of jib, 27 ft. She carries 250 yards of canvas—75 in the foresail, 60 in the mainsail, 45 in the staysail, 40 in the squaresail, and 30 in the jib. To get this great spread of canvas in the fore and mainsails, 8 or 10 ft. "clubs" are used, and two sprits, one to each end of the club of each of these sails, which set with such nicety that when on the wind there is not over 6 in. drift between sail and sprit. The mainsail runs out so far over the stern that an iron V, 4 ft. long, has to be used for the mainsheet. The cost of sails is 50 cents per yard. The canvas is generally furnished by the boatman, the sailmaker doing the work, including roping, for 4 cents per yard.

In a race twelve men will serve for ballast—no dead weight ever being used—and when on the wind outriggers, consisting of two 16 ft. planks, are run out to windward, upon which the men get, one of them being captain of the outriggers, whose business it is to see that the weather bilge is kept just out of water, he using more or less men, and shifting them to windward or to leeward as the occasion requires. It is a great point to keep the sharpie in just this position when on the wind, as she sails faster and holds on better.

The cost of the round stern over the square is $15. The advantages are in looks, no corners to catch the mainsheet; it will not ship a sea so easily when moored by the stern, as boats always are when tonging for oysters. The reasons for so mooring them are, facility in getting at the anchor, and they lie more quiet. The two working masts for 35 ft. boat are 4½ in. diam., and 28 to 30 ft. hoist, and the two spread 65 yds. canvas.

Many boatmen have to go through several bridges in going down river, and as they have to unstep their masts, they are made as light as possible, so as to handle easily, and for this reason they are sometimes carried away at the thwart. A hatchet is provided, so that the stump of the mast can be cut to fit the step when a single reef is put in—not a long operation.

From 150 to 175 bushels of oysters can be carried in a boat of above size, and she will sustain 5 tons weight. The weight of her hull is 2,000 to 2,500 lbs., and it takes ten good men to end her up. The cost of one of these boats, with working sails, is about $250.

They are heavier than one would suppose to look at them. A sharpie built as light as possible for sailing, 14 ft. long, 3 ft. beam, takes two men to load her on a wagon. The stock for this boat, including three coats of paint, was about $6, and the time for building one and one-half days. The price of a boat of this kind is $1 per foot or a little over. They will do well enough to shoot out of on a river or small lake, but are failures for coot shooting on the Sound on account of "pounding," which destroys the aim. When made for rowing, sharpies are considered heavier than round-bottom boats of the same length, made for the same purpose.

They have no hollow water-lines, neither ought the bow to crown up. The sides throw up the bow in bending them, but the forefoot is cut straight away aft. A sharpie's bottom is nearly straight from the stem to midships, or thereabouts, according to the fancy of the builder. What gives the bow the appearance of crowning up is the trim of the sharpie afloat.

## A SMALL SHARPIE

### SEVENTEEN FEET LONG

FOR single-hand sailing and coasting along shore, simplicity and moderate first cost have been aimed at with as much efficiency and power consistent with good speed in a boat of flat bottom. The displacement of an ordinary sharpie has been increased to gain in room and weight. Although the midship frame is kept dead flat on the floor, deadrise from **that point**

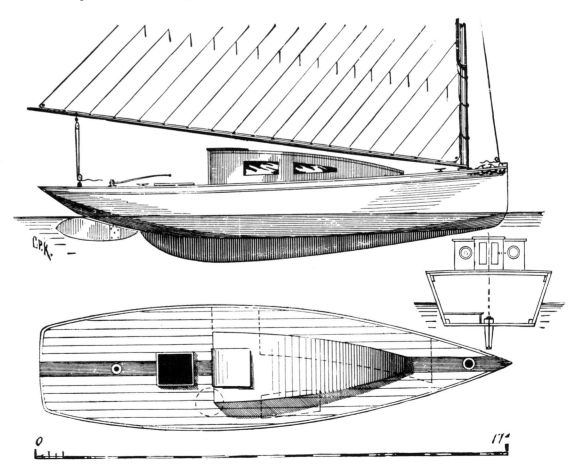

SMALL SHARPIE—GENERAL PLANS

forward and aft has been adopted to conciliate "pounding" at one end and to enable the water to close readily in the run. The floor line along the centre is marked by the lowest line in the sheer plan and the rise of the floor at the side by the line above, the shaded portion between the two indicating the dead-rise of the floor. The total displacement is 22 cu. ft., of which 500 lbs. is represented by ballast. For safety and increasing the sail area an iron keel is

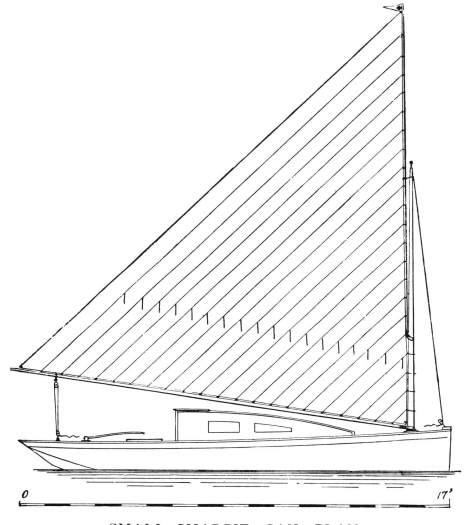

SMALL SHARPIE—SAIL PLAN

attached from below. Should it be desired to ascend a creek for exploration this keel can be disconnected by unscrewing the nuts on the bolts holding it in place. The greatest breadth is located 11 ft. from forward, where the boat is 4 ft. 6 in. wide across deck and 3 ft. 3 in. across the bottom.

There is 4 ft. headroom at after end of cabin hatch. The boat is decked, with a hatch aft to reach the storeroom occupying all the space abaft the cabin bulkhead. A berth and locker have been fitted below on the port side with a swing table opposite. The stove is shown by the dotted circle. Length on load-line is 16 ft., over all 17 ft., gangways each side the cabin hatch measure 12 in. wide. The rig has only one halliard, which first hoists and then peaks up a leg-of-mutton sail bent to a 13 ft. yard, traveling with jaws up and down a pole mast 10 ft. 6 in. above deck, stepped 18 in. from the stem. The boom is 16 ft. over all. Sail area 128 sq. ft., with one line of reef knittles 3 ft. 3 in. above the foot. The boat can be steered from deck or by sitting in the companion hatch. Draft, 21 in. with keel. Least freeboard, 14 in. The cabin is ceiled and finished in bright hardwood; sides of cabin house made of single pieces of ash; hatches and deck fittings of ash and mahogany. Total cost about $270.

## THE BUCKEYE

### PLATE LXXXI

#### FORTY-SIX FEET LONG ON LOAD-LINE

THE Buckeyes, productions of the Chesapeake region, are an exaggeration of the " dugout" canoe, and were developed gradually by the bay shore people, as the necessity for larger boats became apparent. It was easy to get almost any desired length in a single log, but not so as to beam and depth. Very natural it was to add to beam and depth by building up and out with logs bolted to the sides of the long, narrow and shallow dugout. This was done, and masts and sails added to suit the increased size. A large boat required anchors and cables instead of being dragged up on the beach, as with the small canoe. The primitive builder bored two holes, one on each side of the stem, through which to pay out his cables  These were simply two round holes, bored with a large auger, and, when the boat was coming head on, resembled to the fancy of the negroes, the eyes of a buck. The illusion was somewhat increased by the addition of a bowsprit and its attendant gear. The leg-of-mutton sail—the primitive sail of all nations—was adopted with two masts; the bowsprit and jib being a later accession. This is yet the favorite rig of canoes of thirty feet in length and under.

Length being the dimension most easily attainable, the Buckeye was built long and narrow, and being heavy in body but easily driven through the water, with a low centre of effort for her sails, she proved a fast and stiff boat. She was sharp at each end; the greatest beam was about one-third the distance from stem to stern, thence sloping by easy lines fore and aft, giving a clear entrance

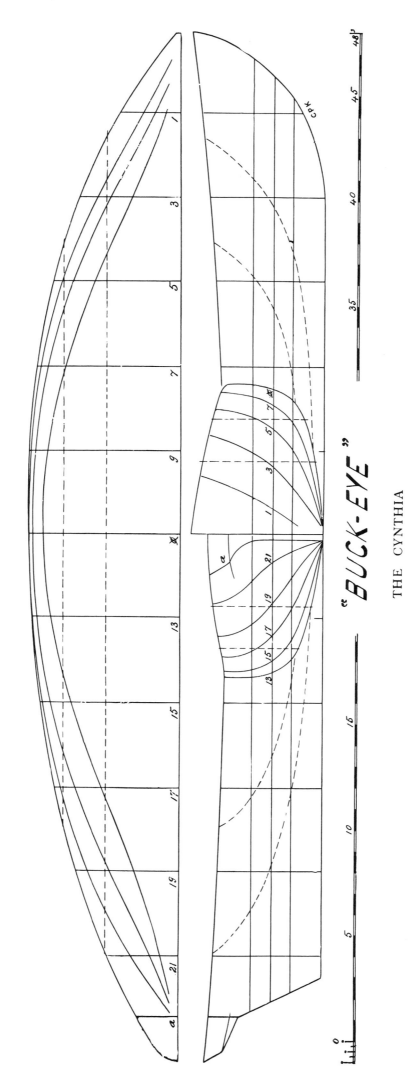

PLATE LXXXI

"BUCK-EYE"

THE CYNTHIA

and good clearance. As to deadrise, it was a matter of choice or convenience. Generally the deadrise was slight. The entire construction depended on convenience and economy. There was no overhang, because it was easier and cheaper not to have any. She had no stays to the mast because it was cheaper not to have any, and besides a "springiness" to the masts was considered desirable, because sudden flaws were not so likely to knock down. A centreboard is always built in, because the Buckeye was intended for the shallow waters of creeks and inlets as well as for the waters of the bay. One peculiarity was the manner of

RIG OF A SMALL BUCKEYE

stepping the masts. The foremast was longer than the mainmast and did not rake so much. To the mainmast was given a rake aft. The negroes say it makes them sail faster on the wind. In small canoes the mainmast is shifted, so as to stand plumb when sailing before the wind. The accompanying sketch indicates the rig and position of the masts. Of late years imitations of the old-fashioned Buckeye have been regularly built, timbered and planked, and the beam has been increased. This has necessitated a larger area of sail, and the schooner rig has been used. Sometimes only the foresail has a gaff. The genuine Buckeye rarely has less than five beams to the length. The modern imitations sometimes have less than four. This puts them on a par with other broad, shallow boats.

The Buckeye has a well deserved reputation for speed and seaworthiness. She pounds somewhat in a heavy sea, but her weight forces her through, if not over, the combers. This makes her a rather wet boat.

Buckeyes often run the coast with cargoes of fruit.

The plans in Plate LXXXI are from an original model of the CYNTHIA, a boat famous as abler and faster than the general run of the family. She represents the latest improvements, and it is not difficult to find good reason for her comparative success in the extra depth of one foot given her beyond the custom, the CYNTHIA drawing 2½ feet, on the depth of 5. She is distinguished likewise by more deadrise, an easier turn to the bilge, and rather longer and finer entrance.

RIG OF A LARGE BUCKEYE

The CYNTHIA and her sisters are no longer the clumsy dugouts of yore, but are built with a frame and regularly planked.

Sportsmen and others on the lookout for a boat which will carry them and a load at good speed on the conditions of cheap first cost, light draft and small rig, with fair behavior in troubled waters, will find in the plans an excellent addition to the collection of useful substitutes for full-fledged yachts.

That she is a swift boat, gauged by a rational comparison of size, few need to be told. With a long body, easy ends and fore and aft sections, with dead-

rise and slow bilge and a fair allotment of ballast to the bulk, boats like the
CYNTHIA ought to be capable of excellent behavior and speedy on all points, falling short only in turning to windward in lumpy water. This the sportsman may
be willing enough to forego for the sake of the economical inducements and light
draft held forth. He will find it quite possible to improve upon her present
equipment and thus exact a higher degree of efficiency by attention to details of
ballasting and rig.

The CYNTHIA is 49 ft. on deck between rabbets, the plans being to outside
of moulds only. Her beam is 14 ft. and draft 3½ ft. with keel in ordinary trim,
or about 2½ if fitted with board. Owing to her ballast she has good weight
for working, some ability in a sea, and shows well in climbing to windward,
where lighter boats fail. She has a round stern, which is locally a matter of
pride and style obtained at an extra cost of about $200. The Buckeye is built
in all the ports along the Chesapeake, and a fifty-foot boat, hull and spars, is
said to cost about $1,000, iron work, sails, gear and joinerwork in cabin being
extra, which $500 may cover.

DIMENSIONS OF BUCKEYES

|  | Length | Beam | Depth |
|---|---|---|---|
| RAVEN | 48 | 13 | 3.10 |
| ANNONYMA | 50 | 12.6 | 3 |
| MINNEHAHA | 56 | 11.2 | 2.9 |
| VIRGINIA G. HOLLAND | 60 | 18 | 5 |

Centreboards are about one-fourth the length in small boats and shorter in
proportion for larger boats. One of the principal builders is Captain Jas. L.
Harrison, Tilghman's Island P. O., Talbot County, Maryland.

## THE SNEAKBOX

FOURTEEN FEET LONG ON LOAD-LINE

THE origin of the boat here illustrated, the sneakbox, of Barnegat Bay,
may be traced back easily to the "sinkboxes" or sinkboats. These
were at first mere boxes sunk in the marsh and covered with a blind, from
which the hunters shot at the flocks of ducks for which the bay is famous. The
box was improved into a scow, or floating blind, and in course of time the boat
shown in our illustration was evolved. In order to float in little water a flat
bottom was necessary, and as the boat had often to be beached and dragged
through the marsh, the end was well rounded up, until the bottom was nearly the

PLATE LXXXII

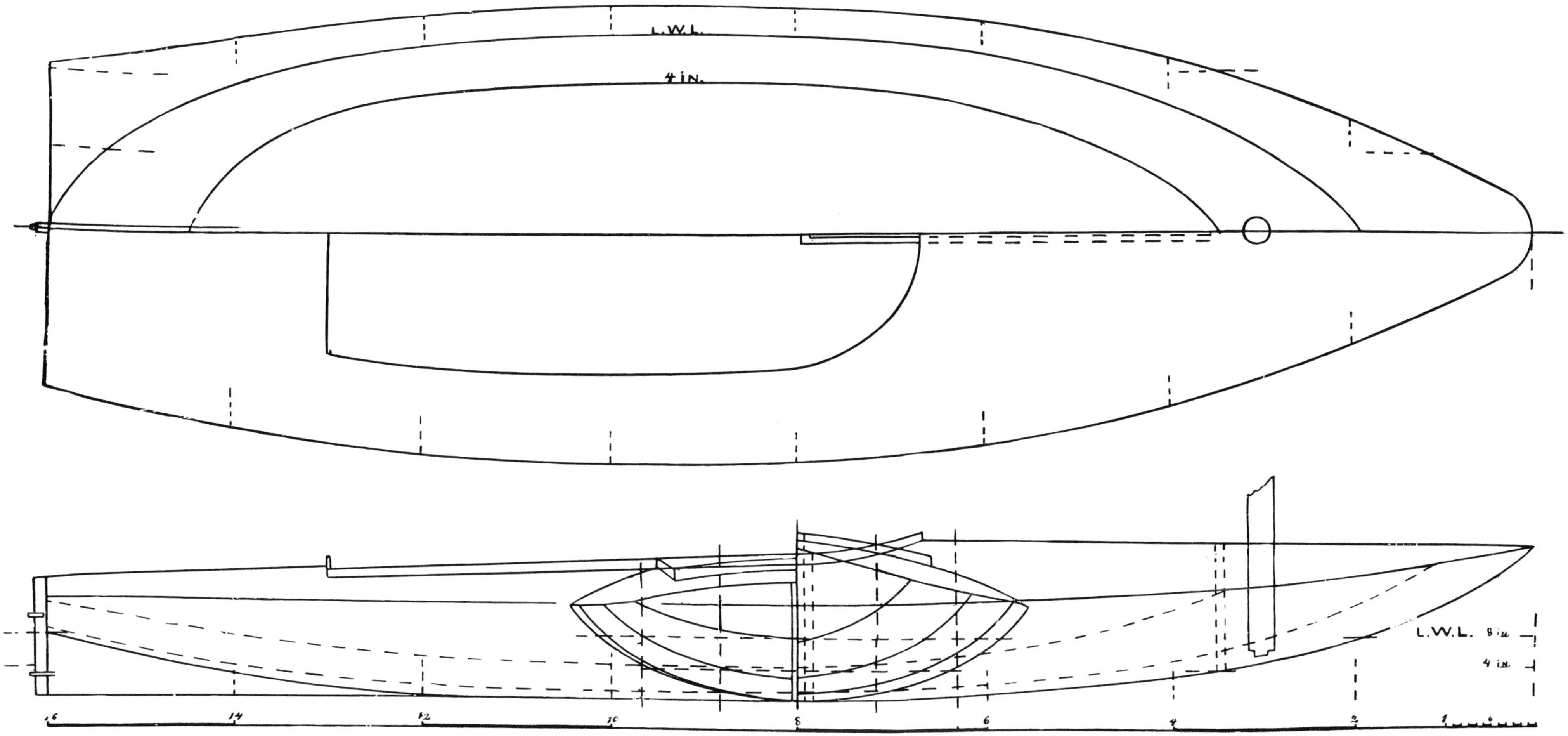

THE CRUISING SNEAKBOX

shape of a spoon. This form also proved easy and buoyant in the rough water often met with on the bay, and, coupled with a well-cambered deck, the little boats were found to be excellent for sailing and fishing, as well as for ducking, being fast, stiff and weatherly. At present they are used in many places besides the Jersey coast, and are general favorites with the duck hunter, the fisherman and the pleasure sailor.

When used for hunting, they may be drawn up on shore, as a sneakbox, being covered with brush or sedge ; or hidden in the same manner, they may be sculled close to a flock of ducks. The stern is usually provided with a rack to hold the decoys, of which forty or fifty are sometimes carried ; therefore they are made wide and full aft.

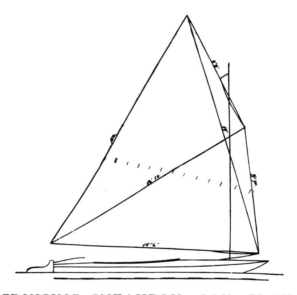

CRUISING SNEAKBOX—SAIL PLAN

The centreboard is either of the usual pivoted type, or else what is called a "dagger" board, narrow and long, curved somewhat like a scimeter, and sliding in a narrow trunk, as a sword in its sheath. The board is not hinged in any way, but is slid into the trunk, projecting down and aft, and giving a good hold on the water. When not in use it is withdrawn entirely, and laid flat on the floor boards. The usual rig is a small sprit sail, and an oar is used for steering and also for sculling ; but when used entirely for sailing, the boat is fitted with a rudder and tiller. Several of these boats, used in the vicinity of New York, are rigged with a balance lug, the same as a canoe, which sail is much superior to the old rig. The boat shown (Plate LXXXII) was built for pleasure sailing only, by J. Kilpatrick, of Barnegat, and is larger than the size used for gunning, being 16 x 5 ft., while the latter are usually about 12 x 4 ft. The cockpit is large enough for three or four persons, all sitting on the floor, as no thwarts are used ; and below deck, and at the sides of the well, is room for stores and cruising outfit. In cruising, a bed for two can easily be made up on the floor, the latter being nearly flat.

The dimensions of this boat are :

| | | | | |
|---|---|---|---|---|
| Length over all | 16 | ft. | | |
| Length on water-line | 13 | " | 11 | in. |
| Beam, extreme | 4 | " | 11 | " |
| Beam at water-line | 4 | " | 4 | " |
| Draft | | | 8 | " |
| Depth amidships | 1 | ft. | | |
| Sheer forward | | | 7 | in. |
| Sheer aft | | | 3 | " |
| Crown of deck | | | 8 | " |
| Mast from fore side of stem | 3 | ft. | | |
| Centreboard trunk, fore end, from stem | 3 | " | 5 | in. |
| Centreboard trunk, after end, from stem | 7 | " | 11 | " |
| Fore end of well, from stem | 6 | " | 8 | " |
| After end of well, from stem | 13 | " | | |
| Width of well | 3 | " | | |
| Height of coaming above deck | | | 2 | in. |
| Breadth of rudder | 2 | ft. | | |

The keel is one piece of oak, 5 in. wide amidships, and 1⅛ in. deep, turned up at the fore end. The slot for the centreboard is 1⅛ in., and the board ¾ in., the latter being of oak, through bolted. The headledges will be also of oak, 1⅛ x 1½ in., with a bolt through the keel and the lower end of each headledge. The bedpieces will be also of oak, 1 x 3 in., bolted down to keel, with painted Canton flannel between, and the sides of the trunk will be of 1 in. pine, well seasoned. The stern is of oak, 1 in. thick, and the planking is 9-16 in., carvel built, with copper nails riveted, if for salt water. The frames are of steamed oak, 1¼ in. sided and 1 in. moulded, spaced 13 in. No gunwale is needed, the deck plank, ⅜ in. thick, being screwed to the upper streak, along the adjoining edges. The deck beams are 1¼ x ⅞ in., spaced 12 in. The deck may be covered with canvas, laid in paint, and thoroughly painted outside. For rowing, oarlocks are fitted to the gunwale outside of the coaming. They are of either wood or brass, and are fitted so as to fold flat on deck, when not in use.

The sail is hoisted by a halliard, with a parrel on the yard to hold it in to the mast. Instead of the tack, as used in canoes, a line is fastened to the fore end of the boom, leading down to an eyebolt in the deck just abaft the mast, thus preventing the tack of the sail from falling forward. The sheet may be made fast to one quarter, leading through a block on the boom, and one on the other quarter, to hand, thus being out of the way of the tiller.

The dimensions of sail and spars are as follows :

| | | | |
|---|---|---|---|
| Mast, deck to hounds | 15 ft. | | |
| Mast, diameter at deck | | 3 | in. |
| Boom | 16 ft. | | |
| Boom, diameter | | 2 | in. |
| Yard | 10 " | 2 | " |
| Yard, diameter | | 1½ | " |
| Foot of sail | 15 " | 6 | " |
| Luff | 9 " | 7 | " |
| Head | 9 " | 8 | " |
| Leech | 20 " | | |
| Tack to peak | 19 " | | |
| Clew to throat | 16 " | 10 | in. |
| Area | 160 sq. ft. | | |

The Barnegat Bay boats usually have a canvas apron or screen forward, fastened to the deck, so as to keep off all spray. Being very stiff, the sneakbox is an excellent boat for young sailors, and also for pleasure sailing on the shoal bays that abound along our coasts.

For the encouragement of sailing in small boats, the Single-Hand Cruising Club, of Ocean County, New Jersey, has lately been organized, and under its

SNEAKBOX, BY RUSHTON, CANTON, N. Y.

auspices the sneakbox is undergoing refinements and improvements to better adapt her for sailing purposes. Captain George Bogart, of Long Beach, has brought out a model which is considered to be the best for general efficiency.

There is more rise or "turn up" to the bow of the best "boxes" than was found in them ten years ago. In addition to the apron, which voided the water from the forward deck while sailing in a head sea, a "shelving" or washboard six inches high is now placed along the edges or sides of the box as well as across the stern, which can easily be removed and stowed inside the boat. This bulwark increases the power of the craft to cope with the sea, and also serves to secure oars, spars, lines, etc., resting on the convex deck of the box. With the washboard and apron this low-lying craft can resist the rough waves of a bay, and can and does cross four-mile "stretches" of open waters during gales of wind that drive 21 ft. catboats into harbor. The safety of the boat will be acknowledged, when it is known that boys from ten to fourteen years old use these boats in rough weather without accident.

As a tow the Sneakbox, without a keel or stem, and with its spoon-shaped bottom and bow, runs easily in the wake of a small yacht; hence, some shooting and fishing yachtsmen have discarded gigs, punts, and canvas folding boats for this strong, serviceable and easily towed craft, which can be sailed as well as rowed.

Even regular culinary outfits are carried in the latest cruisers, being reached through a square hatch on deck aft. Up to 12 ft. the dagger board is in general use, but the cruisers of 14 ft. have yacht centreboards. A 14-ft. sneak will stow two hands. Built in best manner and of good finish, with leathered oars, spars, sail of 29 in. twilled muslin and all fittings, a 14 ft. boat will cost eighty-five dollars and one of 12 ft. sixty-five dollars. Amount of sail, 12 running yards. Ice runners, serving as bilge keels, are attached to the bottom and save the bottom from chafe.


## A LIFEBOAT YACHT

### SEVENTEEN FEET SIX INCHES LONG ON LOAD-LINE

THE history of the Elvira, formerly the Ida, is replete with instruction as to what distant cruising can be undertaken with even the smallest of boats, when modeled with reference to the work. The Ida was built in 1877 by John Roach & Son, Chester, Pa. The hull is of broad sheet iron, riveted along the seams which lap. A set of wooden knees across the keel and a wood clamp with a bilge streak complete the structure, which is in fact very similar to that of an ordinary smooth skin lifeboat, though considerably stouter.

In model she bears resemblance to a beamy whaleboat, with flare in the ends quite prominent to lift her through the coambers. More room inside than might be expected is due to the absence of any framing. The yacht has never leaked, and with ordinary care the hull promises to last many years yet, although eight seasons have passed since her launching. She is a lifeboat in the full sense, being uncapsizable and having air tanks in the ends, enough to float her should she fill, which is, however, practically impossible. When knocked down the cockpit will ship no water, as the quarters are drawn in, there being no counter.

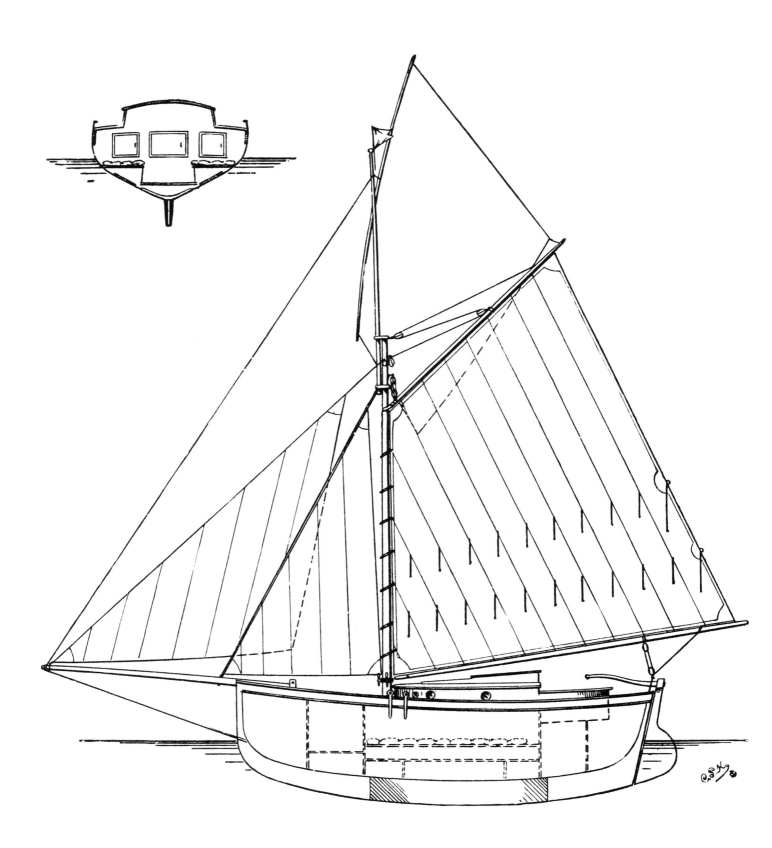

THE YACHT ELVIRA —Scale, ¼ inch = 1 foot

# Yachts of Special Class

After a thorough trial in Chesapeake Bay, the IDA was fitted out for a cruise along the Florida and Gulf coasts, the owner intending to winter in Florida and spend some time in fishing and shooting along the River St. Johns. At Elizabeth City a boy was taken on board to help work the ship, and she put to sea. This was in the fall of '77. All went well for the first few days out, when a hurricane caught the little yacht and carried her far outside of soundings to sea. Here she was put to her best in her desperate struggle with wind and waves, and, as evidence of her possessing the requisite qualities for such a performance, she is still in existence to testify for herself. Finally reaching the St. Johns River, her owner, after a short rest, was successfully driven by the mosquitoes from there to Indian River, where the pests were even more violent, and the trip was pushed further south, to Florida Keys and the Dry Tortugas, and finally northward along the coast to Brazos Santiago, where stores were taken on board, and the vessel returned for winter quarters to the St. Johns River. In the spring she was headed northward, calling at Charleston and Savannah on her way to Norfolk, Va. After leaving Charleston a serious error nearly proved fatal to the voyagers. When off Assateague the course was lost, and the Chincoteague light was mistaken for the Shoal lightship. Owing to this mistake she was erroneously headed for the beach. The wind was fresh and the sea very high at the time. She was soon among the breakers, and one of these unwelcome visitors boarded her aft and swept completely over her. Owing to her good steering qualities, the captain was soon able to bring her by, but before she had actually got round to her work a second breaker caught her broadside and carried her off to leeward; before the next one reached her, however, she was "head on" and riding it safely. She was then filled away, and, carrying full lower sails, worked out into deep water. Calling at various places along the coast, she reached Sandy Hook July 1st, 1879, after a cruise of eighteen months in blue water. She then made a cruise to Newport, R. I., and finally returned to New York, where she changed owners and was rechristened ELVIRA. In the following spring she was altered somewhat, having her rig changed to the cutter; a new cabin was added, and everything done to promote comfort.

The cutter rig was adopted for the reason that it dispensed with one of the masts and gave more sail area, when sailing free, and enabled her to stem the tides of the East River and Sound. After cruising on the Sound for one season a quarter ton of lead was added to her keel and two feet more hoist to her mainsail. Forward she was fitted with a single jib, and the forestay sail was dispensed with, but the bowsprit traveler and housing topmast of the cutter rig are still retained. The keel was rounded up forward and aft, giving it the rocker shape, which greatly facilitates her steering. Her ballast, about 1,800 lbs. of iron and 500 lbs. of lead, makes her a powerful and weatherly craft, considering dimensions. She has been put to all kinds of tests, and in a squall, in June,

1880, under short canvas, she was put broad on to the wind with sheets trimmed flat, until half her cabin house was fairly under water and the waves broke over the weather rail. As soon as the sheets were lifted she righted, her sails were furled, and the anchor let go. After drifting some time to leeward the flukes found a holding ground. During this performance she had not taken in a drop of water below.

| | | | |
|---|---|---|---|
| Length over all | 18 ft. | | |
| Length *L W L* | 17 " | 6 in. | |
| Beam extreme | 6 " | 9 " | |
| Depth amidships | 3 " | 2 " | |
| Greatest draft | 2 " | 10 " | |
| Displacement | 1.85 tons | | |
| Lead on keel | 500 lbs. | | |
| Iron inside | 1,500 " | | |
| Freeboard top of rail | 1 ft. | 9 in. | |
| Hoist of mainsail | 12 " | | |
| Bowsprit outboard | 8 " | 6 in. | |
| Area lower sails | 275 sq. ft. | | |
| Length of cabin | 7 ft. | 6 in. | |
| Depth in cabin | 3 " | 6 " | |
| Width cabin floor | 2 " | 3 " | |
| Width of berths | 1 " | 10 " | |

As an example of masthead iron work some working drawings are here produced. They were designed for a new set of caps for a cutter of three tons, measuring 20 ft. load-line, 24 ft. over all, and 7 ft. beam, with 3 ft. 6 in. draft. For yachts of small tonnage many recommend pole masts as the simplest and most reliable plan, providing the pole extends above the hounds for a length sufficient to swing a good sized topsail, and is regularly stayed by wire to the bowsprit end, and a shroud each side with a backstay in addition, if ballooners are a part of the owner's vanity. But the aforesaid three-tonner was of full cutter rig, with housing topmast of imposing loftiness, and it was necessary to abide by her original rig. She had been fouled at her moorings by some lubber, and had the topmast twisted out of her, the spar holding while the caps gave way at the weld, one of them being wrenched half round, like so much molasses candy.

The internal diameters of the caps were not a matter of choice, but had to be fitted to the spars as they were found, the drawings being intended as general guides, subject to such variations as each case may require. The upper cap consists simply of two rings of $\frac{3}{16}$ iron, stayed the proper distance apart, to give a fair lead to the topmast, by braces of the same thickness, one on each side, welded at the ends to the caps. The depth of the latter should be enough to give good bearings on the masthead, and for the topmast enough to prevent a sharp, razing nip when buckled to leeward. A stout eye is securely riveted and welded to the back to take one of the peak blocks. For want of enough taper or shoulders the upper cap was held from working down by a ¼ in. screw each side, the holes giving shift to one another, as shown. The lower cap is somewhat peculiar. In place of dropping solid over the masthead,

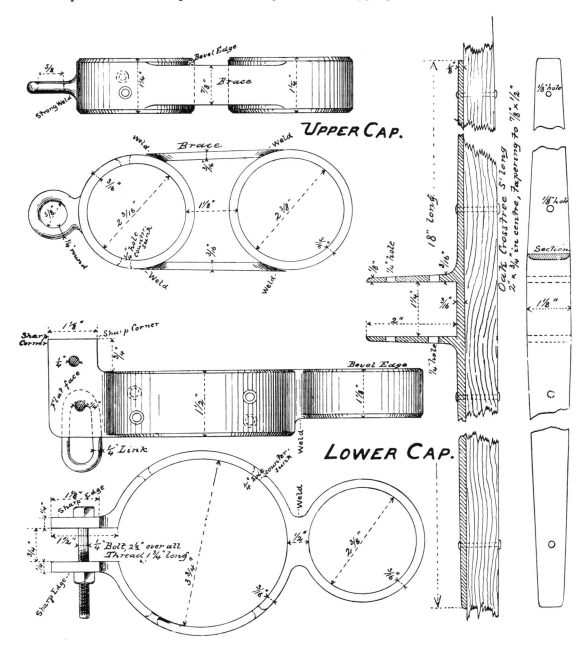

**UPPER CAP.**

**LOWER CAP.**

it had to be slipped over sundry riveted eyebolts for the peak halliards in the masthead, and for that purpose was left open aft and clamped by screws when in place. The hounds or shoulder, on the mast, having been pretty well chafed away, the cap was further secured by four ¼ in. screws. The forward half, for the reception of the topmast heel and fid, was of less depth and secured by a strong weld to the rest. Two horns projected upward ¾ in. on the clamping ends for the accommodation of the crosstrees or spreader. Their object was to lift the crosstrees up clear of the eyes of the rigging, as the oak spreader was cut with jaws in the centre to grasp the mast half way round, for the better securing with extra long wood screws. As a chair or support for the oak spreader a short iron one to go underneath was devised. This was a flat bar, 1⅛ in. wide in the middle, with tapering ends, and 18 in. long over all. Two lugs were "jumped" on this by the blacksmith at a distance of 1¼ in. apart, as shown in the section on the drawings. After the lower cap had been secured, this chair was rested on the horns of the cap, the lugs coming outside the horns and the two ¼ in. bolts passing clear through the horns and lugs. The nuts were then screwed up tight, some thin washers being used between the horns and lugs to make close faying work. This gave a secure foundation 18 in. long, on top of which the oak spreader was held with a couple of ⅛ in. rivets in each arm. The object in devoting more care to the crosstrees than usual was to supply something rigid and perfectly trustworthy, so that a hand up aloft to clear things, for a lookout, or to reeve off gear, would not have life or limb imperiled by a fall from his aerial position through something giving way, and also to keep the crosstrees square at all times. Nothing looks more lubberly to the nautically educated eye than a spreader bent or cockbilled. It should be added that a link was slipped over the lower bolt to take the upper block of the throat. The edges of the caps and iron chair were beveled for neatness and the whole galvanized.

## THE CANOE YAWL

OFTEN it is not desired to go to the expense of a broad or deep yacht of small dimensions, and a good substitute is then sought in moderate beam and draft. This of itself involves a model of specific character, which will partake more or less of a canoe form. Overhang is dispensed with for economy and snugness, and a small rig is sufficient to drive the easy body at her best speed. Although boats of this class have been denominated "canoe yawls," they are not, properly speaking, canoes, for that term denotes a craft which is "paddleable." Strictly, the term "whaleboat yachts" would express the principal features with more distinctness. But their designation as "canoe yawls" having come into general vogue, that title may be retained, in view of the approximation of these small cruisers to canoes in model and arrangement. In type they are closely allied to the sharpie. Given slight deadrise and round to the bilge, the sharpie, with the increased displacement then practicable, develops into the " canoe yawl," as the next step towards yacht-like construction. Very serviceable, cheap yachts these canoe yawls make. The amount of hard work of which they are capable is quite surprising. As sea boats, they have buoyancy and ability in no small degree, and for all-round sailing, except for racing on length measurement against larger and heavier boats, they are not equaled by any other class in proportion to cost and labor in handling. Debarred, through their type, from racing successfully with full fledged yachts under comparison by length, special clubs will no doubt look after the interests of the " canoe yawl " in the

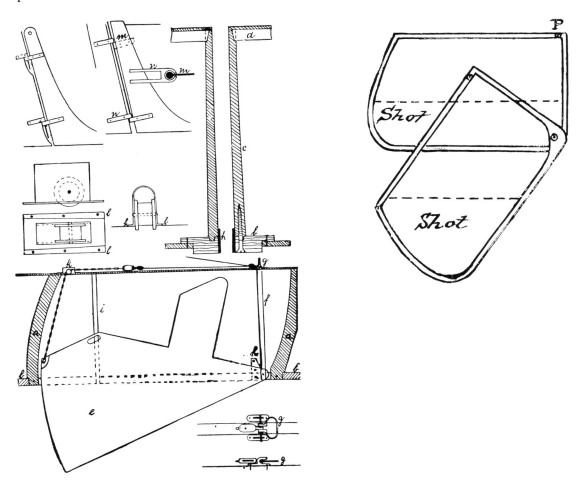

future. To this end some definition of the type needs to be adopted, in which extreme length, beam and depth shall be confined within prescribed limits, in the same way the American Canoe Association has legislated, greatly to the benefit of canoeing interests.

Either centreboard or keel and any kind of rig may be adopted. The centreboard is best of metal, iron or lead, about one-fourth the length of the load-line and placed to balance the sail plan. Usually the pin is well forward, say twenty-five to thirty per cent. of the load-line from stem spars being then stepped to correspond, so that room for stretching in a low berth may be got in the cuddy, though extemporized tents over the cockpit are common. The annexed cuts illustrate a plain swingboard of sheet iron casing filled with shot, which adjusts itself to the lowest position, also a metal board.

The headledges of the latter (*a a*) will be from $\frac{3}{8}$ to $\frac{3}{4}$ in. thick, according to the thickness of the board, and $1\frac{1}{2}$ in. wide, of spruce. They are set into the keel by a jog, as shown in the cut. The sides of the trunk are of well seasoned and clear wood, usually white pine, although mahogany is more durable. A tongue is planed on the lower edge, $\frac{1}{4}$ in. wide and deep, and a corresponding groove is ploughed on each side of the slot. The sides are $\frac{5}{8}$ in. thick on lower edge, for a large board, but may be tapered down to $\frac{3}{8}$ in. at the top, to save unnecessary weight. The sides are tongued on their lower edges, then fastened together, side by side, with a few small brads, and cut to the same shape; then the insides are painted, a strip of brass being first screwed to the inside of each to prevent wear; then they are carefully adjusted, with the headledges in place between them, and a few screws put in temporarily to hold them while riveting. They are then fastened together by copper nails through sides and headledges, about $1\frac{1}{2}$ in. apart, the nails being also riveted over burrs. Two or three pieces of wood, as thick as the headledges, are laid in the trunk to prevent it or the keel from coming together in planking, and are not removed until the boat is finished, or the trunk may close slightly. The grooves in the keel are painted with thick white lead, the trunk is driven down into place and clamped fast, rivets are put through the keel and each headledge, then the holes are bored for the screws. These latter are of brass, $\frac{3}{16}$ to $\frac{1}{4}$ in. diameter and $3\frac{1}{2}$ in. long. The holes are bored full depth with a small bit, then a larger one is run in for a distance equal to the shank of the screw, the latter is screwed firmly in and filed smooth.

Trunks are sometimes made of galvanized iron, but are liable to rust and are not as good as wood. If the sides of the trunk are thick enough, holes are sometimes bored through them from top to bottom and bolts driven down through the keel, preventing them from splitting. In canoe yawls the trunks are usually open on deck, so that the boards may be lifted out.

The heavy boards are usually of plate iron galvanized, and are from $\frac{1}{8}$ to $\frac{1}{2}$ in. thick, the latter weighing 60 pounds. A square board, as is usual in sailboats, would be too topheavy, to avoid which that portion of the board within the case is cut away until only an arm, sufficient to steady the board in the case, is left. The board is first cut to shape out of boiler plate of the required thickness, then it is filed smooth at all corners and angles and reduced to a thickness of $\frac{3}{16}$ in. at the upper after corner where the lifting gear is fastened, and at the lower forward corner where the pin hole is. Next the board is galvanized and then it is ready for the fittings. Sometimes cast iron is used, but it is liable to break.   Muntz metal has also been brought into requisition, but is more expensive.

If the board be fixed in the canoe a brass bolt is put through it and the trunk, on which it turns, but the usual plan is to fit the board to lift out.   The board is hung from a brass rod, or between two brass strips (*ff*), as described for the small board, the top having a handle (*g*) and also a catch to prevent the lifting rod from pulling forward at *h*.   A rivet is also put through the keel to retain the lower end of the rod.   If the board does not weigh over thirty pounds it is raised and lowered by a single pennant of manilla, bent to a shackle or through a hole in the after end of the board and lead through a pulley on deck.

For a heavier board a purchase must be used, a chain made of flat links side by side is fastened to the centreboard by two large links, a rubber ball is then slipped on to the chain to act as a buffer, and a single brass block is lashed to the end of the chain.   The deck pulley (**K**), over which the chain runs, has a sheave with a square groove to take the chain, and is also fitted so as to slide into place on deck, or be readily removed, without taking it off the chain.   A brass block is also lashed to the lifting rod at deck, and the line is rove by making one end fast to the tail of this block, leading through the other block, on the chain, and back through the first block, thence to a cleat.   By taking hold of the chain near the pulley with one hand, and of the lifting handle with the other, the pulley may be disengaged and the board readily lifted out.

Rudders of canoe yawls are hung by common pintles and gudgeons, or by a pin passing through braces, as at *m* in the cut.

As keels, these boats perform very satisfactorily, and with outside iron or lead become practically uncapsizable.   The midship section is much like that of the ELVIRA, but with less rise of floor.   Indeed, the ELVIRA, in type, may be considered a large and rather beamy exemplification of the canoe yawl.   To the same family belong the whale boats, the famous old-time galleys of the Vikings, many life-saving boats, surf boats, the Block Island fishing craft, the Chesapeake Buckeye, the pinkey, and the numerous tribe of double-enders, having about one-fourth their length for beam, long, flat floor with slight deadrise, live sheer, good freeboard, a fair amount of depth, displacement and draft in relation to beam. The water-lines show little or no hollow, being of long, easy spindle form, with the greatest width held at midships or a trifle forward, and with long, flat bow and buttock lines in consequence.

Still another light in which the canoe yawl may be viewed, is that of a cutter, with some of her depth and displacement cut off.   What is lost in ability is made up in the considerations of smaller first cost, less labor and expense in maintenance. and light draft, which, in a very small yacht, are often rightly counted of more moment than the ability and headroom provided in the full cutter model, or the greater speed of the regular catboat on the wind in smooth water and moderate breeze, purchased at the sacrifice of economy, with scarce any other accompanying advantage to cruising adaptability.

The service to which the canoe yawl can be put is almost without limit.

Some idea of her wide range of utility may be gathered from a charming little volume, "Cruising in Small Yachts," written by Mr. H. Fiennes Speed. One of the small craft, skippered in the Thames reaches and about Solent waters, was of the following dimensions: Length, 16 ft; 4 ft. 1½ in. beam; 20 in. deep amidships, with 6¼ in. of keel, containing 3 cwt. of lead. Inside she carried 1 cwt. 10 lbs. of lead. The sail area was 180 ft. mainsail and mizzen, lugs, with jib, the dimensions of spars being:

| | |
|---|---|
| Mainmast . . . . . . . . . . . . . . . . . . . . . . . . . . . . . . . . . . . . | 13 ft. 1 in. |
| Main boom for lug sail . . . . . . . . . . . . . . . . . . . . . . . . . | 10 " 4 " |
| Main yard for lug sail . . . . . . . . . . . . . . . . . . . . . . . . . . | 12 " 6 " |
| Main boom for gaff mainsail . . . . . . . . . . . . . . . . . . . | 8 " 5 " |
| Main gaff for gaff mainsail . . . . . . . . . . . . . . . . . . . . | 8 " 6 " |
| Mizzen mast . . . . . . . . . . . . . . . . . . . . . . . . . . . . . . . | 8 " |
| Mizzen boom . . . . . . . . . . . . . . . . . . . . . . . . . . . . . . . | 6 " 4 in. |
| Mizzen yard . . . . . . . . . . . . . . . . . . . . . . . . . . . . . . . . . | 7 " 4 " |
| Mizzen boomkin, outboard . . . . . . . . . . . . . . . . . . . . | 2 " 6 " |
| Bowsprit outboard . . . . . . . . . . . . . . . . . . . . . . . . . . . | 5 " 9 " |
| Spinnaker boom . . . . . . . . . . . . . . . . . . . . . . . . . . . . . | 10 " 6 " |

Tonnage, "one ton and an awful fraction."

Her well was 5 ft. 6 in. long, and 2 ft. 6 in. wide, with a locker aft for stores, open lockers along the side, and two shifting thwarts, steering with a half yoke on the rudder, and a rod hinged thereto, the motion, of course, being fore and aft. The well was covered completely by a tent.

She was built by McWhirter, of Erith, to her owner's specifications, which, as he gives them, called for " a jolly big canoe; one that will take two people, and sail, and row with a pair of sculls, and look after herself a bit, and one that I can sleep in with a low tent, and move about in without looking in the glass first to see if my hair is parted in the middle." In her, two vacations were pleasantly passed, knocking about, before she gave place to a similar but larger boat, the VIPER.

The VIPER, also from Mr. McWhirter's shop, was built in 1881, for a cruise on the Zuyder Zee. Her sheer plan and rig are shown in the drawing. Her length is 20 ft., beam, 5 ft. 5 in., depth to gunwale amidships, 2 ft. 6 in. Deck has a crown of 5 in., and is of light wood, covered with canvas. Her keel has 19 cwt. 2 qrs. 19 lbs. of lead, with 2 cwt. 1 qr. 18 lbs. inside, and an iron keelson of 75 lbs. The depth of keel is 1 ft. 9 in., and the total depth 3 ft. 4 in. Her cruises were in the Thames and along the south coast of England.

A somewhat smaller boat, on the plan of the Mersey canoes, answers to the following : Length, 17 ft. ; beam, 4 ft. 6 in. ; depth, 2 ft. Oars are used, as the beam is too great to admit of paddling. The deck and well is similar to

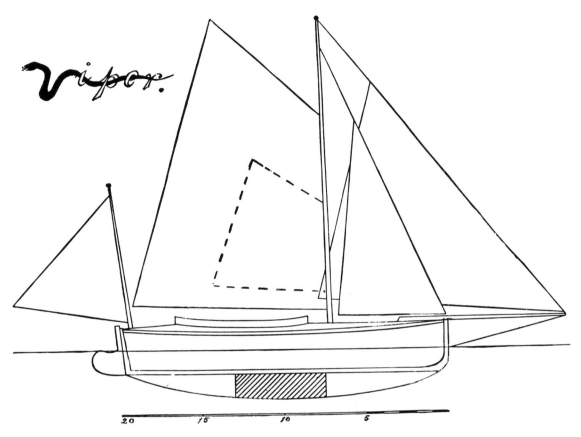

a canoe. Lead ballast is stored under the floors. The rig consists of two lugs, main and mizzen, the dimensions being:

|  | Racing Mainsail Ft. In. | Cruising Mainsail Ft. In. | Mizzen Ft. In. |
|---|---|---|---|
| Foot | 10.00 | 6.06 | 4.06 |
| Head | 10.00 | 7.06 | 2.06 |
| Luff | 5.00 | 2.06 | 2.04 |
| Leech | 14.06 | 10.00 | 6.00 |
| Tack to peak | 14.08 | 9.00 | 5.09 |
| Clew to throat | 10 09 | 7.00 | 4.09 |

As there is no centreboard, the interior of the well is entirely unobstructed, and there is room for three persons, though on a cruise two, with the necessary stores and baggage, would be enough. Berths for two might easily be made up on the wide, flat floor, a tent being pitched over the well, while the thwarts may be removed entirely at night. Under the fore and after decks is ample room for stowage. The steering is done with a deck tiller, as in a canoe.

Stem, sternpost and keel of oak, or the former of hackmatack, sided 1½ in.; keelson of oak, 3 x ½ in.; plank of cedar, 5-16 or ⅜ in. lapstreak; gunwale of oak or mahogany; deck of ⅜ in. pine, covered with 6 to 8 oz. drill laid in paint; coamings of oak, ⅜ in. thick. The ribs, ⅜ x ⅝, spaced 9 in., with floors at every alternate frame.

The sails are rigged as "standing lugs," or a yawl rig similar to the VIPER may be carried. The sails will be of 6 oz. drill, double bighted; rigging of "small 6-thread" manilla; blocks of wood, iron or brass.

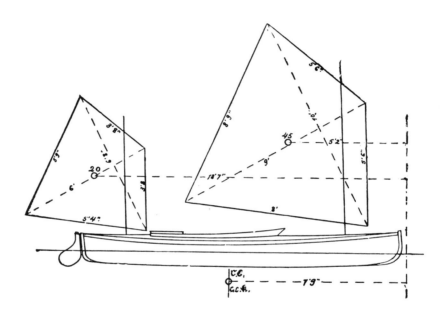

## THE BALANCE LUG RIG

The "standing lug" is similar to the balance. The boom, however, clutches the mast with jaws or has regular goose neck and does not project forward of the mast. The luff runs from the yard above to the jaws of the boom.

Subdivision of sail in the canoe yawl need not detract from speed. It is easy to supply an extra allowance in the total area to make up for deficiency of the yawl or double lug in light winds. These boats, feeling their canvas so much more readily than others of greater beam or displacement, demand changes quicker and oftener to suit varying strength of wind—hence the arrangement in several pieces, which is almost universal. It is also impracticable to travel much about decks for making more sail and reducing, so that rigs under control from the cockpit are preferred. In light weather and reaching, balloon jibs and mizzens of any size help out the speed. The weight of spars aloft, quite an item in small bodies on the length, is reduced, and stiffness and dryness in a chop promoted. Subdivision is justified in the canoe yawl for precisely the same reasons which persuade the builders of sharpies to stick to two leg-of-muttons and jib for racing, rather than copy the heavy stick and single mainsail of the catboat.

When the yawl is deemed too much of a heavy weather rig, the "standing cutter" may take its place. With outer jib stowed or in off the bowsprit,

## THE TYPHIS
### REEFED BALANCE LUG AND BATSWING

and the mainsail close reefed, a very snug reduction is secured. In the worst of weather, the forestaysail may be resorted to. This rig was adopted in the TOMBOY, of Boston, the first regular canoe yawl of modern pattern in American waters, built in 1884 by George Lawley & Son for Mr. Edw. Burgess.

### DIMENSIONS OF TOMBOY

| | | | |
|---|---|---|---|
| Length over all | 18 ft. | | |
| Length on water-line | 17 " | 8 | in. |
| Beam moulded | 4 " | 10½ | " |
| Beam at water-line | 4 " | 8½ | " |
| Least freeboard | | 11 | " |
| Depth at side, amidships | 2 " | 5 | " |
| Deadrise to floor, ditto | 5 in. to 1 ft. | | |
| Sheer forward | 1 ft. | | |
| Sheer aft | 8 in. | | |
| Greatest draft to rabbet | 1 ft. 5 in. | | |
| Draft with keel | 2 " | 2 | " |
| Ballast on keel | 800 lbs | | |
| Area lower sail | 200 sq. ft. | | |

She is smooth built, of ¾ in. plank, with oak timbers ¾ in. square and spaced 6 in., and topstreak and deck of teak, the latter ⅜ in. thick. The coaming is of ½ in. elm, with bulkheads of teak, 5 ft. from either end. The

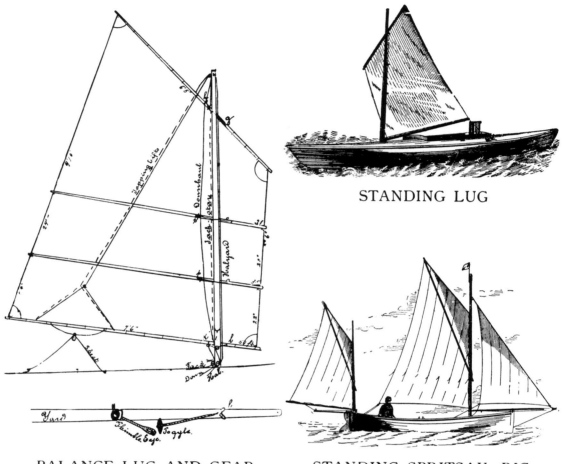

STANDING LUG

BALANCE LUG AND GEAR          STANDING SPRITSAIL RIG.

stem and stern are sided 1½ in., keel sided 3½ in., with 4½ cwt. of lead under it, 4½ cwt. being also cast to fit inside. The draft is 2 ft. 2 in.

The TOMBOY has bulkheads across the ends making her a life boat.


## COMBINATION ROW AND SAIL BOATS

ALTHOUGH the canoe yawl can be propelled by oars to reach an anchorage, she is too heavily ballasted to pull any distance as a regular practice. A lighter boat must take her place. Though a sailing craft, in which sailing is sacrificed to the requisites of rowing, is no longer a yacht within strict meaning, the excellence under sail attained in recent productions places them on a level with snugly rigged catboats and justifies their mention under a special heading.

Yachts of Special Class

framing, holds the tabernacle firmly, and prevents any straining of the boat. The forward side of the tabernacle is closed from the step up to within 8 in. of the deck, so that the mast will not slip forward when being stepped. The heel is slipped into the tabernacle, the mast raised up, falling into the step, and a brass catch, pivoted at one end, is thrown across the after side at deck and fastened with a turn of the thumb nut shown. The sail is a balance lug, fitted with one batten : Foot, 13 ft. ; head, 9 ft. 6 in. ; luff, 6 ft. ; leech, 14 ft. 6 in. ; tack to peak, 15 ft. ; clew to throat, 13 ft. 3 in. ; batten above boom, 2 ft. 9 in. on luff, 3 ft. on leech ; mast at deck, 3 in. ; at head, 1⅛ in. ; mast, heel to truck, 13 ft. 8 in.

### TABLE OF BREADTHS AND DEPTHS

| | STATIONS | 0 | 1 | 2 | 3 | 4 | 5 | 6 | 7 | 8 | 9 | 10 | 11 | 12 | 13 |
|---|---|---|---|---|---|---|---|---|---|---|---|---|---|---|---|
| **Depths** | Gunwale to Load Water Line | 20 | 18¼ | 16⅜ | 14⅞ | 13¾ | 12¾ | 12¼ | 12 | 12 | 12⅜ | 12⅞ | 13¾ | 14¾ | 16 |
| | Load Water line to Rabbet | .... | 3½ | 7¾ | Straight from No. 3 to No. 8. | | | | | | 9 | 8½ | 7½ | 4¾ | .... |
| | Load Water Line to bottom of Keel | .... | 7½ | 8⅜ | Straight from No. 3 to No. 12. | | | | | | | | | | 10 |
| **Half Breadths** | At Deck | .... | 6¾ | 12½ | 17⅛ | 20⅜ | 22¾ | 23¾ | 24 | 23⅝ | 22¾ | 21½ | 19⅝ | 17⅜ | 15 |
| | Load Water Line | .... | 3 | 7½ | 12½ | 16⅞ | 20 | 21⅝ | 22¼ | 21⅞ | 20 | 17¼ | 16⅛ | 9¾ | 2⅛ |
| | No. 2 W. L. | .... | 1¾ | 5⅛ | 9⅜ | 13½ | 16¾ | 17⅞ | 19½ | 19 | 16⅞ | 13⅛ | 7⅜ | 2⅛ | .... |
| | No. 1 W. L. | .... | .... | 2¼ | 4½ | 7 | 9½ | 11½ | 12 | 11⅝ | 9⅜ | 5½ | 2½ | .... | .... |

The mast is square in the tabernacle, above which it is round. The head of the sail is cut with a round of 9 in., the yard being bent to fit it. The sail is hoisted by a halliard running through a strap on the yard just aft the mast, and hooking into a similar strap forward of the mast. Below it is led through a brass snatch block on the heel of the mast, and aft to a cleat on the trunk, within reach of the helmsman. The tack is spliced to the boom just forward of mast, leads through a bull's-eye lashed to boom abaft the mast, and down to a cleat on the after side of the mast. The sail may be easily unbent from the mast and stowed, for rowing, which cannot be done with a boom and gaff sail. The stem, stern and keel are of white oak, the former two sided 1¼ in., the latter sided 4 in. outside and moulded 1 in. The planking is of white cedar, lapstreak, 5-16 in. thick, the upper streak being of ⅜ in. mahogany. The ribs are ⅜ x ½ in., spaced 9 in., being jogged down to the plank and copper riveted ; the throats are of ¾ in. mahogany; rudder 15 in. wide, of 1 in. mahogany, fitted with tiller and yoke. The gunwales, of oak, are

1 × 1⅛ in. at midships and 1 × ¾ in. at ends. The sides of the trunk, which is covered on top, are of dry white pine, 1⅛ in. at bottom and ¾ in. at top. They are set flat on the keel, a strip of Canton flannel, well painted, being laid between, and fastened with 3¼ in. brass screws from outside of keel. The ballast is of gravel, in 30 lb. canvas bags.

Another combination boat of very graceful appearance and excellent qualities is the yawl original to the Alster, a fresh-water lake near Hamburg, Germany, where boat sailing is carried on with a good deal of spirit. The lines of the LELLY, recently built by H. Heidtmann for Mr. F. Kirsten, are given in Plate LXXXVII. She will carry about 300 lbs. ballast, and is usually sailed single-handed in the local races. The rig is a standing lug, but by shifting the mast to after side of thwart, a jib can be used in connection with a bowsprit, the heel of which hooks to a band on the mast and fits down over the stemhead. The Alster yawl has become the ruling type of small sailboat all over Germany. One hand can step or unship the mast, make sail, reef **or** row.

# THE HEATHEN CHINEE

## *PLATE LXXXIII*

### TWENTY-FIVE FEET LONG ON WATER-LINE

THIS boat was designed in 1877 by Mr. Landseer MacKenzie, and built by McWhirter, of Erith on the Thames, England. She is intended for river sailing, being in point of type a step nearer the regular yacht than the canoe yawl. As a racer, and stiff, handy cruising boat, she has met with considerable success. The Chinese batten lugs are very effective in a small boat, especially on a wind in light weather. All heavy tophamper is dispensed with to correspond with the character of the hull. These sails are reefed from the cockpit by hauling down the battens with lines rove off for the purpose, so that tying reef points is dispensed with. There are two centreboards, which permit perfect trim with any variety of sail plan.

| | |
|---|---|
| Length over all | 27 ft. |
| Length on water-line | 25 " |
| Beam extreme | 6 " |
| Draft | 2 " 8 in. |
| Area midship section | 8.4 sq. ft. |
| Displacement | 3 tons |

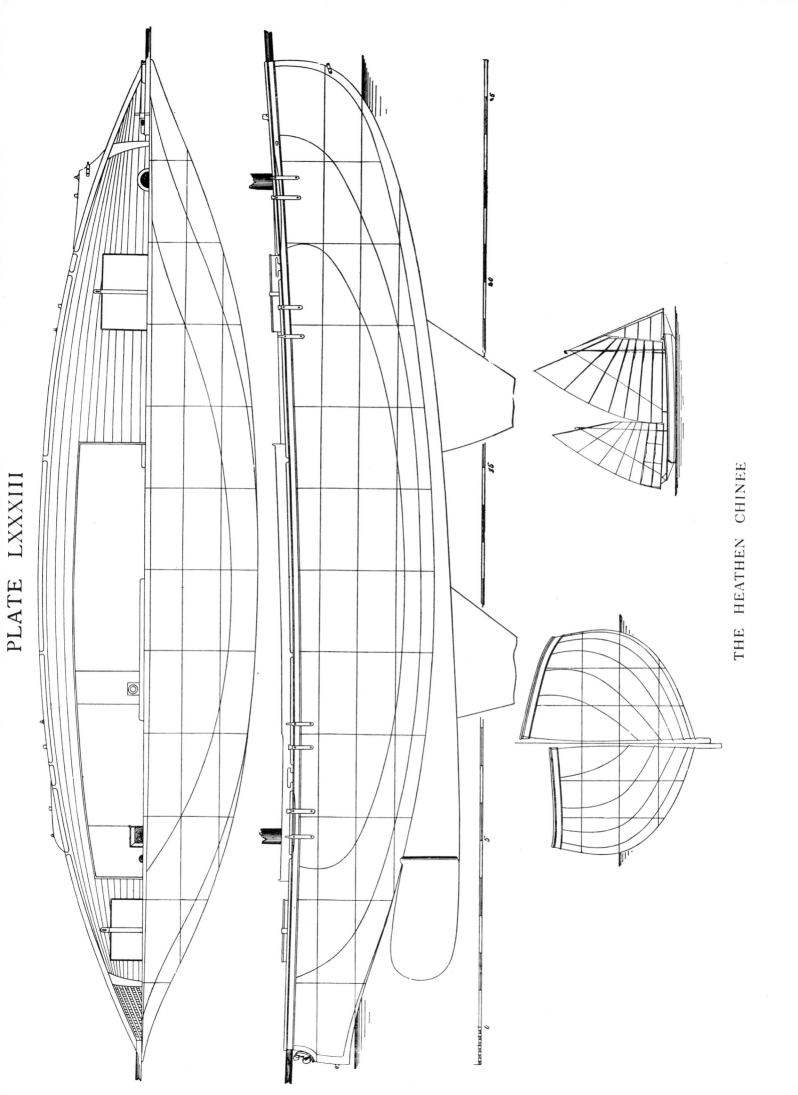

PLATE LXXXIII

THE HEATHEN CHINEE

| | |
|---|---|
| Total ballast | 1,500 lbs. |
| Ballast on keel | 900 " |
| *M S* from end *L W L* | 12 ft. 9 in. |
| Centre of buoyancy from end of *L W L* | 12 " 6 " |
| Centre of lateral resistance from end of *L W L* | 13 " |
| Area both centreboards | 10 sq. ft. |
| Area of sails | 500 " " |

## THE CHESAPEAKE FLATTIE

### *PLATE LXXXIV*

A FLAT-BOTTOM boat known as the "flattie" is in extensive use in Southern waters for carrying loads of produce down shoal creeks to market, and oysters from the flats and bars. This style of craft is easily and cheaply put up, and makes an excellent sporting boat of very light draft, capable of taking the ground without inconvenience. On a large scale the flattie develops into a scow schooner, adapted to carrying cordwood or other

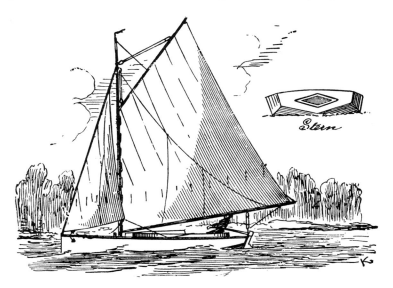

HAMPTON FLATTIE

deck loads. In Pamlico Sound similar craft are used for trawling over flats after terrapin and for clamming in the shoal water of the banks separating the Sound from the ocean. Although not of much account beating to windward in lumpy water, a flattie of good form is not otherwise a dull sailer. She will not compete with a regular yacht, because very snugly rigged, but moderate

PLATE LXXXIV

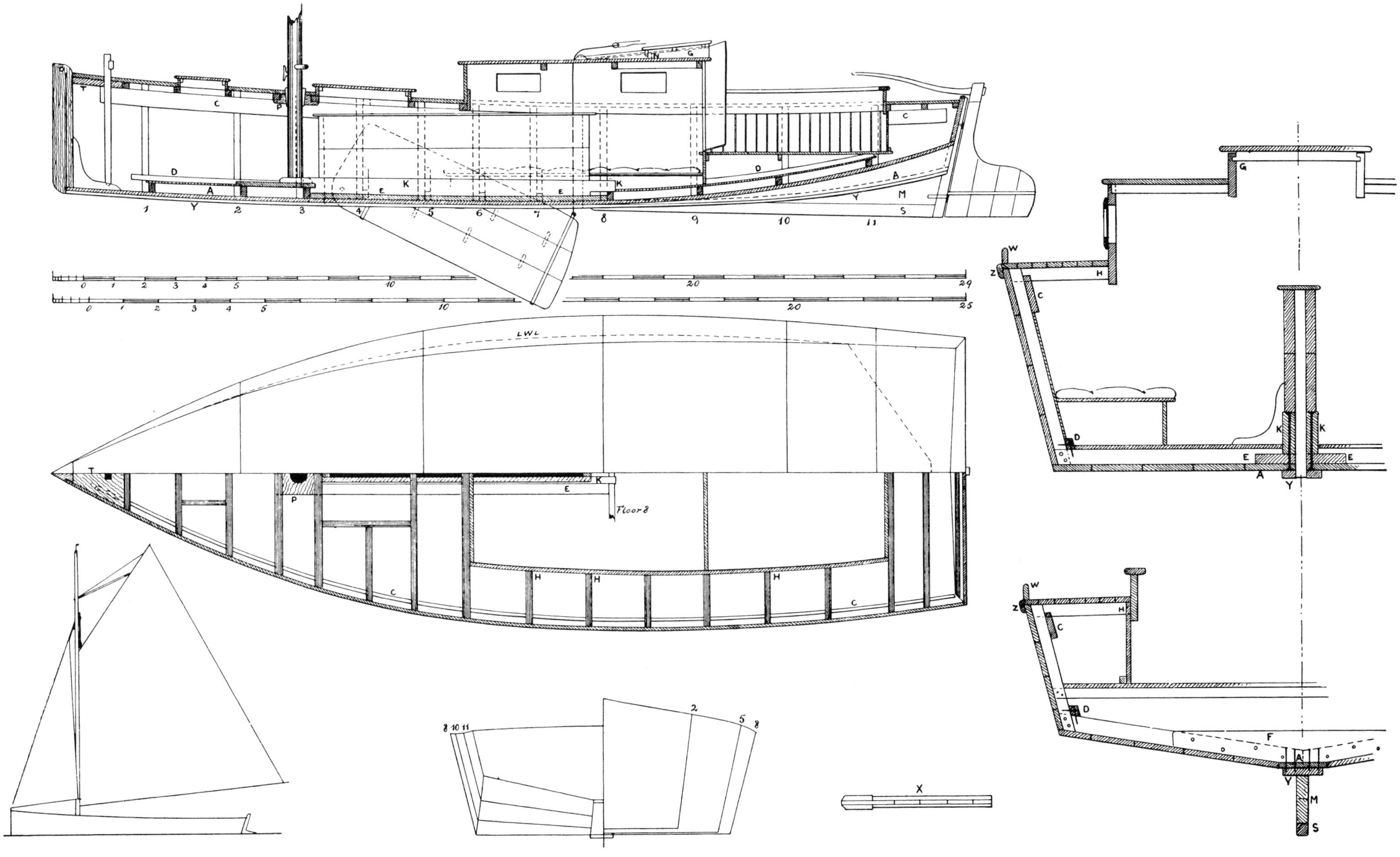

CHESAPEAKE FLATTIE

canvas, beam, high side and flat floor make the flattie a safe boat, which is of more importance for sporting purposes than a high rate of speed. There is not much headroom in a 30 ft. flattie, except under the house, but plenty of room for stowage of decoys and hunting traps of all sorts.

In general she may be described as a beamy sharpie. The bottom has but little camber fore and aft, and the run is helped out by some rise to the floors. With the aid of the plan on Plate LXXXIV any one handy with simple tools can put a keelless flattie together in the following manner:

On the building stocks the keel plank, *A*, is sprung to shape by blocks underneath and shores from overhead. This plank may be 10 to 12 in. wide in wake of centreboard and taper a little toward the ends, although an even width may be preserved fore and aft. The frames 1, 2, 3, 4, etc., are got out by sawing scantling to the requisite lengths obtained from the body plan and uniting their heels to the floors, giving the frames their respective flare, stay-lathing them as necessary. Each frame is then set up in its place across the keel plank and then nailed down. In the run, floors 9 and 10 can be cut out of plank deep enough to allow for the rise on each side. Frame 11 will have the floor in two pieces, the heels nailed to the keel plank and connected by a deep floor plank, *F*, as shown in the diagram. The clamp, *C*, is run round near the heads of the frames, and a piece of scantling, *D*, along the corners of floors and frames as a further tie between them. The sides are then planked up, after putting in enough beams to secure rigidity to the frame. If not too large, the boat can be turned bottom up and the bottom plank nailed on in fore and aft lengths, the inner plank being brought up to the edge of the keel plank to permit tight caulking. The counter has also in the meantime been shut in with cross plank. The rest of the deck framing is then finished, the hatches, house and cockpit built and the deck laid, all of which will be understood from the diagrams. Beams are notched down into the clamp and spiked to it, also nailed through the plank from outside. No fore and aft carlins are needed for house and cockpit, the thick coaming being itself sufficient to support the inner ends of the half beams, *H H*, by nailing. The house can be built up upon the coaming in one or more depths nailed down, or vertical staving can be nailed outside the coaming. The deadwood aft is composed of a filling piece, *M*, nailed up to the keel plank, and a shoe piece, *S*, underneath, with a post aft, the rudder being hung to the latter. For additional stiffness a flooring is laid fore and aft inside. Around the gunwale a chafing batten, *Z*, is nailed, and a low waist, *W*, along the sheer. The deck is laid fore and aft, the outer plank or planksheer being, however, sprung to the shape of the side.

A stout piece of plank crossing two floors, and a block of wood, make the mast step. The partners, *P*, consist of a block let up between the beams.

Forward a solid triangular piece of wood, *T*, fills the eyes of the boat abaft the stem. It serves as a breast hook, and has the bitts or sampson posts down through it. A knee ties the heel of the stem to the bottom plank. This stem is, of course, rabbeted to receive the hood ends of the side plank, as shown in the half breadth plan. The hatch coamings are simply nailed down to the beams. The covers are held in their place by their own cross framing. The companion slide travels in a groove taken out of the coamings, as at *G* in the cross section. A lip under forward end of the slide brings up against a ledge, *N*, nailed down to the cabin top between the slide coamings, when the slide is closed. A clasp from side over the door and padlock secure the entrance, the door being first bolted on the inside by reaching over. The rudder can be nailed up of three thicknesses to avoid bolting according to diagram *X*, or else spiked together out of narrow pieces and strapped by an iron band. To protect the bottom upon grounding, a chafing plank should be nailed on underneath the bottom plank, as *Y*. If carried up to the counter as a strengthening to the keel plank, it must be put on before the dead wood is added.

The centreboard trunk is built as follows: A stout plank, *E*, is nailed to the bottom inside over the slot previously cut. This plank reaches between frames 3 and 8; on top of this fit two fore and aft logs, *K*, jogging the ends over floors 3 and 8 upon which they should also rest. Bolt down through the bottom plank with ¼ or ⅜ iron to tie all together. These logs are intended to tranfer the weight and thrust of the trunk to the whole cross floors of frames 3 and 8, otherwise the weight would fall upon the bisected floors of frames 4, 5, 6 and 7, which are without support in the wake of the slot, other than that derived from the bottom plank. Insert the headposts of the trunk between the logs, *K*, and plank up the sides. The split floors will be supported if jogged over the stout plank, and may also have a knee up the sides of the trunk. It is important that the trunk and boat's bottom be rigid to avoid troublesome leaking.

The centreboard is dowelled together and strapped with light iron at each end. The pin is an ordinary bolt, which should be driven a tight fit to prevent leaking. The pennant for hoisting passes up through the cabin roof, over a half round block of wood, and has a single sheave strapped in the end. A whip is rove through this sheave, one end being fast to the cabin top and the hauling part belaying to a cleat on the after end of the cabin within handy reach. The interior of the cabin can be lightly ceiled over and supplied with transoms and lockers to suit. A drawer under the cockpit will serve as ice chest, and water may be carried in a breaker or small barrel on deck.

The diagrams have scales for 30 and 26 ft. boats, over all length. The cross sections are on double scale. Scantling for a 30 ft. flattie about as follows:

Stem, 6 in. sided; keelplank, 10 × 1½ in.; frames, 2¼ × 2½; floors, 3 × 2¾; clamps, 6 × 1¼ in.; corner tie, 2 in. square; deck frame, 2¼ × 2½; bottom plank, 1¼; side plank, 1¼; deck stuff, 3 or 4 × 1 in.; inside flooring, ¾ in. thick; centreboard bed plank, 8 × 1¾ in. each side of slot; trunk logs, 8 × 1½ in.; siding of trunk, 2 in.; head posts, 3 ft × 2 in.; chafing plank on bottom, 8 × 1½ in.; deadwood, 2 to 3 in. thick; coaming of house, 1¼ in. thick; mast, 5 in. at partners; sails, 10-oz. duck. Caulk with cotton and putty, or pitch the seams. Ballast with stone as required.

It is customary in working boats to bring the tack of the jib to the stem head, but a short bowsprit can be spiked down to the deck, affording more headsail for cruising purposes. By the exercise of some taste, it is possible to model quite a handsome and fairly smart boat on the foregoing ideas. A slight hollow may be introduced in the bow frames and a round to the quarters without resorting to other than straight-grained stuff. The chief point is to give the model good clearance, as dragging water aft is very detrimental to speed. The body plan can be got by squaring across the model block at frame stations, and deducting thickness of plank for getting out the frames. The cost of a flattie should be less than half that of a round-bottom yacht, according to finish of detail.

# XII

# GENERAL INFORMATION

## YACHTS' BOATS

THE skiff, as a tender to small yachts, is in common use. In build, they are generally unnecessarily heavy, and their model admits of great improvement. Their construction will be understood from the chapter on boat building. When built of cedar, lightly kneed, with plenty of flare to the sides, rake to transom and slight hollow forward, a skiff will make a presentable appearance, and be a buoyant, stiff carrier, costing but a few dollars and two days' time to produce. They should be copper riveted, as nailing demands thick sides and heavy construction. Canoe and shell-boat builders are the persons to get out a boat which shall be light and strong. The usual carpenter job is a clumsy affair.

The average round bilged yacht's boat is a cranky affair, distinguished for lacking in the very qualities most to be expected. Real worth, adaptability to purpose, the yacht's boat of the present has next to none at all. She is narrow, high bilged, with much deadrise, great sheer, low waist and small carrying capacity. She pulls easy and fast, but neither is wanted, and should be kept secondary in scheming out her form. As a consequence, most tenders are dangerously tippy, easily swamped, can stow very little, and as life-boats to escape from the yacht, to effect a rescue, or to assist some one in distress, they are of no account.

The first thing an ideal yawl boat should possess is stiffness and dryness. To this end she must be wide, have long, flat floor, small draft and little weight, and above all be high in side, amidships quite as well as in the ends. She must be well put together, of light stuff, accurately fitted, clench fastened with copper throughout. Her stern must be kept broad to carry the bearings well aft. She must be fuller in form than usual. Finally, if possible, air chambers and various minor provisions of a life-boat should be added in her construction. The next thing to be sought is good carrying capacity. A tender is used for the conveyance back and forth of skipper and guests, often also for carrying ice and stores and water, sails and gear, and room and buoyancy are therefore more essential than a fancy mould for speed. In short, service, and not speed, should be the dominating consideration. A small iron centreboard is always a useful appendage, and if placed well forward partly under one of the thwarts, will not be in the way, and often contribute to boxing about harbors, or save labor when anchored a distance off.

For very small yachts an additional feature must receive attention. To tow a yawl boat is tedious and damaging to property. Hence a form must be adopted which can readily be stowed on deck without sacrificing stiffness and good service. This is no easy thing. One of the accompanying plans is a cross between the canoe and " sneakbox," the object being to obtain something narrow enough to fit into the yacht's gangway, ready for use at all times, and also stiff and safe. The features of this boat are a " shovel nose " to facilitate towing, when preferred, rather small beam, well held fore and aft, long, flat floor, quick bilge and high side, with a light deck and coaming, canoe fashion. The shape of the moulds at three cross sections are shown by the dotted lines. She is 9 ft. long, 2½ ft. wide, 1 ft. deep in centre, with a sheer of 2 in., and supplied with an iron centreboard and triangular sail 7 ft. on foot, head and leech. The board is of ¼ in. boiler iron, with 1 ft. vertical drop. The sail is set upon a short stump pole after the plan of the Lord Ross lateen for canoes.

A boat of the ordinary style, but extremely serviceable, is also illustrated with two diagrams. From these it will be seen she possesses great width, with long, flat floor and high sides, tumbling home at the stern and along the side. This

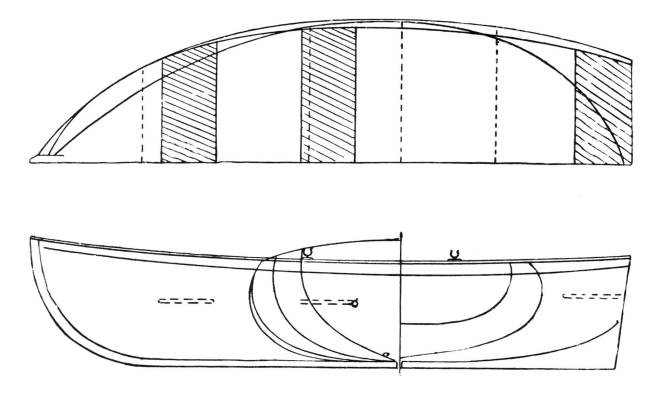

tender belongs to the three-ton cutter, TEAL, and is remarkable for the load she carries and for her stiffness, which makes her a more reliable and useful adjunct than many dingeys twice the length. She is only 6 ft. 6 in. long over all, with an extreme beam of 3 ft. 1½ in. Her fault is towing heavily when sailing fast, and the difficulty of stowing on deck on account of her width. But, on the whole, she is much nearer what a tender ought to be than the imitations of the Whitehall boat.

Skiff building is an art that has received too little attention. Anything is considered good enough for a skiff, yet for small yachts the skiff is better adapted than a round-bottomed yawl. Stiffness, buoyancy, lightness, roominess and low cost are all in favor of the skiff. A simple and commendable method of construction is shown in Plate LXXXV. The shape of the boat will be understood from the Body Plan which is to outside of plank. The frames can be got by deducting the thickness of sides and bottom from the sections of the Body Plan. Or they can be got by taking the inside width across bottom and top on the Half Breadth Plan.

The example in question measures 8 ft. 6 in. over all, 3 ft. beam across the top and 2 ft. 4 in. across the bottom. The depth amidships is 11 in.; at stem, 15 in. The sternboard or transom is 2 ft. 6 in. across top, 2 ft. across bottom and 11 in. wide, including the crown. She will carry two hands on a draft of 5 in. To put up the boat proceed as follows: Get from the mill one ¾ in. board of white pine, 18 ft. long. Have it run through a planer to ⅝ in. A similar board 14 to 16 in. wide for the siding, and some ¾ in. oak for stern, cleats and frames. Also a piece of 3½ in. oak or hackmatack for the stem. Saw the bottom board across in half. Lay the two pieces on the floor alongside one another, and with chalk sketch out the shape of the bottom and trim off to the line. Lay the two pieces on the building stocks. Hold them there by a strut from the shop beam above and block up the ends of the boat's bottom to the required camber. Get out the stem with rabbet and screw it in place. Cut out the cross floors of 1 × 3 in. stuff and slot their ends to receive the heel tenon of the timbers. Cut the latter out of straight-grained stuff to the shape of a stout knee, as shown in the diagrams, leaving a tenon projecting. Drive the tenons into the slots of the cross floors and pin them with a round nail. Also screw the heels down to the floors. When the four sets of frames have thus been put together, with the proper flare, place them in position on the bottom boards and screw them fast from underneath. Bevel off the frames with a spokeshave to receive the side plank. Put the latter in place temporarily, holding it to the frames and stem by clamps. Mark off proper shape of the sheer and the rocker of the bottom, and trim off to those lines. Remember that the sides overlap the bottom, as shown in the cross section of the boat. The bottom boards must therefore be bevelled

PLATE LXXXV

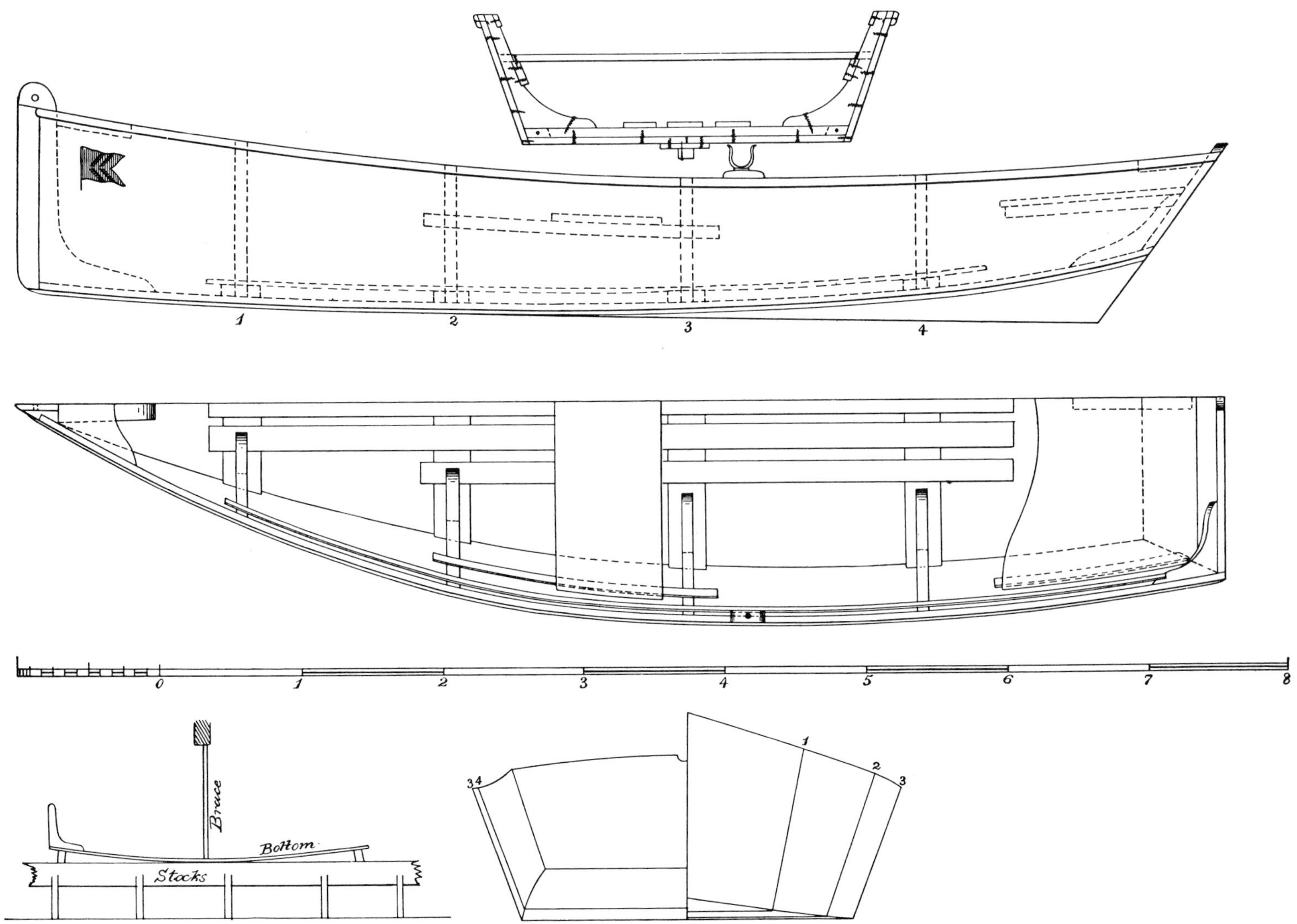

BODY TO OUTSIDE OF PLANKING

YACHT'S SKIFF

Brace

Stocks

Bottom

around the edges with a plane to suit. Screw the side boards in place to the stem, the frames and along the bottom, spacing the small brass screws about 2¼ in. apart, so as to make a watertight job. Cut out the stern board and screw it in aft between the sides and on top of the bottom boards, and also knee it to the sides at the sheer. Fit an oak breasthook in the eyes forward. The boat is now ready for the fittings. Run a light inwale around the heads of the frames to stiffen the gunwale, and nail a chafing batten round outside at sheer height. Screw cleats to the frames and side to receive the thwarts, which, when screwed down, serve to tie the boat together. Fit a centre knee to the transom and lay some foot boards across the floors. Also screw down a suitable oak block bored for the swivel rowlocks. Now turn the whole boat over and screw a strip of oak, 3 × ½ in., fore and aft over the centre seam of the bottom, and nail on what skag you wish aft over that. Bore the stem head for a painter and putty where needed. Then varnish or paint, depicting the yacht's burgee on each bow. The material, oars and rowlocks will cost seven dollars, and three days and a half labor nine dollars more.

THE "COOT'S" TENDER, 7 FT. 3 IN.

Another skiff of the same sort, but only 7 ft. 3 in. long, with the stern board set nearly plumb, is illustrated by the perspective on this page. Breadth across top, 3 ft.; across bottom, 2 ft. 6 in. Height amidships, 11 in.; at stem, 13 in. Made of ½ in. white pine and brass screwed throughout. Weight, about 40 lbs. This boat was towed by the 23 ft. yacht COOT during a voyage of 1,500 miles, and proved a great success in every respect. Although she would carry two in smooth water, one man was enough when it was lumpy. At night she was hauled up across the COOT's quarter. Upon landing she could easily be pulled up on a high dock by the painter and carried to a safe place.

In Eastern waters the Gloucester dory is very extensively used as a yacht tender. The lightness of the dory, and the facility with which she can be

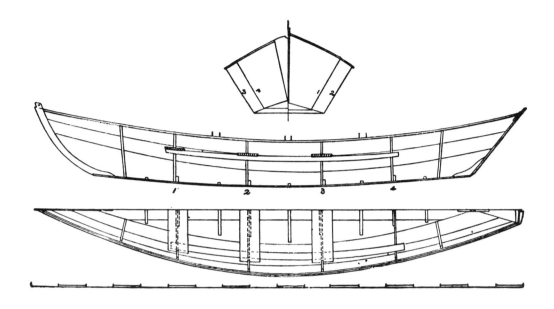

NEW ENGLAND DORY

stowed on deck in a narrow gangway, make her specially suited for yacht service. The dory has a flat bottom with slight rocker or camber fore and aft. The sides flare considerably, terminating forward in a rabbeted stem, and aft in a V-shaped sternboard or transom. Small dories require scarcely any framing. When well fastened there is hardly a limit to their lightness combined with such strength, derived from their form, that they will stand considerable rough usage. They are besides the cheapest style of craft which it is possible to build, and easily put up. In a sea they are extremely buoyant, and for beaching they are unequalled, as the bow can be run out clear of the water for a dry landing. They will "nest" one inside the other, taking up no more stowage room on deck than a single boat.

The diagrams herewith given are scale drawings of a standard 18 ft. dory, as built by Higgins and Gifford, of Gloucester, Mass. The bottom is $7/8$ in. pine. Sides of 9-16 in. pine in three strakes with halved laps. Frames are of oak $1\frac{3}{4} \times 1$ in. and about $2\frac{1}{2}$ in. across the throat. The gunwale is $1\frac{1}{8} \times 1\frac{1}{4}$ in., with a $5/8$ in. cap covering gunwale and topstrake. Thwarts can be lifted out. Smaller dories can be built from the same drawings, but the beam should be relatively increased with decrease in length, to preserve enough stiffness.

Stowing Topsail

# STANDING RIGGING

THE days of rope rigging are past. The yacht is delivered to the owner with wire rigging over the masthead and lanyards set up for a full due. Even these rope lanyards are fast disappearing among small yachts, improved turnbuckles taking their place. The rigger's art in its more complicated and difficult tasks is no longer the requisite it was before wire displaced hemp; and iron bands, eyes and shackles crowded out straps, collars and lashings.

The rigging is now always placed over the masthead in pairs. That is, the wire leads from one deadeye up round the masthead and down to the next deadeye aft on the same side. At the masthead the two parts are seized together, thus forming an eye over the masthead. Where there are three shrouds a side, the third has its own eye turned in with a splice. But up to 40 or 45 ft. water-line two shrouds a side are sufficient. The forestay is put over next and the backstays last, each having its own eye. Putting the backstays over in one piece, simply seizing them together abaft the masthead, is bad practice. Where the topmast is intended to house, the eye in the forestay should be long enough to permit the topmast to pass down through. The special method of fitting the forestay of a cutter is described in the chapter on "Rig and Its Principles." In small beamy yachts the backstays may be omitted altogether, except for cruising in rough water. The shrouds of such boats can be carried further aft than in narrow craft, as they will not interfere so much with squaring off the boom, and act to some extent as backstays themselves. But to prevent the mast being pitched over the bow in a seaway, special backstays are to be recommended. For yachts under 30 ft. water-line, a gun-tackle purchase is all that is required. For larger boats a runner is first rove through a single block in the backstay pendant and the purchase added.

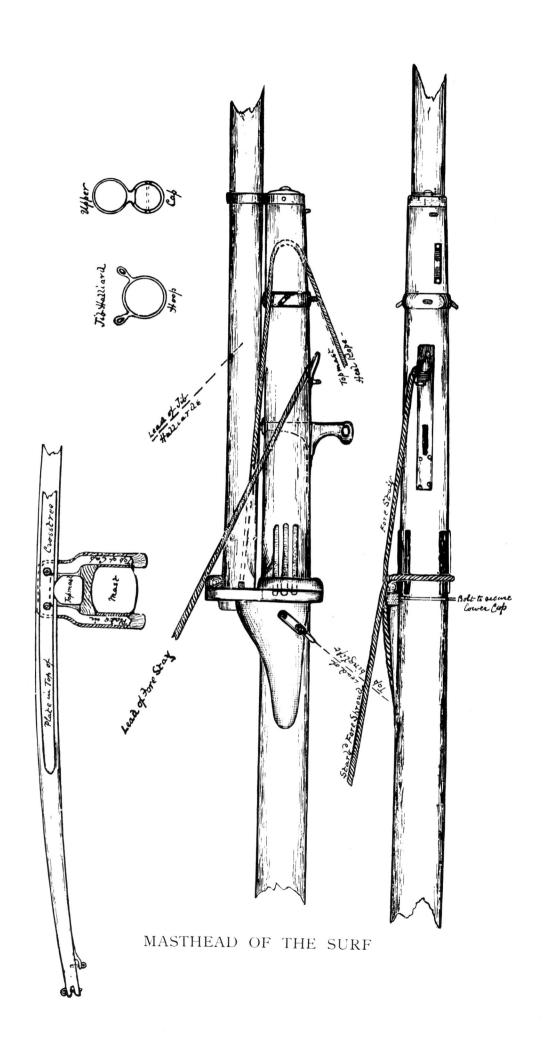

MASTHEAD OF THE SURF

For racing these backstays are of great service, as they hold the mast-head and prevent the slacking of the jibstay upon sweating the jib up to a taut luff.   As all the strain is brought upon the pins of the blocks the latter should be stout and the iron strapping thoroughly reliable.   Iron shell blocks make the neatest arrangement.   The purchases should play very freely through the sheaves, so that upon easing the boom off they can be quickly overhauled. Often the lower blocks are hooked to eyebolts screwed in the rail or deck. But the strain is so great that regular chainplates should be bolted to the yacht's side, like those for the main rigging, or to the stanchions, but some-

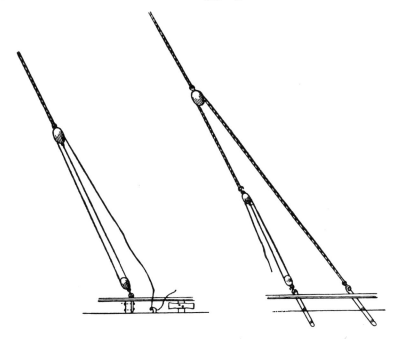

what lighter and at an angle to correspond with that of the backstay.   The plates supply illustrations thereof.   The hooks of the blocks should be of extra size to prevent straightening in the neck.   Belaying cavils riveted into the waist or to the timberheads should be provided in proper place.   The pendant is of wire and the runner of four-strand manilla, often wormed.   The falls of the tackles should be extra stout to prevent stretching and stranding.

The eyes of the rigging over the masthead are usually served over, but this service gradually chafes through and requires renewing.   A better plan is to worm the eyes flush and then cover with stout canvas, and paint or cover with leather.   The nip of the rigging is eased by quarter-round pieces of wood, termed bolsters, screwed on top of the fore and aft trestle trees of mastheads, fitted ship fashion.   But in small yachts the prevailing method is to have an upper and lower iron cap, the masthead being squared or reduced in diameter above the lower cap.   This supplies a shoulder upon which the rigging rests. A leather collar about the masthead, with flaps in wake of the nip of the rigging, will prevent undue chafe. To reduce the masthead is **however** no longer advisable in these days of lofty topmasts and racing kites. Masts are frequently lined out with the same diameter from deck to head, the latter being kept round. On such spars an iron hound-band is shrunk on to support the rigging. Unless a good job is made of this the rigging will **pull** down and give a great deal of trouble.

For setting up the rigging, deadeyes are turned into the lower ends. These are circular clumps of lignum vitæ, bored with three holes, through

which the lanyard is rove. The old plan is to have the deadeye scored out around the circumference. The end of the shroud is taken round the deadeye in this score and spliced or turned up against its own part. A throat seizing is then clapped on close enough to the deadeye to prevent it capsizing out, and two lighter seizings above. The lay of the rope should be preserved round the deadeye. Modern deadeyes are iron strapped, like the lower one in the diagram, the shroud being turned up round a thimble on the pin.

Lanyards should be stout enough not to stretch. Both for safety and for speed the rigging should be set up "taut as a fiddlestring," as there is no advantage whatever in giving spring or "elasticity" to the mast. On the contrary, slack rigging endangers the spar, and in permitting the masthead to work, slacks up everything else to the detriment of high pointing. There is more than enough give to the gaff and canvas, and elasticity in the mast would never come into play until after the impulse of the wind had been cushioned on the sail. The presumed advantages of elasticity to rigging and mast are purely fanciful.

To reeve off a lanyard, turn a Matthew Walker knot in one end, stick the other out through the forward hole in upper deadeye, then down in through the corresponding hole in the lower deadeye, up and out through the middle upper hole, down and in through the lower middle hole, up through third hole above, down through after hole below, the end leading inboard. Slush all the holes well and proceed to set up.

RACKING SEIZING

Clap a selvagee **strap** on the shroud above and hook on a tackle. With the end of the lanyard take a Blackwall hitch round the hook of the lower block and haul taut with the tackle. Secure the lanyard temporarily by a racking seizing applied to the end and the nearest part. Do the same with all the shrouds and allow them to stretch a day. Then get a further and final pull with the tackle all round and secure the ends of the lanyards "for a full due," by reeving first through the eye of the shroud above the deadeye, and then clove-hitching about the shroud, stopping down the end.

Lash on the sheerpoles across the shrouds to keep the deadeyes fore and aft.

Metallic splicing is coming into general use aboard small craft. It does away with the labor of turning in deadeyes and makes a neater job.

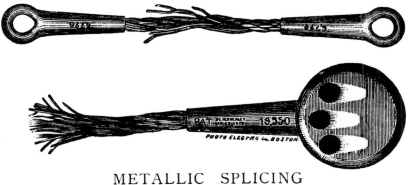

METALLIC SPLICING

This invention is also adapted to the fitting of wire in other respects. Properly made the metallic splice is stronger than the wire itself, as proven by official tests before a board of U. S. officers at the Boston Navy Yard, March 31, 1882. All the splicing of the great Brooklyn Suspension Bridge is metallic. The necessary fittings for yachts are supplied by the inventors at 95 Oliver street, Boston.

Sockets are cast in one piece with the eyes, hearts, hooks, etc. The end of the wire rope is inserted in the cylindrical hole of the socket, and a filling of pure tin or a compound of half lead and half tin is poured round in a molten state, according to the following directions: Melt a sufficient quantity of the filling. Cut out the hemp heart of the wire rope for a length equal to the depth of the socket. Insert the rope in the socket and hold in a horizontal position over a strong heat until a piece of the filling metal will melt when held on the upper side of the socket and passed over its entire length (this heat is required specially at the base of the socket), and until the rope becomes too hot for the hand at a distance of 3 in. from the socket. Have the filling hot enough to ignite a shaving or piece of paper. Now place the splice in a vertical position with the rope in place, and pour the socket full and allow to cool gradually. It is then ready for use.

Turnbuckles are also displacing lanyards of bowsprit shrouds and main rigging. The best pattern is of the cylindrical variety, such as shown on the Lark, Plate XXVII. Hooks should not be allowed, but the ends of the bars should be welded into eyes and connection made by shackles.

The jibstay of a sloop is taken through a hole in the bowsprit end and set up to the stem. The forestay of a cutter leads inboard through a hole in the stem head, and sets up with a lanyard to the bitts when the bow-sprit ships on one side of the stem, or it is set up to an iron bale on the stem head, spanning the bowsprit, if amidships. Sometimes a roller on a pin through lugs in the bowsprit cranze or gammon iron supplies the lead. Hanks for the sail must be slipped over the stay before setting up.

Bobstays of sloops are of iron rod, hooked or shackled to an iron band or muzzle at bowsprit end, and rove through the stem above the waterline, being set up on the inside by a nut and washer. This method is suitable only for the smallest boats. Some means of taking up the stay ought to be supplied. To this end the bobstay rod hooks to the eye of an iron strap rivetted to the stem, and at the bowsprit end is set up with a turn-buckle, so that adjustment can be had. When the bowsprit is of the reef-ing kind, the rod is very short and has a wire pendant shackled to the end. In the outer end of the pendant is a single block for a stout rope fall, and a double block for same shackled to the bowsprit band. The blocks have iron shells and the fall is bolt rope or four-stranded hemp. No hooks should be used in the rig.

It is very common to find the iron strap on the stem one-third the distance up from the water-line, giving to the bobstay a very acute angle with the bowsprit. Much more staying power is got by increasing the angle, having the stem iron at or even below the water-line. Copper is sometimes employed for the stem strap and rod to avoid corrosion in salt water. The stem strap should reach well aft to the rabbet and be through rivetted.

Bowsprit shrouds are of wire. They shackle to bowsprit band and set up with lanyards or turnbuckles to eyes or plates in the boat's bow forward of the chainplates. For reefing bowsprits, the shrouds pass through holes in the bulwarks and set up on deck with tackles. If the bow is too sharp to give good spread to the shrouds, whiskers or a spreader are introduced. The best plan is to reeve a stout piece of oak through a score in the stem, the shrouds nipping in notches cut in the ends. Examples of iron whiskers are given in the plates of the MADGE and YOLANDE.

Foot-ropes for laying out on the bowsprit should be supplied. To use the shrouds for that purpose is apt to slack them. This also applies to the bob-stay. When not in use the slack of the foot-ropes can be hauled in, and no extra gear will be noticeable.

Topmast shrouds are single and go over a shoulder with a hound-band, setting up with lanyards or tackles to chainplates or to eyebolts through the waterways, set up with nuts below. Backstays are rigged in the same way.

In American practice, topmasts are rarely struck, that is sent down on deck. But all lofty topmasts should be fitted to house, or allowed to slide down nearly their whole length, so as to get rid of weight aloft in beating to windward against a sea. The heel should play freely in the caps and not jam. To support the mast when up, a fid or key is rove through a slot in the heel above the lower cap or trestle trees. The weight of the topmast is taken by this fid. To send down the stick, it is necessary to go aloft and unfid, that is pull the key out. To avoid this, various "tumbling fids"

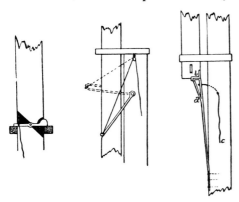

have been contrived. The fid is pinned in the centre and has a tripping line attached to one end. When the topmast has been swayed up a few inches, a pull on the tripping line cants the fid sufficiently to permit its passing down through the cap. Another plan is to hang the topmast by a bale sling hung to the lower masthead and catching a lip or score on the forward face of the topmast. By means of a tripping line the bale can be lifted clear, allowing the topmast to come down.

A simple and effective automatic fid was devised by Mr. Whitehead, of Trenton, N. J., and put into practice aboard the NAHMA with good results. In the diagram, *a* is a piece of light bar iron, the head being turned over in the shape of a triangle and the foot secured to the mast. Under the heel of the topmast the piece *b* is screwed, having a projecting lip below the heel. This piece takes the wear of the spring, *a*. A line through a hole in *a*, and through a diagonal score in the lower mast, serves to haul back the spring *a* snug to the mast, so that the topmast can be lowered. To fid, after the topmast has been swayed up, let go the tripping line, *c*, and the spring will fly out under the heel and take the weight of the topmast.

The spar is lowered and hoisted or "got on end" by the heel rope. One end of this is made fast to the upper cap, then rove down outside the lower cap through a score or "dumb sheave" across the heel of the topmast, and then up the other side through a block hooked to the upper cap and down to deck. A tripping line bent to the heel of the topmast serves to rouse it down. To keep the heel from lashing about, a light wire stay may be set up forward of the mast, having a lizard traveling on the stay. When the topmast is down, secure the heel with the tail of the lizard. If the spar is to be struck altogether, send a hand aloft to slip the rigging off the topmasthead and send it down on deck, or lash it on the upper cap.

Topping lifts for the boom of small craft can be single. Secured at lower cap or masthead and rove through a hole in the boom, belaying to a cleat underneath. Or the standing part can be made fast to the boom, and the hauling part led through a block at masthead. In larger craft a tackle can be added to the hauling end. Many yachts have double or quarter lifts, so that the lee topping lift can be slacked when underway. They are made fast with sisterhooks to the mainsheet band on the boom and lead as already described. They serve also as guides to the gaff in hoisting and lowering the mainsail.

The foretopmaststay should be led inboard through a small block at bowsprit end, so that it can be set up at will.

# RUNNING GEAR

NO precise rules can be laid down for the lead of running gear. What is gained in power is lost in time. Although advisable to have plenty of purchase, it is equally as important that sheets and halliards should run quickly and freely, and that the length of the ropes should not be too great.

For throat halliards the blocks are hooked with sheaves athwartships. The upper block is often hooked or seized to the lower cap, but in larger boats is hung from a crane above so as to clear the cap. The lower block hooks to a shackle pinned through the jaws, with another hanging below for the throat earing of the head of the sail, as shown in the plans of the Coot. In yachts of 35 ft. water-line and above the standing part of the halliards is led down through a sheave and has a tackle in the end to sweat up to a taut luff.

The peak halliards should be distributed through a number of blocks at the masthead, and not all trusted to one block at the upper cap, a common but faulty custom. The gaff has iron bands to suit, though in small craft the standing part is either spliced round the gaff or to an eyebolt. The strain can be distributed along the gaff by hooking to thimbles traveling on rope spans, as illustrated in the sail plan of the Surf. A whip is also rove off in the standing part of the peak in yachts of her size.

Mainsheets are rove as shown in many of the plates. The hauling part should lead from the block on the traveler. In racing craft the sheet is endless, there being no standing part, both ends leading finally through single blocks on each quarter, so that there will always be a hauling part on the weather quarter, no matter what tack the yacht is on.

Jib halliards are seized to the stay at masthead, rove through a single block at head of jib and down through another single block hooked to lower cap. When set flying, or upon their own luff, cutter fashion, the standing part is made fast to an eye in a band half way up the masthead and led down through a block on the opposite side. Chain halliards are not used in small yachts, but a whip in the standing part is very convenient, and almost indispensable to yachts of 30 ft. water-line and over.

Jibs set flying are hauled out to bowsprit end by an iron ring traveler, the outhaul leading back inboard through a sheave in bowsprit end inside of the muzzle band. They are hauled in by an inhaul attached to the ring. The traveler should play freely on the bowsprit, and not be made from too light bar iron, as it is apt to nip. The ring should be covered with leather.

Jib sheets are made fast to eyebolts in the deck nearly abreast of the mast or in the waterways, rove through clump blocks at the clew and aft through fairleaders. The custom of having outriggers over the bow for jib sheets is obsolete.

For single-hand sailing it will be found very convenient to lace the foot of the jib to a light boom and reeve off lazy jacks. The head can then be hoisted to suit any strength of wind, the leech being stopped down to the boom as required, and the slack canvas being held snug by the lazy jacks. This does away with regular reefing, and is much better than "bobbing" the jib, as you do not lose control by the sheets. The boom also greatly facilitates working the jib in beating to windward in a narrow channel.

It is now the custom to have an outhaul to the main clew instead of lashing permanently with an earing. This enables the foot of the sail to be slacked up, or hauled out taut according to the weather. This outhaul is simply a ring traveling on the boom, the clew hooking to the ring and the outhaul coming inboard through a sheave in the boom end and belaying to a cleat under the boom. The ring may be covered with leather and kept slightly slushed with vaseline, which does not stain.

Topsail halliards are rove through a sheave in the masthead. Long topsail yards may require an upper or peak halliard from upper end of yard to keep yard on end while going up, and to steady it when aloft. The topsail tack is single and is got down by swigging off, taking the end to the winch or by clapping on a tackle. The sheet is also single and leads down through a sheave or " bee " at the end of the gaff. The bee is a block of wood enclosing a sheave, and is pinned to the side of the gaff, making a stronger arrangement than slotting out the gaff itself for the sheave. The sheet leads through a block attached to a short pendant from the jaws of the gaff and belays to a cleat near the goose neck at mast.

If a man can be sent aloft, a working topsail is best set flying without any yard by lacing the luff to the topmast as the topsail goes up. In small craft a working topsail is bent to hoops on the topmast and is snugged down to the masthead in a pucker by a clewline. This is made fast at the tack of sail, then leads along the foot through a fairleader at the clew, sometimes also through a "glut" or becket in the centre of the sail and up to the head and down to deck. The sail is first clewed up by this line, then the halliards are let go and the ball of canvas clewed down to the cap. It is not advisable to send men aloft in a small craft, as their weight slacks up the rigging and throws spars out of line, requiring fresh attention to the lanyards, hence yard-topsails sent up from deck are to be preferred.

The spinnaker boom of a small boat is often only a pole, the heel of which is shipped into a grommet strap around the mast at deck. The leech of the sail serves as topping lift and the sheet for after guy, the boom being braced by a lashing at rail. On larger boats the gear is rove off, as shown in the sail plan of the MAMIE, the heel stepping loosely into a conical funnel attached to a swivel goose neck on the mast band.

The gear of small boats should be stouter than the strain requires. Small rope stretches and strands easily and is hard on the hands. Blocks should be large enough to allow the gear to render through easily, even when swelled by the wet. Every sail should come down by the run of its own weight. Lazy jacks, though not smart looking, are of great service to short-handed crews. For the mainsail these can run from double topping lifts to boom at intervals, or from masthead where single topping lifts are used. For a jib lead a line from masthead down along the stay several feet, with a short stick in the end for spreader. From the ends of this stick a main lazy jack can be led to the foot of the jib, and others spliced in as required. When lowering sail these lines snug in the canvas automatically, and prevent the bunt trailing overboard or filling with wind.

When anchoring to the tide with wind abeam, the mainsail can be spilt and lowered with boom off, and trimmed in afterward.

Eye splices and wearing parts should be served with fine marlin. Where the eyes work back and forth, as the standing parts attached to blocks, the eyes should be turned in around thimbles. All ends should be whipped and stopped down. Overhand knots should be turned in sheets likely to unreeve, and lanyards should be set up afresh from time to time. When running gear shows chafe, reeve it off end for end before the rope has suffered. Have as few sizes as possible. Topsail gear should be stout, as it is sweated up so much. Gear which is constantly stretching makes a great deal of useless work and interferes with fine sailing. Appropriate sizes of gear are given throughout these pages.

Spreaders or crosstrees aloft are usually of insufficient strength. They should be made to bear the weight of a hand without being thrown out of line or shape. Light rod lifts from the ends of the horns to upper cap will help to keep them square. Wood spreaders are preferable to iron, but without trestletrees cannot be easily secured. They run across the foreside of the topmast, whereas iron spreaders are usually hooked to the eyes in the lower cap or fastened to after face of masthead.

Small craft up to 22 ft. water-line can show a sufficient sail plan with pole mast only.

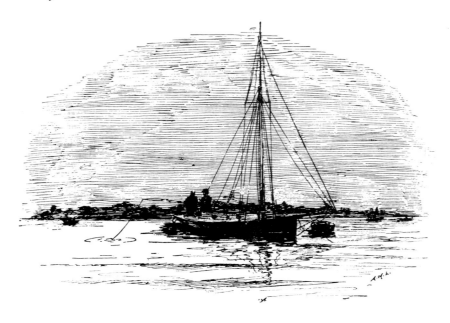

*The Roslyn Yawl*